Linda K. Fuller, PhD

Media-Mediated Relationships:
Straight and Gay, Mainstream and Alternative Perspectives

*Pre-publication
REVIEWS,
COMMENTARIES,
EVALUATIONS . . .*

"**I**n *Media-Mediated Relationships*, Linda Fuller has provided a comprehensive introduction to the myriad ways in which the media of communication are being used to explore and establish relationships in an era made risky through the social construction of sexually transmitted disease. Numerous examples from a variety of media forms are presented in sufficient detail for readers to have a sense of the "character" of the channel. Survey responses from college students provide a useful window into the community of relationship seekers who have come to rely upon these media aids. This book will further challenge the traditionally narrow definitions of media which tend to attract the attention of media scholars."

Oscar H. Gandy, Jr., PhD
*Professor of Communication,
University of Pennsylvania*

More pre-publication
REVIEWS, COMMENTARIES, EVALUATIONS . . .

"*Media-Mediated Relationships* is the first book to take a comprehensive look at how mass media are used in relationships. From 'the personals' to radio station-hosted parties, media mediate relationship initiation. From virtual reality machines to phone sex, media mediate sexual activity. And from television to the movies, these media-mediated relationships are increasingly portrayed as common–though potentially dangerous–liaisons.

Primarily a compendium of information and current research, *Media-Mediated Relationships* raises compelling questions about the nature of relationships in this time of sexual epidemic and electronic wizardry. Will distance dating replace face-to-face encounters as fears of disease and violence rise? Will virtual sex become the safest sex of all? Will relationships with fictional television characters be more real than unmediated relationships?

This book belongs on the shelf of everyone who wonders about the role of mass media in relationships and of those who study interpersonal relationships, mass media, and culture in the age of sexual epidemic."

Nancy L. Roth, PhD
Assistant Professor of Communication,
Rutgers University

"In the last two decades, the study of interpersonal communication has mainly focused on how communication processes affect initiation, development, maintenance, and change of interpersonal relationships in face-to-face encounters. By examining how individuals develop–and even maintain–relationships through alternate and new communication technologies, Fuller's *Media-Mediated Relationships: Straight and Gay, Mainstream and Alternative Perspectives* brings the study of interpersonal communication into the twenty-first century. It examines the role of mass communication in our search for interpersonal connections. The book provides a broad and comprehensive coverage of media-mediated relationships in the print media (books, magazines, and newspapers including 'the personals'), broadcast media (talk radio, soap operas, talk television), communication technologies (computer connections, phone sex, videodating), and music, motion pictures, and games (relationships in music and film, simulations, and board games).

The Haworth Press, Inc.

Media-Mediated Relationships:

Straight and Gay, Mainstream and Alternative Perspectives

HAWORTH Popular Culture
Frank W. Hoffmann, PhD and William G. Bailey, MA
Senior Editors

New, Recent, and Forthcoming Titles:

Arts & Entertainment Fads by Frank W. Hoffmann
and William G. Bailey

Sports & Recreation Fads by Frank W. Hoffmann
and William G. Bailey

Mind & Society Fads by Frank W. Hoffmann
and William G. Bailey

Fashion & Merchandising Fads by Frank W. Hoffmann
and William G. Bailey

*Chocolate Fads, Folklore, & Fantasies: 1000+ Chunks
of Chocolate Information* by Linda K. Fuller

*The Popular Song Reader: A Sampler of Well-Known Twentieth
Century Songs* by William Studwell

Rock Music in American Popular Culture: Rock 'n' Roll Resources
by B. Lee Cooper and Wayne S. Haney

Great Awakenings: Popular Religion and Popular Culture
by Marshall W. Fishwick

The Christmas Carol Reader by William Studwell

*Media-Mediated Relationships: Straight and Gay, Mainstream
and Alternative Perspectives* by Linda K. Fuller

Media-Mediated Relationships:

Straight and Gay, Mainstream and Alternative Perspectives

Linda K. Fuller, PhD

The Haworth Press
New York • London

The Haworth Press, Inc., 10 Alice Street, Binghamton, NY 13904-1580

Library of Congress Cataloging-in-Publication Data

Fuller, Linda K.
    Media-mediated relationships : straight and gay, mainstream and alternative perspectives / by Linda K. Fuller.
        p.   cm.
Includes bibliographical references (p.   ) and index.
ISBN 1-56024-876-9 (alk. paper).
1. Mass media. 2. Interpersonal relations. I. Title.
P91.F82 1995
302.23–dc20   95-14117
                                                                              CIP

Dedication

For X

ABOUT THE AUTHOR

Linda K. Fuller, PhD, an Associate Professor in the Communications Department of Worcester (MA) State College, continues her interest in studying media phenomena. She is the author of *The Cosby Show*: *Audiences, Impact, Implications* (1992); *Chocolate Fads, Folklore & Fantasies: 1,000+ Chunks of Chocolate Information* (1994); *Community Television in the United States*: *A Sourcebook on Public, Educational, and Governmental Access* (1994); and co-editor of the multivolume series *Beyond the Stars: Studies in American Popular Film* (1990+); *Communicating About Communicable Ideas* (1995); and the forthcoming books: *Media-Mediated AIDS; Women's Ways of Acknowledging AIDS; Telecommunications: Implications for Markets, Multiculturalism and Media*; and *Ethnic Images in the Media*. Dr. Fuller has been named a Fulbright scholar, and in 1996 will teach at Nanyang Technological University in Singapore.

CONTENTS

List of Figures   ix

List of Appendixes   xi

Preface   xiii

Acknowledgments   xv

**Chapter 1: Introductory Comments about Media-
   Mediated Relationships**   1

   The Personal Approach   2
   Societal Considerations   2
   Media Considerations   12
   Sexual Considerations   14
   Sexual Orientation Considerations   17
   International Considerations   20
   Theoretical Considerations   24
   Review of the Literature   26
   Methodology   27

**Chapter 2: Media-Mediated Relationships
   in the Print Media**   31

   Books, Magazines, and Newspapers   32
   More Print Media Resources   54
   The Personals   60

**Chapter 3: Media-Mediated Relationships
   in the Broadcast Media**   81

   Radio   82
   Television   95

Chapter 4: Media-Mediated Relationships in Communications Technologies   **117**

Computers   121
Video   130
Interactive Media   133
Broadcasting/Cablecasting Technologies   135
Virtual Reality   136
Telephony   139

Chapter 5: Media-Mediated Relationships in Motion Pictures, Music, and More   **147**

Motion Pictures   147
Media Mediations in the Movies   158
Music   166
And More   168

Chapter 6: Concluding Comments About Media-Mediated Relationships   **171**

Media-Mediated Relationships: A Survey   173
Critical Appraisal   181
Implications   184

Appendixes   **189**

References   **285**

Index   **315**

List of Figures

Figure 1:   Statistics on Singles–by Gender and Age   5

Figure 2:   The Singles Dating Scene   6

Figure 3:   *Together* (Personal Introduction Service)   10

Figure 4:   Indian Arranged Marriages: Criteria   22

Figure 5:   Why Advertise for Dates?   45

Figure 6:   Personal Ad Writing Tips   47

Figure 7:   Tips for Responding to Personal Ads   48

Figure 8:   Place-An-Ad Form   52

Figure 9:   Abbreviation Key for Personals Columns   65

Figure 10:   Titles of Personals Columns   78

Figure 11:   Dick Syatt's Radio Dating Show   87

Figure 12:   WNNZ: The Talk Station/AM 640   96

Figure 13:   Technology Penetration of Selected Media
             in U.S. Households   120

Figure 14:   Computer Hacker "Emoticons"   126

List of Appendixes

Appendix 1:   Correspondence/Introduction Resources   189

Appendix 2:   Business/Agency Resources   201

Appendix 3:   Print Resources   207

Appendix 4:   Magazines and Journals   219

Appendix 5:   Newspapers   225

Appendix 6:   Broadcasting Resources   227

Appendix 7:   Communication Technology Resources   233

Appendix 8:   Telephone Resources   237

Appendix 9:   A Filmography   241

Appendix 10:   Film/Video Resources   247

Appendix 11:   Songs   255

Appendix 12:   *Media-Mediated Relationships:* A Survey   259

Appendix 13:   Survey Comments on Television Dating Shows   261

Appendix 14:   Survey Comments on Relationship Movies   267

Appendix 15:   Survey Comments on 900 Telephone Numbers   273

Appendix 16:   Survey Comments on Electronic Mail   277

Appendix 17:   Survey Comments on Videodating   281

Appendix 18:   Survey Comments on Virtual Reality   283

Preface

If we do indeed live in the Information Age, it is also a truism that it is increasingly difficult to deal with an overload of choices in our search for and maintenance of interpersonal relationships.

Without our necessarily noticing it, we are beginning to pre-empt traditional sources of relationship formation. The family, we learn, is in peril–along with the church, our schools, our streets, our financial and political institutions. As individuals and as a society our response has been to become more insular, to turn to our "safe" friends in the media—whether it be self-advertisements in newspapers or magazines, escapist television-viewing, computer dating, vicariously reading romance novels, dialing 900 telephone talk services, or any other number of media-mediated activities. We also, it is argued, live in a time of reluctant commitments, in a period of playtime—and all this during the Age of AIDS.

In addition to considering the role of mass communication in our search for interpersonal communication, this book seeks to discuss the historical, economic, psychological, and socio-cultural ramifications of our *Media-Mediated Relationships: Straight and Gay, Mainstream and Alternative Perspectives.*

Linda K. Fuller

Acknowledgments

Many people have provided invaluable help in the process of putting this book together. As usual, it is only appropriate to begin with the many libraries and librarians who helped: Krishna Das-Gupta, Worcester State College Library; Judy Gossman, Western New England College Library; and Ardie McEathron, Wilbraham Public Library.

Paul Loukides, co-editor of our Popular Press series of books on American popular film, *Beyond the Stars*, suggested I investigate my observation about the proliferation of the "personals" in film.

Thanks to the students at Worcester State College, who participated in the survey, especially Dharmendra Acharya for the write-up on Indian arranged marriages. Maureen Asten, Bill Byers, Rod Carveth, Tuck Amory, and Richard Sullivan, colleagues at Worcester State College, helped administer the survey. Special mention should be made of the data-inputting skills of Ramsey MacInnes, who went beyond the job description.

Other persons who contributed include the following: Bob Miles Bittner, Publisher, *Singles' Personal Ads*; Robb Carty, for input on the gay musical scene; Alex Fuller, for proofing the entire manuscript; Ed Grossman, Publisher, *Singles Choice*; Michael Harrison, Editor and Publisher, *Talkers*; Laddie Hosler, Editor/Publisher, *The Wishing Well*; Alan Isaacs, Member Services, *At the Gate*; Marjorie Kaufman of the Together Development Corporation; Bobbi Keppel, Unitarian Universalist Bisexual Network; Alix Kruger, for proofing the sections on soaps and sound recordings; Robert and Ruth Leach, Single Booklovers; Matt LeGrant, Co-Chair of the Bay Area Bisexual Network; Dulcey Lester, for introducing me to *Friends*; Ramsey McInnes, for data processing the survey; Andrea McGinty, co-founder of "It's *just* Lunch" in Chicago; G. Jeffrey Provol, Advertising Director, *TV Guide* Classified Mart; John Ramirez, Communications Department, California State University/Los Angeles; Ingrid Schleimer, Consumer Affairs Division, Philip Morris; Michael Schmidt, for input on sound recordings; Charles Shapiro, President of Currents; Dick Syatt, Host, *Hotline Radio Dating Show*; Eric Utne, Publisher of the *Utne Reader*; and the many people who shared thoughts and ideas with me.

A special note must be made of how incredibly enjoyable it has been to work first with John DeCecco, chair of Haworth's Gay and Lesbian Studies program, and then with Frank Hoffmann, chair of Haworth's Popular Culture program, both of whose encouragement and enthusiasm for this project have been steadfast. Having worked with The Haworth Press, Inc. on two previous books, I remain in awe of their efficient and open-minded staff. Bill Cohen originally embraced the idea for a book on *Media-Mediated Relationships*, passing on that inspiration to Bill Palmer and his staff, which has included, at various times, Eric Roland, Patricia Malone Brown, Joan T. Drake, Dawn M. Krisko, Christine Matthews, Peg Marr, Maryann O'Connell, Sandra Jones Sickels, Lisa McGowan, and Susan Trzeciak. Peg Marr has kept on top of copyright consistencies from the start—a sticky but critically important consideration.

As always, I owe a special word of thanks to my family, who allowed me to use a sardonic expression I hadn't been able to use since studying for my master's degree in interpersonal communication: "Sorry, but I can't do that now. . . . I'm working on relationships."

Linda K. Fuller
Wilbraham, MA

Chapter 1

Introductory Comments about Media-Mediated Relationships

The cultural environment is the system of stories and images that cultivates much of who we are, what we think, what we do, and how we conduct our affairs. The cultural environment is our public airways, the media that reflect our world and shape our culture. The cultural environment is the medium into which our children are born and in which we all live and learn. Until recently, it was primarily handcrafted, home-made, and community-inspired. It is not that anymore. We have just begun to take the measure of that transformation.

—Introduction to the Cultural Environment Movement

As we cross the nexus between techno-science and more fundamental disciplines, a phenomenon is emerging in our personal lives: we are beginning to pre-empt traditional sources of relationship formation and are becoming more insular, more cautious. The media play an enormous role in our activities, encouraging us to self-advertise and to screen both ourselves and our prospective acquaintances in newspapers and magazines, to participate vicariously through sexually graphic fantasy books such as *Vox,* radio talk shows and/or television dating programs such as *Studs,* to use our telephones and computers for the ultimate in "safe sex" transactions, to experiment with video dating, and the like.

For straight and gay people alike, the time has come for us to chronicle the omnipresent role of mass communication in our search for interpersonal connections.

THE PERSONAL APPROACH

Perhaps it is only fair for me to begin this book by being up front about its genesis. As a feminist, nearly all of my research in the social and behavioral sciences aims to answer questions posited by Lana F. Rakow (1987, pp. 79-81) relative to underlying motivations, theoretical perspectives, assumptions, methodology, and objectivity and subjectivity in gender studies.

This project began, as so many of mine seem to, in a convoluted fashion. A few years ago, when I mentioned to Paul Loukides, my co-editor of our series of books on American popular film, *Beyond the Stars* (Popular Press, 1990+), how many "personals" were being imbedded in motion picture plots, he suggested that I document them into a report and filmography (Fuller, 1993a). In the process of that research, I began amassing enormous amounts of information beyond the self-advertisement syndrome. Many other media, it turns out, are feeding a need for mediation in relationship formation and maintenance.

Looking at my own life, one might wonder why and how I have become enmeshed with these issues. My husband Eric and I have been married more than three decades now, and have three sons in their 20s, only one of whom is married. We live—really—on Main Street, in the center of a small New England town, and have an active social schedule. Teaching at a college affords me tremendous opportunities to get to know a number of students, those of typical college age and those returning to school, many of whom openly share their experiences and stories. Observing and listening to them, as well as reading and considering both "real life" people and those in the media, have informed this book.

SOCIETAL CONSIDERATIONS

First and foremost, the specter of AIDS surrounds this study. While communicable diseases date to prehistoric periods, with the first true plague thought to date to the Middle Ages (Fuller and Shilling, 1995), they all tend to pale in light of estimates that some 14 million people worldwide are already infected with this disease; consider, further: that number is predicted at 40 million by the end of the century. Along with several other researchers (Seligman, 1992; Sneider, 1992; DeMont, 1993), I would argue that AIDS has—and will even more so in the near future—have a tremendous impact on relationships (Roth and Fuller, forthcoming).

This is not to say, however, that persons with AIDS (known as PWAs) have to halt their relationships; rather, they tend, like all of us, to weigh various options regarding intimacy. Seligman (1992, p. 56) notes:

> When the epidemic began a decade ago, people got sick so fast that romance was low on their list of priorities. Now, with earlier diagnosis and better drugs to prevent and treat symptoms, men and women who are HIV-positive may live for many years with the virus, often looking good and feeling fine.
>
> Whether they are homosexual or heterosexual, they frequently go through a period of celibacy while adjusting to their diagnosis, but eventually recognize the need for companionship and intimacy. Faced with an uncertain future, they are unwilling to accept a present bereft of relationships.

"Singles" as a demographic variable continue to command the attention of advertisers and media consumers alike. Growing 85 percent since 1970, approximately 49 million Americans today aged 25 and older are never-married, divorced, or widowed (DeWitt, 1992, p. 44; Surra, 1990). Those numbers increase even more when one considers nearly another 20 million single younger adults, aged 18 to 24. (See Figure 1. *Statistics on Singles—by Gender and Age*, p. 5.) So much for worries about the dreaded man shortage (Faludi, 1992).

Composed predominantly of three distinct groups, each with its own unique attitudes and behaviors, singles typically fall into these categories:

1. *Never/not-yet marrieds*—Typically between the ages of 18 and 24, 98 percent of whom have never been married, this group

makes up just less than one-third (29 percent) of all singles. By 1991, according to the U.S. Bureau of the Census, this category contained more than 41 million American adults. The population of never-married women aged 20 to 24 rose from 36 percent in 1970 to 64 percent in 1991, while for never-married men that age it rose from 55 percent in 1970 to 80 percent in 1991.

2. *New second-wave baby boomers*—The largest cluster (37 percent), accounting for more than one in three singles, are persons aged 25 to 44. While some two-thirds of these baby boomers have never married, and another third are divorced, they constitute the prime target for dating services.

3. *Middle aged to elderly*—Mostly widowed, mostly women, singles aged 45 to 74 account for some 24 percent of the niche.

"One in five Americans is single and searching for a mate," claims sociologist Paula Mergenhagen DeWitt. For their purposes, dating services are thriving, numbering nearly 2,000 by the late 1980s according to the International Society of Introduction Services in San Francisco. (See Figure 2. *The Singles Dating Scene*, p. 6.) Ehrenreich (1993) has speculated, "Americans love marriage too much. We rush into marriage with abandon, expecting a micro-Utopia on Earth. We pile all our needs onto it, our expectations, neuroses and hopes. In fact, we made marriage into the panda bear of human social institutions: we loved it to death." We also populate a world described by Kidder (1992) as, "a global popular culture that uses nudity and prurience as advertising tools and promotes lust and violence as 'entertainment.'"

Claiming they're "picky, picky, picky," John Tierney (1995, p. 22) points out that some 47 percent of Manhattan households are made up of people living alone, with a fifth of the women over age 45 having never married. His reasoning: they are afflicted with what he calls the "Flaw-O-Matic," a kind of barometer that encourages finding that fault in potential mates. No doubt we are living out the "cocooning" phenomenon predicted by futurist Faith Popcorn.

FIGURE 1. Statistics on Singles—by Gender and Age. (Numbers in millions, according to 1990 census.)

	Number	Percent
<u>Single Men</u>		
18 to 24	10.6	85%
25 to 29	5.2	50
30 to 34	3.8	35
35 to 44	4.5	24
45 to 54	2.3	19
55 to 64	1.7	17
65 to 74	1.6	20
75+	1.3	30
Total	31.0	36%
<u>Single Women</u>		
18 to 24	9.4	73%
25 to 29	4.1	39
30 to 34	3.1	28
35 to 44	4.9	26
45 to 54	3.2	25
55 to 64	3.5	31
65 to 74	4.7	47
75+	5.4	75
Total	38.2	40%

Sources: *Information Please Almanac,* 46th ed., 1993; *Statistical Abstract of the United States*, 112th ed., 1992 (U.S. Department of Commerce, Economics and Statistics, and the Bureau of the Census).

(Note: Details may not add because of rounding. Data are most recent available.)

FIGURE 2. The Singles Dating Scene[1]

Q (asked of unmarried and noncohabiting adults):
HOW OFTEN WOULD YOU SAY YOU DATE PEOPLE OF THE
OPPOSITE SEX—OFTEN, OCCASIONALLY, OR NEVER?

A:	Often	Occasionally	Never
Women	20%	35%	46%
Men	39	40	21

Q (asked of respondents who date):
HOW IS THE DATING SCENE?

A:	AGREE		DISAGREE	
	Women	Men	Women	Men
It is very difficult these days to find new people to date.	75%	57%	23%	39%
Most of the single men/women I meet are unwilling to make a serious commitment.	65	43	25	48
Most of the single men/women I meet don't know what they're doing with their lives.	57	51	39	43
Most of the men/women I'm interested in going out with are already married.	29	24	60	65
The demands of my job give me little time for a social life.	34	39	48	52
I'm happier than most of my married friends.	57	59	29	27
Being single is a lot easier than being married.	60	80	32	24

---

[1]Printed with the permission of Philip Morris Incorporated and the Roper Organization, from the 1989 Virginia Slims American Women's Poll.

Consider:

• Great Expectations, a videodating enterprise that was initiated in 1976, claims more than 135,000 members at its 42 centers nationwide, over 400 of whom have met and married through its services; its slogan is: "We make meeting (single) people easier." As *California Business* has reported,[1] the videodating giant has persisted despite the recession. *The Cincinnati Business Courier* (Peale, 1992) has profiled local franchise owner Don Schumacher who, at age 62, has found his own "date with destiny" as an entrepreneur for the agency, precisely called Great Expectations Creative Management, Inc. See also the wide range of *Correspondence/Introduction Resources for Media-Mediated Relationships* in Appendix 1.

• Fund-raisers such as my local March of Dimes chapter's annual "Bid for Bachelors Auction," where eligible tuxedoed volunteers are made available to the highest bidder (Mitchell, 1993).

• "Plump Partners: Connecticut's #1 Introduction Service for Full-Figured Folks & Their Admirers" suggests their clients have "more to love." Offering personalized matchmaking services at two different locations (Hartford and Newington), the organization has specials, including a spring cruise on the Carnival Fantasy. Their telephone number is an easy 800/34PLUMP.

• Teenagers, reports *The New York Times* (Henneberger and Marriott, 1993, p. 1+), are either not dating or not admitting to it if they do. Citing a 15-year-old male saying, "Nobody wants a relationship except the girls. The guys don't want to look soft to their friends," the authors are concerned about young men's apparent desire to disrespect, even abuse, the young women. Their interviews with 50 teenagers turned up the fact that many of the girls seem to be passive about romantic relationships, consider them rare, and mostly not worth the trouble. Consider, too, the recent Louis Harris and Associates survey for the American Association of University Women Educational Foundation that found more than two-thirds of the girls surveyed reported having been touched against their will.

• Certain target markets are particularly well suited to matching services. There is, for example, The Science Connection (Nicholls,

1993), a dating agency for persons of scientific bent; Friendship Exchange (Schemo, 1992), a matchmaking service for mentally ill couples; a San Diego matching/dating service geared to nonsmokers (Crabtree, 1992); Sports & Recreation Singles Connection in Baton Rouge (Alexander, K., 1991); the Sacramento service helping older women meet younger men (Graebner, 1991).

• Reinstitution of the traditional Jewish matchmaker, or "renta yentas," as Kim Nauer (1991, p. 35) calls them, is a reaction to concern about the growing number (60 percent) of interfaith marriages (Maio, 1992). Bruce Greenbaum, an associate rabbi in Denver, recently started Social Network, limited to Jews; within months, his dating profile process had attracted up to 300 individuals. It works this way:

An aspiring member fills out a form listing first name, interest, activity, religious identity (Reform, Orthodox, or Conservative), occupation, age, height, weight and the type of person he or she wants to meet. No last names, addresses, or phone numbers are given, but applicants are given the option of enclosing two photographs of themselves. . . .

> Each member is assigned a code number. Their forms are kept in the synagogue library, where other members can look them over.
> A man may select the code number of a woman he thinks he would like to meet. He puts his first name on a preprinted postcard and leaves it with the synagogue. Greenbaum pulls the woman's form from a locked safe, looks up her name and mails the interested man's card to her.
> The woman sends a postcard back, checking one of two boxes: "Presently unavailable" or "interested." (Halverson, 1992)

• "Date Checking" is listed as *Rolling Stone*'s Hot Neurosis: "It's no longer necessary to wait until you're couple No. 3 on *The Newlywed Game* to find out about the sordid past of your beloved. These days, eligible singles seek professional help—in the form of a private eye. According to Heritage Investigations, whose date-check caseload has tripled since 1982, dating partners—particularly single females—often employ private detectives to check into their prospects' pocketbooks, sexual pasts, or employment records when suspicions arise."[2]

• The International Directory of Bisexual Groups is available for a minimal cost from ECBN, PO Box 639, Cambridge, MA 02140.

• New London (CT) Adult & Continuing Education offers a one-night course in "How to Write & Respond to Personal Ads, Successfully." Charging $10 for residents, $15 for non-residents, its description reads this way: "Explore the World of Personal Ads. Learn to comfortably respond to the ones you like. A great way for busy people to meet someone new."

• "Together," a personal introduction service in the western Massachusetts and northern Connecticut area since 1974, bills itself as "a classy, dignified service . . . for commitment minded singles." Its advertisement includes a number of "facts." (See Figure 3. *Together,* p. 10.)

• Even the staid (pre-Tina Brown) *The New Yorker* included a profile relevant to relationship issues: about psychoanalyst Dr. Barbara Chasen, a leading matchmaker for Jewish professionals, and founder of the Introductions Club, said to be in response to "the dating crisis of the nineties."[3] In its "Vows" column, featuring a particular marriage each Sunday, *The New York Times* quoted a recent groom's experience moving from a quiet farm in Palmyra, PA to the Big Apple: "At first, his dating life was about as slow as the airport in Palmyra. 'One of the things which disturbed me was that everyone in New York wore sunglasses, had headphones and read newspapers,' Mr. Clark recalled. 'It seemed impossible to talk to anybody.'"[4]

• "Being Alive" is a dating service in Los Angeles geared solely to adults who have AIDS or who are HIV-positive (Hall, 1991; Meyer, 1991). Other related groups include Friends for Life, a social and support group; Bay Area Youth Positives, for teens and those a bit older; and Blood Brothers, a gathering at New York's Comeback Club in the West Village that draws some 200 HIV-positive men on Thursday nights (Seligman, 1992, pp. 56-57).

FIGURE 3. *TOGETHER* (Personal Introduction Service)[1]

• "It's *just* Lunch," a Chicago dating service founded by former advertising executives Andrea McGinty and Margaret Kunkler in January of 1992, quickly grew to a clientele of nearly 1,000. Ranging in age from 25 to 55, subscribers are screened through questionnaires and a detailed interview; once they "pass," they then can choose between paying $400 for six months of blind dates, or $600 for a year for the matchmakers to set up lunches—making reservations, clearing the match, and handling all the details except actually getting the client to the lunch, which is dutch treat. No phone numbers, last names, or employment statistics are exchanged before the meeting, and the understood wisdom is that lunch is the perfect time of day in terms of actual and fabricated constraints. With a number of success stories under their belt, McGinty and Kunkler recently opened a second office in the Chicago area and plan to have others in New York City, Los Angeles,[5] and other areas of California. And just think about it; Neela Banerjee reminds us: "It can't get very romantic if you have to go back to work" (1993, p. B1).

• The Massachusetts Teachers' Association newsletter runs an advertisement under "Single Activities" for LunchDates, a service since 1982 that claims more than 10,000 members, with a 20 percent discount for MTA folks; the drift: "Meet people you'll like one-to-one over afterschool drinks or dinner in nicer restaurants . . . . It's safe, fun, and confidential." Brunch Buddies, which can be reached weeknights from 7-11 pm at 800/2-FIND-US, is a dating service for lesbians (extension 1), gay men (ext. 2), and HIV+ men (ext. 3).

• Even the venerable *Christian Science Monitor* now has a classified advertising section. Someone was recently looking to share accommodations in a Chicago suburb: "Straight SWM to share fully furnished 3-bedroom, 1 1/2 bath house. $350/month + 1/2 utilities. No smokers. No drugs."

• Various travel magazines feature a number of "clothing-optional" vacations in their classified sections, like Caribbean Travel Naturally, Sunshine Company, or Cypress Cove Nudist Resort.

No clothes don't automatically mean no holds barred, however. We live in a time when individual choice is valued above all else, when even abstinence has become fashionable. " 'Non' is more than a prefix," claims Molly O'Neill (1990, p. 1). "It has become a life style." As membership in the number of 12-step "Anonymous" programs (e.g., Alcoholics Anonymous, Gamblers Anonymous, Overeaters Anonymous, Sexaholics Anonymous) has doubled in the last decade, O'Neill asserts that, "The red circle with the slash has become the country's all-purpose problem buster." For potential relationships, the current mating call has become, "Nonsmoking, nondrinking prince seeks sober princess." Small wonder that self-help and recovery movements have become "our new gospel, our latest try for faith in a secular age."[6] Given the climate of our socio-cultural times, many of us are, in the words of Anne W. Egan (1993), "running on Velcro."

At the corporate level, "relationship marketing" is the buzz word for the 1990s. The mandate: "Learn everything possible about your customers; make them love you, and if their loyalty wanes, fight like hell to keep them" (A. Stern, 1993). Meant to fill an untapped void, the idea is to develop long-term bonding strategies with customers—such as special services, newsletters, and the like—making them feel good about the company and their connection to it. Far be it from business to miss the phenomenon of relationships matched and maintained through the media. (See Appendix 2.)

Business/Agency Resources

In a way, it is curious to talk about business and relationships in the same breath; yet, as will be considered from a media perspective, that is what much of matchmaking in the 1990s is all about. None of it comes cheap (Thomas, 1991); for example, *The New York Times* (Fanning, 1990) has profiled headhunter Robert M. Davis, who sets up relationships for busy executives and can arrange a spouse for $10K. Appropriately, Justine Kaplan (1992) has consigned Cupid's current tune to be, "Buy, buy love." Far be it from communications entrepreneurs to miss out on a needed niche—what Peter Wilkinson (1990) calls "The meet market."

MEDIA CONSIDERATIONS

"If one looks at the mass media as institutions which deliver symbolic content to an audience," wrote sociologist Herbert J.

Gans (1972) over two decades ago, "there are three major and interrelated areas of study: the institutions themselves, the content, and the audience" (p. 697). This study investigates not only media messages about relationships that are out there, but also various interpretations of them by individual audience members.

Davis and Kraus (1989), investigating possible connections between social variables, such as frequency of social activity and subjective loneliness relative to media usage, stress studying both the context as well as the content of media exposure. While the issues here are complex, the notion of "loneliness" hardly helps explain interactions between individuals and their media choices.

While most research on mass communication and sexuality has focused on issues such as pornography, gender, and "sex and violence," sexual socialization has received scant attention. Massey and Baran (1992, p. 31) have called for examination and documentation of significations of sex in the media:

> New methods, enriched perspectives, and growing public and scholarly awareness of the potential influences of media portrayals of sex will mean little in our attempts at understanding how young people mature into competent sexual entities as long as our media producers, audiences, and scholars remain afraid of S-E-X.

Our consumer culture has certainly not missed an opportunity to take advantage of our search for relationships. Advertising, the basis of practically all our media in the United States, perpetuating both the marketplace and its hegemony therein, has every reason to appeal to singles. Sut Jhally (1987) faults the advertising image-system for being a propagandistic process aimed at economic growth, while Mary Tannen (1995, p. 53) writes off recent copy featuring clean, nonaggressive males as partly reflecting fear of AIDS and partly reflecting concern for seeming overly sexual in light of what might be construed as harassment circumstances.

The romance of couples—if recently not necessarily heterosexual ones, has long been a motion picture staple. Responding to more modern ways of constructing reltionships, Virginia Wright Wexman (1993, p. 183) has noted that, "Ideas about marriage itself have evolved so that the companionate model has come to be viewed less as a lifetime partnership and more as a means to achieve an ephemeral ideal of personal fulfillment."

Voyeurism, a long-time media specialty, also figures into this discussion. While a number of motion pictures based on the concept will be cited throughout this study, a *Newsweek* cover story on Madonna's coffee-table book *Sex*—packaged in a Mylar bag warning "Adults Only!", priced at $49.94, selling 150,000 copies the first day it was released—considers "the safest sex around" to be media-inspired:

> Call it the new voyeurism: the middlebrow embrace, in the age of AIDS, of explicit erotic material for its own sake. From Mapplethorpe to MTV, from the Fox network to fashion advertising, looking at sex is creeping out of the private sphere and into the public, gentrified by artsy pretension and destigmatized out of viral necessity. Canny marketers exploit it; alarmed conservatives, joined by many feminists, are trying to shut it down. (Leland, 1992, p. 95)

SEXUAL CONSIDERATIONS

Intimacy, according to Anthony Giddens (1992), has evolved into a "plastic sexuality"—decentered, and freed from the needs of reproduction. With origins in the late eighteenth century, when a movement began to limit family size, and later enhanced by the spread of modern contraception and new reproductive technologies, relationships today are viewed as having sexual and emotional equality. "In the pure relationship," Giddens considers, "trust has no external supports, and has to be developed on the basis of intimacy. Trust is a vesting of confidence in the other and also in the capability of the mutual bond to withstand future traumas" (p. 138). Goldberg and Phillips (1990) are concerned about implications of intimacy for and from mass culture, while some feminists see the invention of Western romantic love as an antidote to so many centuries of misogyny.[7]

Sex in the 1990s has received a fair amount of press, albeit with different interpretations. Coming on the heels of public trials about rape, sexual harassment, spousal abuse, and marital infidelity, opinions like that of Paula Kamen, author of *Feminists Fatale: Voices From the Twentysomething Generation,* ring clear: "People today are much more cautious about making a commitment, perhaps so cautious they just can't sit back and let romance take over. There are too many things that can go wrong and maybe destroy your whole future or kill you."[8] While the World Health Organization (WHO) estimates acts of human sexual congress numbering more than a hundred million globally each day, the quality of those encounters is often mirrored in the media at less than always consensual and enjoyable.

In what at first blush seems like a humorous "Hers" column of *The New York Times Magazine,* Susan G. Hauser (1992, p. 20), who bills herself as a "DWF who lives in Portland, Oregon with two children, one dog and nine guinea pigs," worries that she is becoming like her 96-year-old grandmother, who continually refers to not having "known a man since 1953." She confesses: "Come to think of it, I don't know anybody with a sex life. Most of my girlfriends are divorced, like me. (My married friends have the decency not to talk about sex in front of me, in the same way that polite children don't eat cookies in front of those who have none.) When my friends and I do discuss sex, the conversation usually begins, 'If memory serves me right. . . .'"

There appear to be a whole new set of rules at play, requiring a certain new sexual literacy, which South African writer Mike Lipkin bemoans (1993, p. 74):

> The burgeoning power of women and their recently acquired status as equals if not superiors to their male counterparts has turned sex, love and romance into potentially emotion crippling experiences.
>
> For one thing, it's become a lot harder to meet a suitable mate. Then, if you're lucky enough to connect, there are all the strange new mating rites to figure out—the strategies, power plays, manipulations, crossed signals, hidden agendas, confusions and conflicts arising from the tyranny of sexual politics. What's more, there's the charming reality that you could pick up a killer virus in the process.

The Alan Guttmacher Institute released its report on sexual practices in the March/April, 1993 issue of its journal, *Family Planning Perspectives,* billing it the "first scientifically valid survey of its kind" (Adler, 1993, p. 55). Based on responses from 3,321 American men in their 20s and 30s about their sexual practices, the results were surprising in their conservatism: their median number of sex partners over a lifetime is 7.3, median age for losing virginity is 17.2, and median frequency of sexual intercourse is slightly less than once per week. Only 2.3 percent of the interviewees reported any homosexual contacts in the last 10 years, just over 1 percent declaring themselves gay—statistics that have caused quite a bit of controversy as to their verifiability and/or their applicability.

A landmark study of sexuality in the United States, hailed as the most comprehensive survey of sexual behavior ever undertaken, was recently reported on by the National Opinion Research Center (NORC), based at the University of Chicago. Reporting on 90-minute face-to-face interviews with 3,432 randomly selected adults aged 18 to 59, the $1.7 million study appears in two books: *The Social Organization of Sexuality: Sexual Practices in the United States* (University of Chicago Press, 1994) and *Sex in America* (Little, Brown, 1994). The media seemed to be the most surprised to find that, "Most of America's singles aren't swinging these days—not unless they're living together" (Nordgren, 1994, p. 1). One of the key points the researchers underscored was that people tend to select sexual partners who are like them, even in the "sexual marketplace" of personal advertisements (Obermiller, 1994).

"The new sexual revolution: Liberation at last? Or the same old mess?" was the featured special topic for the *Utne Reader* in summer, 1993. While five years earlier its findings were that, "Sex for pleasure was about as popular as a spring vacation in Antarctica," today, despite AIDS and the rise of other sexually transmitted diseases, "sexual revolutionaries have pioneered new philosophies, techniques, political movements, and equipment to restore our battered sense of eros" (Walsh, 1993, p. 59). Witnessing that the sexual "If it feels good, do it" explosion of the 1960s has turned into the sexual implosion of the 1990s, Walsh bemoans, "Today it's sex with machines, sex with cathode rays, sex with latex gloves, sex with vibrators, sex with floppy disks, and, coming soon, thanks to the wonder of 'teledildonics,' sex with robots" (p. 64).

Newsweek ran a feature article on "sexual correctness" in its October 25, 1993 issue, questioning whether it has gone too far. There is Katie Roiphe's controversial *The Morning After: Sex, Fear and Feminism on Campus*, arguing that date rape reduces women by making them into helpless victims needing protective codes of behavior, as well as Antioch College's much-publicized rules governing sexual intimacy, asking for consensual approval every step of the way. Concludes Crichton (1993, p. 56): "Not all boys turn into Glen Ridge, Spur Posse, Tailhook-grabbing beings. But when it comes to human sexuality, the messages that are being sent to kids—male and female—remain cloaked in myth. In 1993, girls who want sex are still sluts, those who don't are still teases."

Regarding "political correctness," lately there appears to be something of a popular cultural backlash. Even with their Standards and Practices departments severely pared down, the television networks still walk a fine line toward scared sanitizing of practically all programming fare; yet, as they become more Disney-like, almost anything goes on many of the cable channels. Despite all the hoopla MTV's *Beavis and Butthead* received when it was named the culprit for an Ohio five-year-old setting his house on fire—killing his younger sister—the show remains on the air, albeit apparently somewhat cleansed of allusions to fun with fire and moved to a later hour. On radio, shock jock Howard Stern has never enjoyed more popularity and press. As we sashay along wondering what is satire and what is just plain silly, media representations of gender and the role(s) between and among the genders call into question their own parameters.

SEXUAL ORIENTATION CONSIDERATIONS

As the subtitle of this book indicates, it seemed only natural to incorporate populations other than "straight" in a discussion of relationships in the 1990s. When one considers how recently bisexuals, gays, and lesbians[9] have moved through stages of "coming out" (of the closet) to "acting up" and even "outing," it is important to recognize, as do Jeffrey Escoffier (1992, pp. 1-3), publisher of *Out/Look,* and Lillian Faderman (1992), the importance of this inclusive research.

If civil rights marked the 1960s, there is no question in many people's minds that gay rights belong to the 1990s. While gays in the military was a disappointing first issue testing Bill Clinton's presidential promise for a constituency that showed such powerful political clout, at least it underscored both their presence and their prescience of advocacy issues that would be looming. John D'Emilio (1993, p. 69), author of *Making Trouble: Essays on Gay History, Politics, and the University,* has stated:

> Today, we remain beleaguered by AIDS and shaken by the ferocity of the Christian Right's attacks on us, especially in the last electoral campaign. So we sometimes don't notice how change, *which we have made,* has snuck up on us. But the Clinton victory, and the hope that it brings, has made the depth of our accomplishments more visible than ever. We are re-weaving the social, cultural, and political fabric of this country with boycotts of the Boy Scouts and Colorado, fights over the public-school curriculum, an endless stream of gay and lesbian military personnel coming out, domestic partnership benefits in some corporations and universities, the FBI compiling anti-gay hate-crime statistics (instead of arresting us for our "crimes"), and Sandra Bernhard playing an out lesbian character on *Roseanne,* the most popular network television show.

Learning about groups such as the National Gay & Lesbian Task Force, the Gay Academic Union, the International Gay Travel Association, ACT-UP, the Gay & Lesbian Alliance Against Defamation (GLAAD), amongst others, the country began to take notice. For one thing, there has been an obvious "growing political involvement over gay rights at the federal level" (Knickerbocker, 1993, p. 4).

Gay rights have been playing out on a number of agendas, ranging from "special rights" for minorities to child custody and adoption cases for "domestic partners"[10] to fairness in the workplace. Yet, at the same time that schools for gay students are being started and supported (Dobnik, 1991), academe argues over policy rights for hiring and diversity issues. My own particular concern has been over the issue of hate crimes (Fuller, 1992b), a homophobic theme taken up by others ranging from the Southern Poverty Law Center to the entertainment industry (Gross, 1991; Farber, 1993; Fejes and Petrich, 1993). John P. DeCecco, professor at the Center for Research and Education in Sexuality (CERES) at San Francisco State University, blames it on St. Augustine: "He made the flesh something that was the embodiment of corruption and said we simply cannot save ourselves from our corrupting sexual desires without the church."[11]

Consider: Gay Games, which draw more than 15,000 participants from some 40 countries; Doug Stevens' group "Outband," the world's only known gay and lesbian country band; gay-only cruises (Wade, 1992); Gay Ski Week; McCormack & Associates, the first executive search firm specializing in gay and lesbian talent (Noble, 1993); and "Community Spirit," a long-distance calling program introduced by Overlooked Opinions, Inc., the country's first opinion polling group dedicated to the 12 million bisexual, gay, and lesbian households in the United States. ManMate, an introduction service for professionally oriented gay men, has been in business since 1985; its motto is "Take Charge of Your Love Life" (Hall, 1991).

Certainly the marketing world has taken note. "No one doubts college-educated gays and lesbians with no children have money to spend," writes Mathews (1992) citing a 1988 Simmons Market Research Bureau survey of readers of eight gay newspapers that found "gay readers drank 2.7 times as much vodka and had 4.6 times as many American Express gold cards as the average American." *USA Today* devoted a feature article "Courting the gay market" (Moore, 1993, p. 2B) to pointing out what an attractive market gay consumers are: "They've got money: The average household income is $51,624 for gay men and $42,755 for lesbians, vs. the U.S. average of $37,922. They're educated—58% are college graduates, vs. 21% of all Americans. And they are brand-loyal and appreciative." The appeal is apparent everywhere:

At the same time marketers are going after gay consumers, gay imagery is spreading into mainstream advertising. Androgyny and sexual ambiguity are all over fashion and liquor ads, not to mention playing at the multiplex in *The Crying*

Game. Ads with gay themes appear in the general press—Banana Republic pared two men in *Vanity Fair* last year. Mainstream ads strike homoerotic themes, like Calvin Klein's Marky Mark underwear ads. It is now running in gay publications. And some ads—like bus-shelter posters for Levi's SilverTab jeans that show a sculpted, shirtless, jeans-clad man—are so popular with the gay community that they keep disappearing. (pp. 1-2B)

"We are in the midst of a second gay sexual revolution," declares Michael Callen in the now-defunct *QW*.[12] "After nearly a decade of AIDS-induced sexual shell shock, the '90s are witnessing the emergence of a new, in-your-face, radical, creative, friendly, hot, group-based sexuality reminiscent of the best of pre-AIDS sexuality." Ann Powers (1993) has witnessed the emergence of a phenomenon she calls "queer straight," which she defines as "that testy love child of identity politics and shifting sexual norms." Part of a rejuvenated gay and lesbian movement, neither the historical, political, economic, nor sociocultural implications of sexual orientations should be overlooked.

Perhaps it is also appropriate to note that The Haworth Press, Inc. has long been a leader in gay and lesbian publications. Publisher of the *Journal of Homosexuality*, The Haworth Press, Inc. is also responsible for the three most relevant books for this project: John DeCecco's (ed.) *Gay Relationships* (1987), which deals with where and how to look for lovers, whom to choose, and how to maintain gay relationships; Wolf and Kielwasser's (eds.) *Gay People, Sex, and the Media* (1991), a comprehensive collection on both interpersonal and mass communication processes; and John DeCecco and John P. Elia's (eds.) *If You Seduce a Straight Person, Can You Make Them Gay? Issues in Biological Essentialism Versus Social Constructionism in Gay and Lesbian Identities* (1993).

INTERNATIONAL CONSIDERATIONS

Typically, we associate mediated relationships in other countries with the practice of matchmaking. Carrying on a practice that began in the Old World, "Marriage brokers' work continues an American tradition that dates back to the days when lonely frontiersmen in the Old West corresponded with adventure-seeking women from the Eastern cities," Henneberger (1992) tells us. "The practice died out as the West became populated, but was renewed, the brokers say, in the 1970's, when men who considered themselves casualties of the American women's movement began looking overseas for more traditional wives."

While young people in rural Morocco have traditionally been expected to marry first cousins on the father's side as a means of keeping landholdings in the family, Australian Aboriginal communities feared the effects of Western films on practices of prearranged marriages, and Gelman (1993, p. 61) reports on anthropological findings that, "Among the polygamous farmers of southern Kenya, a man almost always married first for practical reasons." (See Figure 4, p. 22, for Dharmendra Acharya's report on *Indian Arranged Marriages: Criteria.*)

While matchmaking globally is on the increase (Foot, 1990; Gransden, 1991; Shenan, 1992) in 1991, some 100 mail-order brides came to New York alone—mostly from the former Soviet Union, beating out rivals from Poland, Peru, Korea, China, the Philippines, and other places where women want to change their lot. The *Wall Street Journal* (Hudson, 1990) has discussed Valentine videos prepared by Moscow matchmakers between Russian brides and potential Western beaus. Bridal agencies put together lists, photos, and various catalogs, which they sell to prospective grooms. There are also, it should be added, mail-order husbands—specialties of "Alaska Men USA" and the Florida-based "Bachelor Book."

Canadian Business has reported on an executive service charging $100,000 for worldwide spouse searches (Bernstein, 1984); at the time of the article, the company was claiming a 53 percent marriage rate. And in Beijing, according to the *Far Eastern Economic Review* (Smith, K., 1990), and *Beijing Review*, "TV programme helps in finding a spouse" (1990) singles are into hi-tech, turning to computers and television for matchmaking.

Japan has had a particularly intriguing turnaround in the matchmaking world. While dating services are available to help hesitant bachelors (Cullison, 1992), dates can also be derived from vending machines—a unique ploy for shy would-be courters: "A man can

FIGURE 4. Indian Arranged Marriages: Criteria

Since ancient times, when parents were arranging marriages for their children, they tried to make sure that the boy was at least seven years older than the girl, who was usually about 11 or 12. In the twentieth century, however, the boy (the average being aged 22-25) should be about three to four years older. This was due to the fact that women mature faster than men do. Neither the girl or the boy have the freedom to date. This helps prevent the children from falling in love with someone the parents don't approve of.

In arranging a marriage, the male has to be equally or more educated than the female. This is because he is the head of the family and he will be the bread earner of the family, while the female is usually at home with the children. Even with no children, the women would still be at home, cooking/cleaning/shopping and maintaining social contacts.

Both children should be of the same caste. Very rarely do the parents arrange marriages outside a caste. In the lower caste, the age of arranged marriages was still lower. Sex is hardly a factor.

In appearance, the girl should almost always be shorter than the man, because the girl will have seven years of growing to catch up on. The couple also has to look good together. One cannot be very attractive and the other very ugly; they should be on the same level.

The parents' background is also very important; they should hold good positions in society. Both sides of parents have to be socially acceptable. For example, if on one side the daughter had an affair or ran away, then the other parents would see this as degrading or a blow to their reputation and social standing. Thus there would probably be no marriage.

Neither the boy or girl, which should be the same religion, are considered important. It is the parents' role that is important. This is so they can bring pressure on the boy and girl if there is any conflict in the marriage. So it would result in divorce and in turn ruin both sides of the parents' reputations. Marriage for love is a fairly new idea, and in today's Indian society, marriages have been updated to the point of placing ads in newspapers and magazines.

Dharmendra Acharya

pay the equivalent of a few dollars to have his particulars—including the kind of car he drives—printed on strips of paper that are dispensed to women who put a few coins into the machine seeking a date" (Sterngold, 1992, p. 12). As men continue to outnumber women in Japan, and as the remaining women are getting more aggressive about their own rights, a new profession has sprung up: "consultants who teach men how to talk to women, how to dress, and how to be a considerate husband" (Moffatt, 1990). The *Arts & Entertainment* network aired a fascinating feature story on Japan's problems with its bride shortage,[13] showing how the country has been reduced to looking elsewhere—particularly the Philippines. According to Yamaguchi (1993), Japanese espousal of bride importation is a double-edged sword:

> Mail-order marriages with Chinese brides are growing increasingly popular, despite the high risk of failure and complaints from human rights groups that brokering foreign brides is akin to a slave trade.
>
> The number of Chinese, mostly women, who entered Japan with spouse visas jumped to 1,779 in 1991, nearly triple the 670 in 1990, according to the latest figures available from the Immigration Office. Entries on spouse visas from the Philippines and Korea totaled 1,080 and 744 respectively in 1991.

While most brides are upfront about accepting marriage proposals not for reasons of love but to gain freedom and better economic situations, another way to look at it is this: men get wives, women get out of even worse situations, and families hopefully get children.

China itself has similar problems, with the state statistical bureau reporting that of the total population of 1.2 billion persons, about 205 million over the age of 15 are single (Shenon, 1994, p. 20); of that number, there are some three men for every two women, with single men over age 30 outnumbering women ten to one. A popular Beijing matchmaking television show called *We Meet Tonight*, billed as a cross between the *Dating Game* and a talent show, typically features men trying to woo those scarce women. The country's stricture of one child per family, added to the technology for ultrasound to determine gender and abortions to allow for gender preference, are notably responsible for the predominance of Chinese males—an ironic twist to this whole scenario.

No matter what the country, or who the players, Michael A. D. Reid (1991) reminds us, matchmaking is an art, not a science.

THEORETICAL CONSIDERATIONS

At the heart of this study is an extended version of the notion of "cultivation analysis," a term most associated with the work of George Gerbner (1980, 1986) and his colleagues out of the Annenberg School for Communication at the University of Pennsylvania. While most of their research focuses on the effects of television viewing, prompted by a content analysis of Prime Time that dates to 1967 (Gerbner, 1969), its applicability here comes from the attention that cultivation hypothesis places on developed images of "reality" concomitant with media usage, a mythology that then subsequently plays a role in viewers' perceptions of and responses to actual environments.

The operationalized social construction of reality, according to Gerbner et al., includes a media overrepresentation of certain populations, such as white males and professionals, and a concomitant media underrepresentation of others, such as various minorities and blue collar workers; similarly, cultivation analysis concentrates on certain behaviors, like violence and aggression, rather than on particular value structures. The researchers claim that heavy television viewers, defined as those watching four or more hours per day, construct a world view that is more comparable to that of television content (e.g., distortions such as more crime, fewer women, minorities and the elderly, and occupational discrepancies) than to the actual world in which they live.

Extensive use of electronic media, then, can "cultivate" a distorted social reality. One of the results for these viewers is a world view that is more fearful of, and more alienated from, the actual society in which they are living; typically, this "victimization" paranoia manifests itself, believe it or not, in yet more television viewing—with household doors and windows carefully secured. Another manifestation of cultivation theory is the "mainstreaming," or general, culture-wide perspectives developed among common audiences, regardless of similarities or differences in their demographic and/or psychographic profiles. Currently, Gerbner is in the process of founding an organization he is calling the Cultural Environment Movement (CEM), described this way:

> CEM is the emerging coalition of media, professional, labor, religious, environmental, health-related, and women's and minority groups working for liberation on the cultural front; for a reversal of the concentration of control over both old and new communications technologies; for a halt to the increasing commercialization, conglomeratization and globalization of ownership; for an end to formula-driven homogenization of content; for investing in a freer, fairer, and more diverse cultural environment; and for broadly-based participation in cultural decisions that shape the lives of our children.[14]

While cultivation theory has its detractors, notably P. M. Hirsch (1980, 1981a, 1981b), it still makes a very cogent argument in many areas of application. Potter (1993) has made some suggestions for reconceptualizing cultivation indicators, extending the effect and the relationship, developing a typology of effects, considering the context of other simultaneous influences, providing analysis over time, and examining the process of influence on both individuals and messages; yet, he is still thinking of cultivation mainly for television. This book's emphasis on extension of the cultivation concept includes many media configurations.

As early as 1956 Horton and Wohl suggested that electronic communication, such as occurs in the unidirectional process of broadcasting, has the capability of creating special relationships between senders and receivers unparalleled in the print media. Labelling this interaction "parasocial," Horton and Wohl argue that although the results are mediated, the fact that these processes are face-to-face gives them a psychological advantage. While the theory of parasocial interaction has been applied to a variety of media, particularly television (Rubin, Perse, and Powell, 1985; Fuller, 1986b; Auter, 1992; Turner, 1993), researchers continue to be interested in its concomitant interplay with interpersonal communication as well. Certainly it helps explain why star newscasters oftentimes become bigger than the stories they report, or why soap opera villains tell about being spat upon by fans who see them passing along the street, or why Jerry Seinfeld and his friends, as well as the cast of *Friends*, are being claimed as personal acquaintances by practically every college student.

REVIEW OF THE LITERATURE

While there are a number of publications that seemingly deal with the topic of *Media-Mediated Relationships,* many of which will be dealt with within the confines of this study, to date none has taken the objective tack that underscores the basic approach here of describing a phenomenon.

Cate and Lloyd (1988), Adelman and Ahuvia[15] (1991), Hendrick and Hendrick (1992), Dolan (1993), and Ehrenreich (1993), for example, take as their premise that people are actively involved in mate-searching. Austin (1985), Bernikow (1986), Davis and Kraus (1989), Bell and Roloff (1991) put it down to loneliness. Goffman (1959) and Fogel (1993) consider the individual's personal development through relationships, focusing on the process of communication in learning about self and culture.

Foa and Foa (1980), Avery and McCain (1986), Lindlof and Meyer (1987), Massey and Baran (1992), and Perry (1992) are concerned about ongoing interpersonal processes, while message mediation and its effects on the content of mass media form the inquiry undertaken by Shoemaker and Reese (1991) and Tuchman (1993). Only Wood and Duck (1995), however, are concerned with unusual relationships: long distance, nonmarital cohabitation, and computer mediated.

Wanting to factor in the effects of computers on human relationships are studies by Dutton, Rogers, and Jun (1987), Chesebro and Bonsall (1989), Mosco (1989), Emerson (1992), Lea (1992), Perse et al. (1992), Walther (1992), Walther and Burgoon (1992), Joe (1993), and Lewis (1993), while Rice (1984), Meyrowitz (1985), Rapaport (1991), Gattiker (1992), and Markoff (1992) question the wider role of technology in general. Nimmo (1990), Ganley (1992), and Larson (1994), meanwhile, appropriately wonder about the political power of personal media.

Most of all, the consensual bottom line in most of the literature appears to be that no one really wants to be single. With maybe the exception of Susan Faludi (1992) or William K. Rawlins (1992), people today are prodded by books such as B.I. Murstein's *Paths of Marriage* (1986), Ruthe Stein's *The Art of Single Living: A Guide to Going It Alone in the '90s* (1990) or probed with notions such as Milton Fisher's *Haven't You Been Single Long Enough?* (1992), Harville Hendrix's *Keeping the Love You Find: A Guide for Singles* (1992), or Sharon Wolf's *Guerilla Dating Tactics: Strategies, Tips and Secrets for Finding Romance* (1993). In a Valentine's Day article in *The Washington Post* profiling various persons who have used dating services, Howard Schneider (1993, p. F1) refers to them as members of the "low expectations dating club."

Through it all comes a critical concern from communications researcher Oscar H. Gandy, Jr. (1993) regarding the role of personal information, and how our privacy is being continually eroded and pried upon. Who has access to the data we might input into video dating profiles of ourselves? Who knows what television pay services we might subscribe to? Who can (over)hear our 900 telephone calls? While this book could hardly be classified as one dealing with political economy, it echoes, nevertheless, issues raised by scholars such as Gandy, Meyrowitz (1985), and Wasko and Mosco (1992) on the role of electronic media in expanding financial and social control over our lives.

At the 42nd annual conference of the International Communication Association, held in Miami in 1992, a leading group of researchers (Ronald Rice, Robert LaRose, James Katz, Joseph Walther, and Willard Rowland), with Herbert S. Dordick as chair and George Gerbner as respondent, discussed how the concept "mass media" should be replaced with the term "personal media." The key point is considering how new forms of media confound conventional theories, now placing individual communication needs and interpersonal communication behavior centrally in the study of mediated communication.

METHODOLOGY

The approach of this book involves an attempt to trace media-mediated relationship issues through the print (books, magazines, and newspapers), broadcast (radio and television), film, and new communications technologies media. Yet, the reader certainly will recognize that there will be enormous symbiosis here between and among the various media sources.

Concerned with the tools and foundations of qualitative research in their study of audiences, Lindlof and Meyer (1987, p. 1) begin with this proposition:

> Many questions regarding the forms and consequences of mediated communication require research procedures that are unusually sensitive to the manner in which information is made available and diffused in advanced technology cultures. . . . Advances in scientific understanding are as much due to the stimulative effects of new research technologies as to insight or ideation alone. Ethnograpy and related qualitative approaches comprise a set of procedures that may be very well suited to the highly situated and rule-bound features of mediated communication, and make it feasible to gain access to the meaningful constructs of media users.

Toward that end, as it was determined that it is important to put a face on the issue of media-mediated relationships, a report is given in Chapter 6 on a survey administered specifically to test some of the theories outlined here.

NOTES

1. "Love is not a luxury in this recess," *California Business*, Volume 27, No. 10 (October, 1992), p. 16.

2. "Hot Neurosis: Date Checking," *Rolling Stone* (May 17, 1990), p. 120.

3. "Matchmaker," *The New Yorker*, Volume 67, No. 49 (January 27, 1992), p. 24.

4. Lois Smith Brady, "Vows: Tanya Gibson, Brian Clark." *The New York Times* (October 31, 1993).

5. See also Al Martinez, "Lunch as a way of life," *Los Angeles Times* (March 4, 1993), p. B2.

6. Michael Vincent Miller's review of Wendy Kaminer's *I'm Dysfunctional, You're Dysfunctional* (Reading, MA: Addison-Wesley, 1992) in *The New York Times Book Review* (May 17, 1992), p 1+.

7. See R. Howard Bloch, *Medieval Misogyny and the Invention of Western Romantic Love* (New Haven, CT: Yale University Press), 1991.

8. Comment in John Nordheimer, "No. 1 activity of today's lovers? Worrying," *Union-News* (March 2, 1992), p. 14.

9. For convenience, the term "gay" will often be used as an encompassing one in this book.

10. According to Katrine Ames (1992, p. 62), "The number of Americans living together outside marriage has increased more than 400 percent since 1970. Almost 3 million of the country's 93 million households now consist of unmarried couples. . . . Domestic partnership is often perceived as a gay issue."

11. Natalie Angier, "Bias Against Gay People: Hatred of a Special Kind," *The New York Times* (December 26, 1993), p. E4.

12. Michael Callen, "Come together: Hailing the second gay sexual revolution," *QW* (May 10, 1992). See also: Greenburg, 1991.

13. "Matchmaker, Matchmaker" aired on *A&E* on April 3, 1992, produced by David Jones and directed by Peter Cannon.

14. Letter from George Gerbner to advisors and friends of the Cultural Environment Movement (September, 1993), p. 3. As a member of the Board of Directors of CEM, I serve as chair of its by-laws.

15. Adelman and Ahuvia begin their journal article with this statement: "Involuntary singleness can be a profound source of pain for many adults."

Chapter 2

Media-Mediated Relationships in the Print Media

> *Or whether (as some sager sings)*
> *The frolic wind that breathes the spring,*
> *Zephyr with Aurora playing,*
> *As he met her once a-Maying,*
> *There on beds of violets blue,*
> *And fresh-blown roses washed in dew,*
> *Filled her with thee, a daughter fair,*
> *So buxom, blithe, and debonair.*
>
> John Milton, *L'Allegro* (1645)

The print media—books, magazines, newspapers, and the like—provide classic examples of what people are using to help mediate their relationships.

Probably the most noticeable area in the print media falls under the category of classified self-advertisements, or "the personals," a growing phenomenon that initially formed one of the key reasons this book came about in the first place. Although the personals have been a media staple for well more than a century, their current exponential gain in popularity—a response, it is argued, to the growing number of singles who have forsaken bars, computer dating services, and/or various enterprises seeking to target market them, such as health or fitness clubs, travel agencies, laundromats, museums, even deli check-out counters. Variously called "introduction," "companion," "one-on-one," or "relationship" ads, print personals have become ubiquitous.

As the first media perspective on the topic of the personals, this book will discuss the phenomenon historically (pre-eighteenth century), content-wise (codes, cliches, and exotic examples), economically (a very lucrative and continually growing business), socio-psychologically (including a literature review, plus privacy issues), and media-wise, from the plain brown wrapper for the raincoat trade to acceptance in the mainstream press.

BOOKS, MAGAZINES, AND NEWSPAPERS

Books

While bookstores are filled with how-to volumes about overcoming co-dependency, loving too much and/or not being able to love, the Peter Pan principle (men who can't grow up), or the Cinderella principle (women who can't give up looking for Prince Charming), none try to unravel the phenomenon of our concern for relationships. As was demonstrated in Chapter 1's literature review, most of the books take as their premise that no one wants to be single.

Clearly, too, while porn shops (a.k.a. "adult bookstores") have long been a lucrative business, new ones seem to be springing up with regularity—depending on zoning and community standards. Some books that might be considered appropriate for those repositories, however, are now appearing in the huge bookstores, such as Barnes & Noble and Book Warehouse, that represent a whole new approach to the field. For example, Susie Bright, founder of the lesbian erotica magazine *On Our Backs* and author of the "sexpert" erotic travelogue *Susie Bright's Sexual Reality: A Virtual Sex World Reader* (Cleis Press, 1992) might be found next to radio talk show personality Dr. Ruth Westheimer's *The Art of Arousal* (Abbeville Press, 1993), a coffee table history of eroticism in classical art. Definitions of pornography become ever more difficult to find.

"Yesterday's smut is today's erotica," writes Walter Kendrick (1992, p. 3) in his review of Nicholson Baker's best-selling novel, *Vox* (Random House, 1992), a recounting of sex by telephone:

Though Mr. Baker's tireless phonemates do no writing, they rank among the most "verbal" characters in recent fiction, and the stories they tell are, at least by old-fashioned standards, pornographic. Blunt Anglo-Saxonisms abound; organs and secretions are dwelt upon in lewdly luscious detail; at the end, Abby and Jim achieve their sole aim—guilt-free (and nearly simultaneous) orgasms.

Whether the reader joins them is the reader's choice. But *Vox* doesn't discourage orgasmic response. Its trim size and slight weight tailor it to be held in one hand; for all Mr. Baker's style and wit, if *Vox* had been published 20 years ago, it would have gone among the "stroke books" it archly resembles.

The ultimate in safe-sex erotica/pornography, *Vox* is particularly relevant to this study, combining as it does the print media and telephone technology in its content, as well as print and broadcasting in its promotions. Deborah Garrison (1992, p. 94) calls the book "heady drafts of sex packaged for the literary audience as real writing—or, perhaps more accurately, heady drafts of writing foisted on the unsuspecting best-seller buyer as real smut," perfect timing for this "era of safe sex, of (at least in terms of lip service paid) the New Monogamy, of jollies vicariously gleaned from televised public scandals." Caryn Brooks (1992) envisions the book as print hand jive: "Recent signals point toward a veritable Age of Masturbation. In the shadow of AIDS, and in the spirit of self-exploration, many people are choosing to jerk off as a means of sexual expression. . . . (When the two characters in *Vox*) get together via fiber optics they begin a new kind of hands-on relationship." Baker's next book, *The Fermata* (Random House, 1994), was narrated by a man who can secretly freeze moments in time, thereby allowing him to control his personal relationships from a distance by means of a kind of otherworldly magic voyeurism. Consider also sex therapist Avodah Offit's *Virtual Love* (Simon & Schuster, 1995), billed as "the first E-mail novel," where the main characters begin a relationship via cyberdialogue.

Romance novels, a hot item since Avon's 1972 *The Flame and the Flower,* by Kathleen Woodiwiss, today constitute 46 percent of all paperback book sales. According to Carol Stacy, publisher of *Romantic Times* magazine, a Brooklyn-based industry that sells more than 135,000 copies each month, "Today's typical romance reader reads 10 to 30 novels of the 120 romance titles published each month."[1] *Forbes* reports that romance books constitute a $750-million annual business. The oldest type of women's narrative, romance novels are probably best exemplified by Harlequin, a Toronto-based enterprise which has published more than 2,300 titles since 1958.[2]

The self-help book industry, which Grodin (1991, p. 404) claims as concomitant with the "second wave" of the women's movement, is considered a valuable resource for persons evaluating issues of identity and relationships. Analyzing the genre as both information source and therapeutic fare, along with co-dependency and recovery literature, she cites research indicating that women tend to read and purchase more psychologically oriented self-help books than men. She concludes on a sad but relevant note:

> The social change that women are experiencing today is both exhilarating and painful. Readers express delight with the crumbling of society's traditional structures, yet simultaneously feel dislocated. Surviving dislocation may require being comfortable with exclusion, being able to separate from the whirl of social pressures, and being able to create more functional connections. A fruitful area of continued research will be an examination of the ways women and others are establishing such connections. (p. 417)

There is even a how-to book about approaching the self-advertisement industry: Susan Block's *Advertising for Love: How to Play the Personals* (Quill, 1984). Calling it a game, Block outlines the personals' players, fans, rookies, timing, winning and losing, scoring, hitting, team sports, switch hitters and swingers, and where to play. Her research method was to flexibly contact various people who had run classified self-advertisements:

> I wrote to the ones who piqued my interest, asking them to contact me. I placed ads of my own, calling for personal-ad stories. I asked friends and acquaintances and found, to my surprise, that the majority of them had either played the ads themselves or knew somebody who had. I asked strangers I met in trains, planes, bars, theaters, and at parties and found

that almost everybody—even if they didn't play the game—had at least read the ads and wondered, as I did, who was behind them and why. (p. 16)

From there, Block identifies two stereotypes of "typical" personals players (p. 31):

1. The beautiful, smart, busy types who are liberated enough to play the ads despite what their uptight acquaintances may say.
2. The ugly, stupid, desperate, clinging types who consider the first date a major commitment, since it's probably the first date they've had since junior high.

A few current best-sellers deal with the topic of the personals, all associated with crime and murder, notably:

1. John Lutz, *SWF Seeks Same* (St. Martin's Press), 1990. Advertised with the warning "Life in New York Can Be Murder," it deals with a young woman who finds a roommate through the personals—"only to discover she's gotten more than she bargained for!"
2. C. K. Cambray, *Personal* (Pocket Books), 1990. The paperback cover, featuring a fuzzy frightened face in the background, is superimposed with a classified advertisement: "Redheads wanted for coffee and conversation. Box A-126," headed by the warning, "Some women are dying to meet Mr. Right." The story centers around Amanda, a single parent trying to cope with demands of work and family pressures while simultaneously remaining on the lookout for a significant other. Although she still had her doubts about playing the personals, her friend had found someone through them:

> Two months ago Pam had arrived for dinner waving a copy of the Hartford *Reformer,* the onetime counterculture tabloid. By now its sixties anger had been replaced by eighties Scandinavian furniture ads. Its personal ads, she said, had undergone similar changes. "The kinky stuff is all gone, Mandy. Now it's real people, like yuppies and all. And an ad only costs a couple bucks. People just pick up copies of this thing free everywhere. *Thousands* of guys read the ads." Some of her friends had tried the personals and met nice men. She, Pamela, was

going to try them. "It's the latest and greatest how to meet men game." (pp. 4-5)

It was a dilemma: "To reply seemed a confession of desperation, an exercise in if-all-else-fails. It wasn't her style to broadcast the condition of her heart to consciously put herself in a one-woman lineup for a strange man's scrutiny," she hesitated. "Yet she had been in Hartford for almost four years, and while she had met some men she liked, nothing had come of the relationships." What happened when she did respond, then, to the call for redheads? As you might imagine, it began with taunting, threatening phone calls, followed up by murder and madness.

3. Mary Higgins Clark, *Loves Music, Loves to Dance* (Simon & Schuster), 1991. Bearing a familiar warning—in this instance, "Meeting Mr. Right can be murder . . ."- the lure depicts a personal advertisement reading: "Single Male, 40, Professional—who loves music SEEKS ATTRACTIVE FEMALE 25-30 who also loves music, loves to dance." This book was made into the motion picture *Single White Female*, starring Bridget Fonda, which will be discussed in Chapter 5.

4. Paul Theroux, *Chicago Loop* (Random House), 1991. Reviewed as a "study in dementia,"[3] it tells the story of a man who places ads in the personals—"each ad slightly different, each coded to appeal to the hunger, the need, the secret prurience of some special reader, somebody who's just asking for it. The personal ads are his undoing."

Interestingly, especially in light of the recent University of Chicago sex study mentioned in Chapter 1, books about marital bliss have become fast sellers—books like Dr. Harold Bloomfield's *Love Secrets for a Lasting Relationship*, Lonnie Barbach and David Guisinger's *The Erotic Edge* (for marrieds), Patricia Love's *Hot Monogamy*, or Joan Lloyd's third collection of helpful hints for monogamous couples, *Come Play With Me*. Are we feeling safer, or are we just scared about that wider world out there?

Magazines

A whole industry of publications aimed at singles has been springing up, such as *Singles Scenes* (Larson, 1987); *Intro Maga-*

zine of Studio City, CA, a national monthly that bills itself "The Single Source for Single People;" *Single Life* (Bloomfield, CT); *Person-to-Person,* a "personal-contact" directory; *Chocolate Singles Magazine;* and *The Personals* (from The Customart Press) as shining examples. *Sweet 'n' Sexy Seniors,* a bimonthly magazine out of La Jolla, CA, runs a "Ladies & Gentlemen" column geared to the elderly. See Appendix 3: *Print Resources for Media-Mediated Relationships* for a more extensive, if still partial, listing—more magazines continue to appear. Also, Appendix 4: *Magazines and Journals* lists the many critical resources included in this study.

Match Book, billed as the magazine version of television's "Love Connection," recently hit the newsstands in the New Haven area featuring data on several hundred singles who had filled out questionnaires, many attached with photos. Distribution points include local health spas, lounges, beauty salons, and other businesses. Anka (Radakovich) writes a monthly dating column in *Details,* for which she is billed the "sexual affairs correspondent" (della Cava, 1993). But although the subject is sex, she really is romantic: "People in their 20s want everything. Hot sex, love, someone beautiful, intelligent, fun. But they're not getting it. AIDS is largely to blame. So they're hopeful but helpless. The least I can do is entertain them."

The *Utne Reader,* a magazine that deals with the alternative press, includes some particularly interesting avenues in its classified Introduction Services, such as "The Right Stuff," that provides an 800 number for graduates and faculty of the Ivies, Seven Sisters, MIT, Stanford, Northwestern, University of Chicago, UC Berkeley, and Duke who might want to "date someone in your league"; that Stargazers might want their own astrological personals newsletter; or that spiritual partners might want to subscribe to "Soulmate News."

Called "the magazine equivalent of public-access television"[4] for their irregularity, "zines," or mini-magazines that are singular in theme and idiosyncratic in style, are becoming fashionable. "Magazines aimed at the 20-something crowd are coming of age," declares Kerry O'Neil (1993), citing more than three dozen magazine geared to that generation, with new ones appearing all the time, like *Vibe,* on urban music, Benetton's *Colors,* or Time Warner's *Raygun,* an alternative-rock music magazine.

Several major cities in the United States with monthly city magazines are incorporating personals columns—notably, *Miami Magazine, Los Angeles Magazine, The Berkeley Monthly, Baltimore Magazine, The Washingtonian, St. Louis Magazine, Boston Magazine, Monthly Detroit, Atlantic City, Philadelphia Magazine, New York, D Magazine* out of Dallas, and *The Progressive* of Madison, WI.

Some are surprises. *High Times,* a national magazine dedicated to arguing about the positive aspects of marijuana, provides personals as a free service to its readers. *Mensa Bulletin,* a monthly magazine for members with demonstrably high IQs, also contains gratus personals columns. Since chocolate lovers have much in common,[5] *Chocolate Singles'* "Person-to-Person" provides a good way for them to communicate. *Whole Life Times,* a national ecology magazine out of Brighton, MA, makes matches through its personals.

The gay community also has quite a list of population-specific publications. Joy Morrison (1994, p. 4) has noted that gay and lesbian magazines such as *Advocate, Out, Deneuve* and *10 Percent,* with circulations of approximately 80,000 for the two former, 20-40,000 for the latter, are available at newstands in major cities and have wide subscription circulations in the gay community. Concerning travel, there is the newsletter *Out and About,*[6] offering evaluations on destinations popular with gays. *Our World,*[7] which began in 1989, serves some 18,000 subscribers. And *Out,* the first national general interest magazine for homosexuals in competition with mainstream publications, was voted "Hot Magazine" by *Rolling Stone*; a clever promotional ploy was giving charter subscribers a copy of the CD "Get Out," featuring Lou Reed, David Byrne, k. d. lang, (Steven) Morrisey, and others. Lately, there has been an explosion in gay-oriented publications. According to Jay Mathews (1992), "The new magazines *Out* and *Genre,* the refurbished national bi-weekly *The Advocate* and the New York weekly *QW,* and the new catalog *Shocking Gray* are beginning to draw unprecedented attention in what has been a back-of-the shelf fringe of the publishing world." Further, he adds, "The news publications have better writers and more money than their pulp predecessors, due in part to an infusion of talented gays from general-interest publications."

Anything That Moves,[8] the world's only full length feature magazine regarding bisexuality, discusses its name choice on page 1:

We deliberately chose the radical approach. We are creating dialogue through controversy. We are challenging people to face their own external and internal biphobia . . . . *ATM* was created out of pride; out of necessity; out of anger. We are tired of being analyzed, defined, and represented by people other than ourselves—or worse yet, not considered at all.

The 60 plus page publication consists of an Open Forum for letters, a number of articles and editorials, political and advocacy reports, poetry, photographs, cartoons, information on sex clubs, book and film reviews, quotations, and a listing of "Bi Community & Resources," as well as a classified section.

Houlberg (1991) undertook a content analysis of the monthly magazine of a sadomasochism club to determine what issues are important for its more than 700 members, finding seven subject categories: organizational reports (40 percent), fantasy and real S/M stories (17 percent), S/M photography (14 percent), S/M "how-to" (12 percent), S/M issues (10 percent), S/M poetry (5 percent), and S/M media reviews (2 percent). Stressing the importance of the publication as the club's only record, and underscoring the importance of confidentiality throughout, he concluded that the magazine served its purpose of creating "shared meaning" for the club members—or, as he humorously calls the publication, it is truly a "tie that binds."

Even as venerable an American institution as *National Geographic,* founded in 1888, has recently come under scrutiny and deconstruction by anthropologist Catherine A. Lutz and sociologist Jane L. Collins. Analyzing some 600 randomly selected ethnographic photographs that had appeared in the magazine between 1950 and 1986, the authors conclude that editorial decisions have been based on a basic humanism designed to have us see similarities among peoples. Lutz and Collins describe "an ideological magic," according to Greenblatt (1993, p. 113): "In their account, the smiles, the complacent registering of 'progress,' and the easy embrace of transcendent values mask the reality of racial and class violence and do the work of colonialism." Looked at another way, *Reading National Geographic* demonstrates yet one more example of our vicarious pleasure from print:

National Geographic offered a kind of *Wunderkammer,* or cabinet of curiosities: a heterogeneous archive of natural specimens, both generic and peculiar, a collection summing up the Creation for the pleasure and instruction of its readers. But it also masked, under its high-minded pursuit of scientific knowledge, a thrilling prurience about other people's bodies, a fearful inquisitiveness about tribal rites and customs, a thirst for the primitive and the exotic.[9]

Advertisements also have long appealed to our voyeuristic natures. Witness, too, the continually growing use of underwear ads in mainstream catalogs, the androgynous titillations inspired by Versace that are crossing over into other media representations, and the bolder statements, both visually and print-wise, embedded in commercial messages. Robert Goldman argues in *Reading Ads Socially* (1992, p. 2) that they make ideal sites for observing how the logic of the commodity form expresses itself culturally and socially, a visual ideology framing meanings and how we react to them:

But there is a great deal more at stake in reading ads than simply whether or not to buy. Advertisements have sociocultural consequences and repercussions that go beyond the corporate bottom-line, even though it is that bottom-line which motivates and shapes the ads. This critical reading of ads seeks to excavate the social assumptions that are conventionally made (and glossed over) in the split seconds that it takes us to decipher an ad and move on to the next. Reading ads in terms of the social knowledge necessary to their interpretation enables us to isolate and detail the ideological codes that animate the ads. Suspending the taken-for-granted attitude that accompanies the reading process can turn the reading of ads from depoliticized diversion into a political act.

Performing a content analysis on profiles, or self-advertisements, from *Living Single* magazine, Bolig, Stein, and McKenry (1984) wanted to identify categories of exchange used by men and women, with findings supporting the traditional social exchange dating notion for men but not women. While men's profiles tended to emphasize physical attractiveness and other expressive qualities, women tended to focus on career and education. The authors write:

> The increase in number and variety of informal and organized, nonprofit and profit-making services addressing the needs of singles has paralleled the dramatic increase in the number of singles. Although the lay public and even some social scientists tend to view both the increase in singles and singles' services as symbolic of the loneliness and alienation of society in general, the development of singles' services could more accurately be viewed as a healthy and innovative adaptation to rapid social change. Use of diverse and unique means to find persons with whom to relate, date, and possibly mate, may indicate a more purposive and rational approach as opposed to the 'game playing' of romantic love. (p. 587)

Entertainment Weekly reported on the buzz in Tinsel Town over who placed the personal ad in the magazine *ASAP* describing himself as a "Wealthy Hollywood Bad Boy" who abhors "the idea that humans are naturally monogamous" and seeks an "exotic and special (woman) to be the star of my personal movie."[10] The 300-word ad, costing $1,800, cast glances in many places but was written off as a hoax by any number of suspects.

In an attempt to deconstruct romantic love in terms of how it is shaped by the public discourses of late capitalism and mass media, Illouz (1991, p. 234) analyzed women's magazines[11] in terms of three broad issues: (1) the main themes, (2) the metaphors by which romantic love is constructed, and (3) the normative logic underlying the romantic discourses. These general rhetorical orientations emerged:

> The first, prescriptive articles, give recipes for attaining a successful relationship, rejuvenating romance in marriage, obtaining a date, etc. The second category, normative articles, involves material on romance standards such as on relationships with forbidden or unsuitable persons (e.g., a boss or a married man). The third category, analytical articles, examines the meaning of love. This category includes polls and popularized sociological or psychological work about love.

Broad metaphorical love fields issue forth: love as intense force, as magic, and as hard work. "The practical rationalization of romantic love has an ambivalent political bearing," the author concludes. "On one hand it has contributed to framing romantic relationships as an equitable contractual exchange within which women could assert themselves as equal partners. On the other hand, because the rationalization of romantic discourse has been mostly geared to women, it may have had the effect of consolidating the old idea that women are in charge of emotions and relationships" (p. 246).

The magazine *Utne Reader* has established an intriguing service that is relevant to this study: neighborhood salons, meant to bring together people in a specific locale to gather for discussions about "anything and everything they are thinking and obsessing about." With more than 300 such groups across the country, made up of some 20,000 participants, here is a sampling of their self-descriptive reports:[12]

- A diverse group with sufficient iconoclasts to stir the wits and rattle the conventional wisdoms. Our members span five decades of ages, all alert, sometimes feisty, seldom personal, and always ready to participate.
- The Roller Coaster salon . . . we rise and prosper and attack and sink, gather strength and renew ourselves. Discuss current issues and ethical and philosophical issues. We have a few members who are happy with the world the way it is. We hope to arouse them to an attractive level of discontent.

For a one-time charge of $12, the lifetime member can also participate in the recently launched global network of international mailing lists, called E-mail Salons. National Salon Association members receive a list of interested neighbors and the booklet "The Salon-Keeper's Companion: How to Conduct Salons, Councils and Study Circles." And, it is worth noting, the phenomenon has been catching on—yet another example of our reaching out to connect with others similar to ourselves.

Newspapers

The first print column to the lovelorn appeared during the Victorian era—in 1898's *New York Journal,* written by Beatrice Fairfax, a.k.a. Marie Manning. A popular addition to the newspaper during the heyday of yellow journalism, within two months the newspaper was receiving some 1,400 letters each day.

While the personals have long been accepted in, oftentimes being an integral part of, alternative newsweeklies like the *Tucson Weekly News, L.A. Weekly,* the several *Advocates* (Hartford and New Haven, CT, Springfield, MA, San Mateo, CA), *San Francisco Bay Guardian,* Washington, D.C.'s *City Paper, Illinois Times, Detroit Metro Times, Twin Cities Reader, Maine Times, The Boston Phoenix, Worcester Magazine, Providence Eagle, Ithaca Times,* and Philadelphia's *ELECTRICity,* gradually they have infiltrated into more mainstream media, like *New Republic* out of Washington, D.C., the *Des Moines Register, The New York Review of Books,* my hometown newspaper, the (Springfield, MA) *Union-News,* the *Chicago Tribune,* and many more newspapers that will be cited in this study. For researchers interested in mass communication as a barometer of the times, the personals provide an important case study. See Appendix 5: *Newspapers,* listing just the ones cited in this book.

"The Social Connection," sponsored locally by the *Union-News/ Sunday Republican,* a Newhouse newspaper for Greater Springfield, MA holds events such as a Halloween masquerade ball, but also puts a great deal of emphasis on the senior population. Billed as "a new way for single people who are 60 or older to meet," the newspaper emphasizes that it is free, easy, and confidential—and a good way to attend local jazz concerts, dances, sporting events, and the like. Some examples from their personals include: "Vibrant, youthful & energetic lady. Activities: biking, tennis doubles & skiing. Professional retired teacher. Spiritual (*The Road Less Traveled*)"; "WM, 61, enjoys dining out, movies, riding in the country, TV. Loves animals. Would like to meet WF 60-70+ who is honest & sincere." According to David Firestone (1994), senior centers become ideal places for singles to share companionship; he states: "Love in later life is a distillation of love, a reduction to the essence of human need" (p. 44).

A pilot study performed by Lazier-Smith in 1987 on the use of personal classified ads in newspapers of capitals cities around the country found them quite prevalent even then. The leading category of personals was found to be dating/mating by individuals, followed by dating clubs, and then escort/adult entertainment, religious, and psychic personals. The authors suggested that newspaper consumers were using print media as a replacement for previously recognized social institutions, such as clubs, churches, and taverns, to meet friends and companions. Still, it seems quite amazing to have *The New York Times,* for example, include an article by famous cook Marian Burros (1990) on eligible bachelors who can cook, or discuss self-advertisement in its Sunday marital "Vows" section (Brady, 1992):

> (The bride) answered personal ads in Connecticut and New York magazines. "Most of the personals are filled with 'love to ski,' et cetera," she said. "I shied away from people interested in sports; I'm deficient in that area. My idea of a sporting event is Christmas caroling in an open convertible."
> Her search had its low points: many men her age told her she was about 20 years too old.

There are also a number of newspapers devoted solely to classified self-advertisement, such as *National Singles Register,* a national biweekly tabloid out of Norwalk, CA; *Intro Magazine,* with its "RSVP" feature; *Single Life's* "One-to-One"; *Person-to-Person,* in Laurel, MD; or Customart's *The Personals,* which features both personal and matrimonial ads. *The Worcester Phoenix* has a separate Adult Entertainment section that typically runs a dozen pages, offering variations (e.g., "BOTTLE BABY? Nice BM, 34, seeks clean, drug-free nursing mom, any race, for warm, cuddly moments"; "GUYS SPANKED by Dad, 41, over my knee in your t-shirt & socks"; "Young couple wish to make home video. Can you help us?"), adult services (e.g., straight and gay chat lines, strip-o-grams), and escort services.

Serving Chicago and northwest Indiana, *Singles Choice* claims a circulation of 140,000. Responses can be by letter or voice mailbox, as well as several 900 party lines, like 900/FOR-LUCK ("Hot-N-Sexy Chicago area Ladies looking for a good time!") or 900/FOR-SOUL (Black Chicago singles, including interracial dating). The publication offers a convincing argument, available in Figure 5. *Why Advertise for Dates?* (p. 45) It also includes specific information on its own operation:

FIGURE 5. Why Advertise for Dates?[1]

Across the country, there are literally hundreds of ways for singles to meet—dating services, matchmakers, video dating, your Aunt Bertha fixing you up with her bridge partner's cousin, and even radio disc jockeys, just to name a few. But, the fastest growing, most popular, most successful method by far, is *personal advertising.*

The reasons for the popularity are many. Not only is it convenient and efficient, but one of the most economical ways to reach the largest number of people. *Through advertising, you can meet more people in a short time than you might be able to meet in a lifetime;* and it's FUN! You can reach thousands of singles, many of whom share your interests, background, life objectives and moral outlook. Also, since response indicates interest, advertising greatly reduces the fear of rejection and sense of competition which seem to go hand in hand with trying to meet at singles bars and parties. All this, plus the excitement of messages left for you in your private voice mailbox and letters discreetly sent to your home, forwarded from interesting people answering your ad make it clear: IT PAYS TO ADVERTISE!

In these pages, you will discover many single men and women, much like you, searching for friendship, companionship, and even that someone special. People who advertise and those who respond to ads are mainly intelligent, thoughtful, hard-working people. People not desperate to find a date, but smart enough to know that using personal ads is the most efficient, economical way to connect with like-minded, eligible singles.

The identity of every advertiser remains confidential. Names and addresses are never revealed. All ads are coded, and mail is forwarded to advertisers through our office. Voice messages are left in private, secure voice mailboxes, where the advertiser can call in with total anonymity, using a unique passcode, to listen to his or her messages.

Personal ads can be the most efficient, fastest, most rewarding means of meeting other terrific, eligible people, and may be the best way of meeting your SOMEONE SPECIAL! Be brave! With a personal ad in *Singles Choice* Magazine, your social life can do only one thing: IMPROVE!

---

[1]Printed with permission from Ed Grossman, Publisher, *Singles Choice.*

- ANONYMITY—All *Singles Choice* magazine personal ads are assigned a 5-digit code number that is printed at the end of the personal ad. Attractive, eligible singles wishing to meet you respond by letter by addressing a note to your special code number. We forward the note to you. The people responding never know who you are. VERY CONFIDENTIAL!

- CONVENIENCE—With your own personal ad in *Singles Choice* magazine, Chicagoland's highest circulated singles publication, once you send us your personal ad, you can sit back and wait for the written responses to be sent to you in the mail, and can call in at your convenience to your private voice mailbox, to listen to messages phoned in. IT'S EASY!

- FUN—Wouldn't it be fun to come home from work everyday and check your mailbox for letters forwarded to you from attractive, eligible singles wanting to meet you! Wouldn't it be fun to call in to your voice mailbox and listen to all those people interested in meeting you tell you in their own voice about themselves! A GREAT TIME!

- LOW-COST—Personal ads are a cost-effective way to screen potential dates and expand your social contacts. For example, in *Singles Choice* magazine, your 28-word personal ad, run 5 times, would cost just $7.40/issue! A GREAT DEAL!

- SECURITY—When you place your own personal ad in *Singles Choice* magazine, your name, phone number, and address are never given out to those responding to your ad. YOU decide of those responding to your ad, whom to contact. YOU decide after contacting those people you are interested in, who you want to know your name and phone number. VERY SAFE![13]

Also, publisher Ed Grossman has constructed helpful tips for playing the personals. (See Figure 6. *Personal Ad Writing Tips,* p. 47, and Figure 7. *Tips for Responding to Personal Ads,* p. 48.)

In addition to the standard personals seen in most news sheets, *The Dating Page,* out of Lynnfield, MA, also intersperses some jokes (e.g., "Men are all alike. Yeah—men are all I like, too," or

FIGURE 6. Personal Ad Writing Tips[1]

1. USE THE VOICE MAIL FEATURE WITH YOUR PERSONAL AD! The relatively small cost of retrieving your messages on our $.69/min. retrieval line is FAR outweighed by the increase in number of responses your personal ad will receive. The average ad using the voice mail feature gets 5 times the number of responses than the same ad without the voice mail feature! The more responses you get, the better your chances of meeting that someone special you've been waiting to meet! (When you opt to use the voice mail feature, your ad can be answered by EITHER a phone call OR a letter.)

2. Include your age in your ad—or at least an age range of the person you would like to meet.

3. Spend more time in your ad describing your own interests, hobbies, character traits, and less time describing your ideal date.

4. You limit your number of responses when you request a photo. Lots of terrific people wishing to respond to your ad do not have a photo available.

5. Keep in mind you are selling yourself. Make your ad positive and upbeat. Don't list things you don't like, but rather, those things that you enjoy, have a passion for, or would like to try.

6. Use one of the special "highlight" features available—your ad in bold letters, italics, or a box around it—or any combination of these to make your ad really stand out!

7. If you are having trouble figuring out what to say in your ad, try reading trough both the male AND female ads in this issue for ideas and "catch" phrases. Men, pay particular attention to how the ladies are describing the person they would like to meet and women, read what the guys are looking for in a date. Use those words or phrases in your ad to describe yourself.

By following these simple suggestions you can increase the number of responses to your ad and maximize your chances of meeting someone terrific! Place your personal ad today!

---

[1]Printed with permission from Ed Grossman, Publisher, *Singles Choice*.

"What is the official Slobovian mascot? The litterbug") and advertisements for everything from plastic surgery to international match-ups. *Friends* magazine, published in Connecticut and Rhode Island since 1987, touts events such as its birthday party celebration or the 50/60 Singles Dance, as well as Singles Night at the teletrack, a local hotel's Sheepskin Singles for college grads, Christian

FIGURE 7. Tips for Responding to Personal Ads[1]

The goal of responding to a personal ad is to get the ad writer to call you. Only then will you be able to effectively communicate with him/her, enabling you to ascertain whether or not you want to set up a time and place to meet in person. Keeping in mind your goal, there is one simple adage to remember: First impressions are everything.

Responding to an ad with a phone call:
You may respond to personal ads with this (#) symbol after them, by using your phone. When calling, speak clearly, and slightly slower than normal, directly into the phone. Tell the ad writer why you selected his/her personal ad to respond to, give a brief description of yourself, and tell the ad writer your hobbies, interests and goals. Then, and most importantly, leave your name, phone number (work number if you prefer), a best time to call, and if you like, your address. Repeat your name and number again, slowly.

Responding to an ad with a letter:
Don't:
1. Don't send photocopied "generic" letters designed to answer any personal ad.
2. Don't write on a piece of paper torn out of a spiral notebook and don't write on hotel/motel or your company stationery.
3. Don't write about things you dislike or hate doing—Don't be negative.
4. When sending your envelope for forwarding, avoid folding it by using a larger outside envelope to enclose it in.

Do:
1. Respond on a neat, clean sheet of paper, stationery, or greeting card. Make a point to write neatly and legibly. Print if necessary.
2. Tell the ad writer why you liked his/her ad, and describe yourself in 3-6 paragraphs.
3. Keep your letter positive and "upbeat."
4. Enclose a photo if you have one to spare—and make sure it is a flattering photo of you.
5. Include your name, phone number (work number if you prefer), and your address if you like. Also include a best time to call.

Remember, first impressions are everything, and you only have one chance to "sell" yourself when responding to a personal ad. Also, don't "put all of your eggs in one basket." Respond to a number of ads to help increase your chances of meeting someone special.

---

[1]Printed with permission from Ed Grossman, Publisher, *Singles Choice.*

Singles Outreach, Single Parents of Southeastern Connecticut, or the Singles Theatre Network.

Friends and More, a West Springfield (MA) magazine "Dedicated to Serving the Singles Community," has offered a free trial membership. It is one of the few similar publications that includes actual articles in it—albeit ones such as "Overcoming Those Mental Barriers to a Dating Service" or "The Road to a Successful Long-Distance Relationship." "Respectable Personal Ads" are the province of Tallahassee's (FL) *Singles Connection,* which provides this caveat: "Proper use of the ads in this publication have enabled many people to find new friends, companionship and in several cases, a partner in marriage. However, one must remember, a worthwhile relationship takes time and caution on the part of both parties."[14] At $3.75 per issue/$25 for a year's subscription, the publication is significantly more costly than most (many of which are free), and much smaller, with only about three dozen advertisements; yet, the self-descriptions are quite detailed, as well as quite dignified, and *Singles Connection* is a quick seller, they tell me, at its several Florida outlets. Here are a sample of entries:

- M39: Handsome white Christian gentleman, good build, loves to dance and gardening and attends ALL FSU football games. I like to travel and take cruises. I am seeking a long term to permanent relationship with an attractive lady with a good figure and personality. I'm a good person who is as pretty inside as out.
- F: Petite blonde lady, 65 years young, 5'2", 103 lbs, with good values. I am a nonsmoker, and a social drinker. Picnics, movies, walks on the beach, animals appeal to me. I work a part time job. Seek gentleman 65-70 years, with similar interests for friendship and companionship. Please respond. I would like to meet you.

Singles' Personal Ads, serving parts of New England but calling itself "America's Largest," typically includes more than 1,300 ads in each bi-weekly issue. Boasting that 50-word self-advertisements are free for four issues—"No tricks, no surprises, no retrieval fees"—the magazine also has a unique gimmick to facilitate ad writing, where would-be participants simply circle appropriate phrases about themselves and who they would like to meet. (See Figure 8. *Place-An-Ad Form,* p. 52.)

Most newspapers containing personals sections are entertainment-oriented, using the self-advertisement sections as a cross between conversation pieces and revenue sources. These might include, in addition to the many free alternative weeklies and monthly city magazines mentioned here, as well as those continually springing up, the following: *Lifestyle,* out of San Francisco; Atlanta's *Creative Loafing*; the *Boston Phoenix* and the *Worcester Phoenix*; Rochester, NY's *City Newspaper*; Cleveland's *Scene*; Seattle's *The Weekly*; New York City's *Metropolitan Almanac* and, most of all, *The Village Voice.*

The pre-eminent personals precursor of all newspapers, *The Village Voice* not only set the original standards when it began selling the ads in 1958, but has continued as a lucrative newspaper source even in the soft economy (Case, 1992). Almost any of its issues contains personals that are classics; to wit:

- A GREAT GUY (Really!) Can't believe I'm doing this! I'm handsome, 30, 5'10", drk hr/lt eyes, athletic build. Funny, successful, thoughtful, sensual, musical, diversified interest. Sks F complement. Non-smkr.
- Dominant F seeks M who always wanted to be disciplined like a naughty little boy.
- ALIMENTATION. From Alison's to Zoe's, masculine bon vivant, professional WM 46 can give good company & great intimacy to a good-natured, virile solvent WM 18-34. Are you he?
- 7-DAY CARIBBEAN CRUISE. GM, I won a cruise for 2. Care to be my bunkmate?
- A KNIGHT TO REMEMBER. Let this tall handsome successful SWM, in shining armor sweep you off your feet, w/cndlit dining, exotic travel, romance, adventure & pamp'g.
- Howard Stern Fan seeks uninhibited F to review his "Private Parts." SWM 39 seeks sensuous, bright F, IQ at least 79.
- EXPERT ORALIST. Handsome SBM 44 seeks a leggy F. Clean & attractive a must.

- Are there any females with hairy legs & stretch marks, D&D free, as I, for this male black 30s, for discreet sexual meetings?
- SUBMISSIVE WOMAN WANTED. Do you want to be financially secure, treasured, and cherished? SWM, 38, very rich investor, wants to share your dreams and fantasies. You must want to give complete submission.
- GBF, 26, feminine, pretty, seeks physically fit, soft but stern bitch.
- ALL HIRSUTE FEMALES (any age, weight, race). Generous WM, 39, 6'2", blond, firm, wants to spoil you. Pref unshaven.
- A Christmas gift to me & my wife: She is 27 slim attractive hot & very bicurious but shy. Let's surprise her. Any race.
- SWM, 28, Musician. Semi Home boy, Elvis Costello type. Aspiring massage therapist. Bored w/clubs & nightlife. Seeks open minded attrac. fit SWF who walks talks laughs & more. No 90210 freaks.
- Exotic Brazilian. Well endowed M looking for sexy 30 plus couple for ultimate pleasure. Uninhibited & exhibitionist a plus.
- HERPES IN REMISSION. Young businessman, gorgeous sks young (over 18), attractive, slim F for solid relationship.
- TV/TS WANTED BY MWM. Must be passable, drug & disease free. Discretion assured. New Jersey.
- WHIPPED CREAM AFFAIR. I am looking to meet lady who enjoys the sensual feeling of being covered with whipped cream then licked clean. I'm attractive MWM 40yr. Serious answers only!!!

In addition to mentioning specific ethnic, racial, and/or religious groups, as well as nearly every imaginable sexual fantasy in its personals, *The Village Voice* also advertises a number of adult services. Here is just a sampling: The Asian Connection, Hot & Horny Street Sluts, Live Dreamgirls, Sex Connect, The Exotic Dateline, Down & Dirty Penetration, Hot-Hunk, Call Your Mistress, and many more.

Meanwhile, the lovelorn are still turning to newspapers for advice. Ann Landers has published to her wide readership this warning from a woman who only signed herself "Portsmouth, Ohio":

FIGURE 8. Place-An-Ad-Form[1]

NAME:
ADDRESS: CITY/STATE/ZIP:
PHONE NUMBER (optional):
SEX: Male____ Female____ FREE VOICE-MAILBOX? Yes____ No____
AGE (exact recommended, but other OK):____RACE (optional):____
HEIGHT (optional):____ WEIGHT DESCRIPTION (optional): ____
HAIR COLOR (optional):____YOUR PROFESSION (optional): ____

ABOUT ME: I AM: (Circle words/phrases that are appropriate) Custodial parent-non-custodial parent-Never had kids-Want to have kids//Non-drinker-Light Drinker-Social Drinker-Ready for AA// Never married-Divorced-Legally Separated-Widowed//Smoker-Non-Smoker-Looking-To-Quit-Smoker//Outgoing-Talkative-Quiet-Somewhat Withdrawn//Energetic-Laid Back-Energetic AND Laid Back//Conservative-Moderate-Liberal//Very Attractive-Moderately Attractive-Average//Show Affection Greatly-Average-Attractive-Moderately Attractive-Average//Show Affection Greatly-Average-Not Much//Into Fitness Because I Enjoy It-Into Fitness Because Everyone Else Is-I'm Fit So I'm Not Into It-I'm Not Fit But Would Like To Be//Snappy Dresser-Very Fashion Conscious-Above Average Dresser-Average Dresser-Blue Jeans Type of Person-High Fashion Can Go To Hell-I Dress Conservatively-I Dress In 60's Style//I Follow Trends-I *Make* Trends-I Ignore Trends//Serious Nature-Moderately Serious-Non-Serious Except For Relationship-Non-Serious Almost Always//Very Adventurous & Daring-Moderate-Not Much/I Make Waves-Ripples-Nothing//Stimulating conversationalist-Average-Don't Say Much// Very Responsible & Dependable-Average//Sensitive (Easily Hurt Feelings)-Average-Tough//Macho-Non-Macho//Libber-Non-Libber//Active With Causes-I'll Let Others Do Causes//Witty Sense of Humor-Average-Not Much Humor//Cheerful-Average-Intellectually Cynical//Into Personal Growth & Awareness-I'm Aware Of Myself, So I Don't Need It//I'm a Great Cook-I *Need* a Great Cook//I Believe The Man Should Pay For Nights Out-We Should Go Dutch// Aggressive-Average-Passive//EDUCATION: High School-Partial College-Bachelors-Masters-MD-PhD//POLITICAL: Liberal-Middle-Conservative//

I ENJOY: (Circle words/phrases that are appropriate)
TRAVELLING: World Wide-Caribbean-USA-Cape Cod-New York City-Any Coastline-Canada-NH/VT Mountains; OTHER ACTIVITIES: Anything Outdoors-Being Close To Nature-Normal Walking (Hand-in-Hand?)-Jogging-Skiing-Bicycling-Motorcycling-Camping Out-Children-Tennis-Golf-Live Theatre-Country Fairs-Antique Shops-Flea Markets-Day Trips-Weekend Trips-Beaches-Animals/Pets//Dancing, Dining In-Dining Out-Picnics//Movies In Theatres-Movies On VCR; TYPES OF MOVIES: Supernatural-Sci-Fi-Romantic-Old-Comedy-Adventure; MUSIC: Classical-Urban-Light Contemporary-Rock-Country-Jazz, New Age-New Wave-Top 40; READING: Classic Novels-Romance Books-Stephen King-daily newspaper-Trade & Tech. Periodicals-Comic Books; TV: PBS-Game Shows-Soaps-Sitcoms-3 Stooges; OTHER: Going Out Often-Going Out Occasionally-Enjoy Warmth Of Home Fireplace-Cuddling With the *Right Person*; SPORTS: Enjoy Immensely-Moderately-Hardly At All-Spectator Only//Bicycling-Basketball-Hockey-Racquetball-Underwater-Soccer-Golf-Skating-Running-Board Games-Hiking-Football-Tennis-Volleyball-Skiing-Other___//Other:

---

[1]Printed with permission from Bob Miles Bittner, Pub., *Singles' Personal Ads*

Dear Ann Landers: Please advise women who are looking for male companionship or husbands not to waste time responding to personal ads in papers and magazines.

I am a widow in my early 60s, and I have answered at least 25 of those ads. They are all a bunch of baloney. Men who run those ads do not really want to get married. They are just looking for someone to sleep with or somebody who will take care of them.

One man who advertised himself to be 70 confessed that he was 83 but thought he LOOKED 70. His wife had been dead three weeks. He said upfront that he has no interest in getting married because he has four children and wants to leave everything to them, but he would like a woman who is "friendly." He made it plain that in spite of his age he was still capable of "a lot of friendship."

Please, Ann, warn women about these skunks. Tell them they are better off alone. If you print my letter, do not use my name because I would not want anyone to know I had been so foolish as to answer an ad.

(Permission granted by Ann Landers and Creators Syndicate)

Ann Landers' response? "Thanks for the alert. Every now and then I get a letter from a reader who says he or she found someone wonderful through an ad, but those who were disappointed, disgusted or embarrassed outnumber the others 100 to 1."

In February of 1994 my local newspaper (*Union News, Sunday Republican*) in Springfield, MA ran a three-part series called "Sex Sells." Despite the widespread economic problems that our area has been undergoing, the authors pointed out, its sex staples were booming—part of the multi-billion dollar adult entertainment industry. The first focus was on strip bars, where owners and strippers—male and female alike are prospering while so many other businesses are struggling. Tips, it was reported, can range from $100 to $300 per evening. "More than 300 men paid $5 each at Monson's Magic Lantern 11 nights ago to watch five women strip for a $500 prize as part of an amateur contest . . . among the bar's largest crowd in six years, its owner said," according to the front page article (Kelly, 1994). According to an editorial accompanying the initial discussion of "The Illusion of Sex," these ventures thrive for two reasons: "First, because one segment of society enjoys engaging in these activities, and is willing to pay for them; and second, because those who believe such activities should be banned are hampered by America's constitutional freedoms."

Obscenity issues have been discussed here, the reporters remind us, ever since the Bay State banned John Cleland's *Fanny Hill* in 1821—making the expression "Banned in Boston" synonymous with titillating media fare. Part II of the series took up adult video stores, reputedly a $4 billion industry in the country, finding that some 73 percent of the video stores in this area carry XXX-rated tapes. Customers at Bookends, for example, "Can build a wardrobe of edible clothing, select magazines, books and videos, choose from a lineup of inflatable surrogates (including a latex fat lady), pick among 100 vibrators or from a display case of ball gags, ankle straps and other sadomasochism equipment" (Macero, 1994, p. 6). Finally, Part III zeroed in on sex by phone and/or computer; wrote Diane Lederman (1994, p. 1), "Like sex over the telephone, people in the age of AIDS can have safe sex, or a sexual fantasy without physical contact. Just be prepared to pay."

MORE PRINT MEDIA RESOURCES

Newsletters

As can be seen in Appendix 1: *Correspondence/Introduction Resources for Media-Mediated Relationships,* there are a number of print resources out there relevant to this study. Some emphasize pen-pal writing exchanges, such as Australian Singles, Currents, Friend Finder, OK Letters International, the various Penfriends groups, Sunshine International Penpals, and Transatlantic Penfriends. Others cater more to finding special interests, for example, the aforementioned gay travel publication *Out and About,* Artistic Connections, Jewish Single Line, The Movie Lovers Club, Single Booklovers, or The Single Gourmet.

At the Gate,[15] a "contact network for socially responsible singles interested in the many aspects of green living," began in 1985. Its diverse membership, representing people from the United States, Canada, and other parts of the world, joins those interested in sharing "a global consciousness influenced by holistic philosophies, green politics, and a willingness to explore the mind, body and spirit." Sharing 5 percent of its profits with groups like Greenpeace, Amnesty International, Oxfam America, People for the Ethical Treatment of Animals, and other smaller grass-roots groups, it joins people concerned about "ecology and the environment; human rights, equal rights, and animal rights; peace and justice; health and natural living; spirituality and personal growth." And most of all, it boasts a number of members who have married or at the least have developed lasting relationships. Enrollment is conducted through private code, and members can meet one another if they want to by responding to various posted profiles, such as these:

FEMALE

1. *KANSAS, Lawrence: Beth, 27, 5'5", hourglass figure, brown-eyed girl, writer, vegetarian, creative, amusing, affectionate, passionate, intelligent, sexy, loves music, cooking, camping, animals, romance. Can go from wild child to earthy homebody. Looking for my Man! Must be: All listed above plus honest, motivated, playful, rational, emotionally stable. Prefer but not necessary: brunette, medium build, longer than average hair.*
2. *MASSACHUSETTS, Boston: DWF, 61, into social action, personal/spiritual growth, art, theatre, movies, music, dancing, acting, laughing. Called warm, vibrant, attractive, younger looking but like those who do not find older women "anathema," but who can appreciate potential wisdom and other cultivated qualities coming with life's experience and seasoning. Responses from my own age range and geographical location preferred but not necessary. Will respond to all.*

MALE

1. *WISCONSIN, Racine: Carl, 50, 5'10", ocean blue eyes, DWM, Millwright, non-smoker: I am honest and active, with a positive attitude and a reincarnated soul. I was born curious and in search of life's teachings. Interested in para-psychology, sailing,*

nature, fine arts, sports cars, and chocolate. Seriously seeking soulmate for adventure, fun, and romance. Photo please.
2. COLORADO, Denver: Russ, 29, 5'10", 190 lbs., S. Bartender/photographer: Aspiring photographer & poet who understands the necessity of money in life, but prefers experience & exploration; Sensual & Searching; B.A. in psychology, with some Grad-School; Rachmaninoff to Rolling Stones to Red Hot Chili Peppers; Mapplethorpe to Monet; I believe in the human spirit; Seeking woman with girlish spirit for pen-pals, friendship, and . . . ? Photo please.

Single Booklovers, started in 1970 by widower Bob Leach and today maintained by him and wife Ruth, whom he met through the organization, publishes a monthly newsletter "for the express purpose of helping cultured single, divorced, or widowed men and women get acquainted in a dignified way."[16] Members get to provide a two-line sketch about themselves, such as these:

- Woman—Adrian, MI. "5'2" editor/writer, non-smoker seeks warm, caring, humorous friend with strong desire for marriage and children. Reading, travel."
- Woman—Portland, OR. Divorced 5'8" non-smoker "Reubenesque; loves fine art, fine music, fine food. Is comfortable conversationalist. Would love to hear from you."
- Man—Crofton, MD. Divorced 5'10", 180 lbs non-smoker "Attorney, communicative, dynamic, interested in Dali, jogging, Shakespeare, basketball, travel; The Good Earth, Lonesome Dove."
- Man—Rome, GA. Separated 5'6", 160 lbs "Computer consultant, prefers non-smoker, light drinker; morning person with no children. Acts/directs community plays."
- Woman—Los Angeles, CA. Widowed, 5' "RN, vivacious blonde with balanced mind and body seeks same. Loves dining out and dancing, reading, laughing, discovering."

Estimating more than 500 marriages that have resulted from group introductions, Single Booklovers has received quite a bit of press. *The Daily News* has written about the membership: "All 50 states are represented and so are all age groups. There are teachers, professors, writers, computer programmers and nurses. There's also a nuclear physicist, a farmer, a professional woodworker, a research scientist, a pharmacist and a pilot."[17] Reporting on one couple who met through matched profiles, *The Wall Street Journal* quoted a husband hooked by an aesthetic correspondence: "We finish each other's sentences, or anticipate each other's thoughts. Even my friends who seem happily married don't have as much in common as we have."[18]

Recently, *TV Guide*—at a circulation of more than 17 million copies, the Number One weekly general consumer magazine—recently began its own "Classified Mart." Appearing in the first and third issues each month of the magazine's Top 25 markets, reaching more than 20 million readers—billed as having a median age of 37.2, a median household income of $33,140—its promotional appeal cites: "*TV Guide* reaches more adults who made purchases by phone or mail in the past year than any other weekly magazine. Additionally, a recent 900# reader poll generated more than 150,000 calls in the first two weeks plus nearly 6,000 responses via fax and mail!" Prototypically mainstream, examples of the expensive $39.95 per word "personals" include the following:

- EXCITING SINGLES NETWORK. Touch tone callers can place ads to listen to talking personal ads nationwide by area code. Call Now, Date Tonight. 1-900/226-0609 $2.95 per min. Must be 18 or older. Maja Ent., Ottawa, IL. Info. 312/509-8130.
- AMERICA'S LOVE CONNECTION. 1-900/773-4446. $2.50/min. 18+ Meet singles in your area. CCI Boca, FL.
- NEED A DATE TONIGHT? Meet single men, women in your area. 1-900/787-4587 Ext 225. $2.00/min 24 hours.

Not at all a dating service, the Unitarian Universalist Bisexual Network has this as its mission: "To create acceptance, inclusion, safety, and support for Bisexual people through education and change in the UUA."[19] Founded in 1991 as an association of bisexual and bifriendly people, it concerns itself with all sexual minorities, including those in the transgender community. In a May, 1993 *UUBN Newsletter,* one member shared some thoughts on intimacy and partnership diversity as an answer to the quest for a more inclusive terminology:

> We were l/b/g/and hets interested in overcoming social & cultural gender stereotypes & limitations on intimacy, partnership, & friendship— supporting diverse lifestyles of friendship, intimacy, partnership and sexuality. This includes l/b/g & straight relationships as well as celibacy, polyfidelity, polyintimacy, non-traditional straight couples (e.g., not legally married & thus stigmatized & discriminated against in housing, etc.), alternative intentional &/or extended families & communities & friendships & child-raising, bonding in other than sexual ways, intimacy & affection between 2 straight men or 2 straight women or "best friend" relationships instead of a sexual one between a straight man & woman, etc., etc. All sorts of alternatives & possibilities & variations could be thought of that would come under this concept.

Since 1974, *The Wishing Well,* a publication of Laddie's Ventures 11, has been "specifically designed for women-loving-women who have no other way to locate their sisters, as well as for those who simply want to broaden their horizons beyond their local areas."[20] Members, either individually or as couples, can be code-matched with similar women who live near them—with privacy protected. At a 10-word minimum, $1 per word, classified advertising reaches some 5,475 readers in 50 states and worldwide, including "music/theater/drama lovers, book buffs, outdoor enthusiasts, travelers, spiritualists, environmentalists, entrepreneurs, writers, naturalists, and buyers of personal products."

Cartoons

Just as more media have been incorporating articles about and advertising for mediating relationships, so too have humorists not missed the phenomenon. A proliferation of cartoons have appeared, especially about the personals. Here are some examples:

- *The New Yorker,* traditionally a barometer of popular parlance, has increasingly included the personals theme in its cartoons.

One of my favorites is D. Reilly's post-date woman at her door saying, "I've had a lovely evening, Keith, and may I say that I found you every bit as caring, sensitive, warm, witty, emotionally available, open to commitment, eclectic, values-rooted, stable, cultured, centered, fit, sincere, adventurous, unglitzy, down-to-earth, spontaneous, and fun as your ad promised you would be."

• Levin's mustached man in a dress and beads sitting across from the bemused preppy, with the confession, "My mistake, really. I thought your ad said you were into cross-training."

• The older, elegant gentleman raising an index finger to the secretary taking down his stats at the Metro Singles Group, adding, "Oh, and she should be into Mozart, long walks, whales, Fats Waller, Thai cuisine, Richard Nixon, self-hypnotism, the Poconos, commodities options, Zoroaster, and spelunking."

• Victoria Roberts' two goofy-looking characters revealing, "I didn't put this in my personal ad, but I'm synonymous with Belgian cuisine."

• The two bathroom towels Mankoff has drawn, the left one reading "Fantastic, fit, fortysomething exec, interested in culture, athletic pursuits, and gourmet food, seeks intelligent, dynamic, thirtysomething beauty for evolving relationship, leading to marriage"; hanging next to it is "Vivacious, 30-plus career woman with beauty and brains wants to enjoy the arts, fine dining, and fitness with successful, 40-plus man who is not afraid to contemplate the 'm' word."

• Winillar's witch reading the palm of an equally scraggy old man, joyfully commenting, "Gee, you didn't mention your wart in your personal."

Etc.

Besides billboards, balloons, scrawled messages in telephone booths and bathrooms, print media about and begging for relationships actually is ubiquitous. I had fun dedicating my article on film personals to our three sons: "To FWF IV, KKF, and ASF—SWMs who are adept, bright, creative, dauntless, enterprising, fun, genteel, handy, imaginative, joyful, kindhearted, loving, manly, nimble, open-minded, perceptive, quick-witted, real, sportsmanlike, talented, unique, versatile, witty, (un)xenophobic, yogurt- and Yorkshire Pudding-eaters, and zany."[21]

THE PERSONALS

A longtime media staple, print self-advertisement, better known as "the personals," are emerging with both new vigor and new content in the "safe-sex" era of the 1990s.

A Brief History of the Personals

We might wonder just how Cleopatra got Julius Caesar to come meet her, but history has documented that, "In 1727, a brave British spinster named Helen Morrison placed a personal in the Manchester *Weekly Journal,* whereupon the mayor promptly had her shipped off to the local looney bin" (Block, 1984, p. 29). A longtime front-page feature of the *London Times* in the nineteenth century, personal advertisements were known as "the agony column."[22] Edmund Wilson, recalling a former English instructor, now a book publisher, in his 1942 *Memoirs of Hecate County,* discusses this feature in the *Booklover* :

> (It) originally had some connection with various kinds of literary business. We had sometimes used to read it for amusement, and when I had looked at it in its earlier days, it had seemed to consist mainly of appeal from "gentlemen, cultured, traveled, fiftyish," desiring correspondence with ladies who "loved books and fireside chat," and "women of refinement, conversant with the arts, fond of theater, concert and opera," who wished "to banish ennui by interchange with mature well-bred men, free from philistinism and provinciality." But of late years, I was now told, a new element had been seeping in, and the page was almost as full of advertisements by "gentlemen of robust constitution" in search on "nonprudish ladies responsive to the new dance rhythms," "Ganymedes who were at home in French and Italian and enjoyed European travel," "watchers to the Well of Loneliness" and

"alumni of Dr. Birch's School," as one of those Paris journals that is openly devoted to pimping. And now a terrible thing had happened. The American Purity League, a vice-hunting organization, had recently got wind of this and were about to bring the *Booklover* into court for carrying indecent advertisements. (p. 359)

Recall, too, that in the early days of this country, mail-order brides and matchmakers were commonplace means of arranging companionship. Yet, while the personals have been included in *The Village Voice* for some four decades, it is only recently that they have become a more acceptable, more frequent choice for meeting people of similar interest. Only recently have they been acceptable, also, to the mainstream media.

"In the middle of the social ferment of the 1960's and the self-actualization movements of the seventies, personal ads started making a comeback," writes Susan Block in her 1984 book *Advertising for Love: How to Play the Personals* (p. 29). "With skyrocketing divorce rates and fewer opportunities to find mates within the traditional church and small-town social structures, people had to start making matches for themselves. Gradually, the socially stigmatized 'advertising for it' became transformed into an acceptable way to find new friends."

Labelling the personals "an odd and compact art form, and somewhat unnatural . . . like haiku of self-celebration," essayist Lance Morrow (1985, p. 74) has observed:

The sociology of personals has changed in recent years. One reason that people still feel uncomfortable with the form is that during the '60s and early '70s, personal ads had a slightly sleazy connotation. They showed up in the back of underground magazines and sex magazines, the little billboards through which wife swappers and odd sexual specialists communicated. In the past few years, however, personal ads have become a popular and reputable way of shopping for new relationships.

When magazine founder, publisher, and editor Suzanne Douglas of Los Angeles decided to put out the slick, sophisticated monthly

Intro ("The Single Source for Single People") in 1981, she based her hunch on a pervasive loneliness in our society. "Love is a big seller," she explains. "What we've done is revive the art of the handwritten love letter."[23]

Citing a dramatic increase in the number of singles in today's society, Steinfirst and Moran (1989, p. 129) try to explain why self-advertising has come "out of the closet," becoming not only more acceptable, but actually fashionable:

> In the 1980s, when leisure time is at a premium for today's working young people, personal ads have become an acceptable and comfortable alternative to the conventional methods of meeting persons (generally) of the opposite sex. Instead of going to a singles' bar or arranging for a blind date, individuals, both male and female, compose an advertisement describing themselves and their desires and sit back and wait for a response.

As of about the mid-1980s, emphasis in those descriptions has been less on seeking sex, more on seeking traditional, long-time relationships (Astor, 1991). *Advertising Age*[24] claims the personals have gained new respectability because of our "efficiency-minded" times: "Readers and advertisers reply to whom they choose; cool selectivity is th name of the game."

Content of the Personals

"By their nature, of course," writes media critic Caryn James (1989, p. C19), "personals reflect not only the writer's sense of humor, but also how he or she wants to be seen." Keith D. Mano (1987, p. 52) has called the personals columns "sub-pornographic: voyeur and exhibitionist maintain their anonymity. And their control. Society has discouraged perversion by isolating it. Personal columns unstring our social fabric by allowing isolated men and women to find each other without risk across a wide circulation."

While you are probably aware that S = Single, M = Male, F = Female, W = White, B = Black, and that D = Divorced, did you know that J = Jewish, C = Christian, G = Gay, H = Hispanic, Bi = Bisexual, ISO = In Search Of, or POSSLQ = Persons of the Opposite Sex Sharing Living Quarters? Regular readers of personals know the codes and cliches better, such as that PIX is requesting a photo, S&M = Sado-masochism, B&D = Bondage and Discipline, and that TV = Transvestite, TX = Transsexual. See Figure 9. *Abbreviation Key for Personals Columns*, p. 65, which may just contain some new terms—such as G/S = Golden shower and W/S = Water sports, both of which have to do with urination, or what you might have thought of as ethnic shorthands, for example, Gr = Greek or Fr = French, which in personals parlance stand for kinds of coitus.

Kathleen Fury (1987, p. 192), a regular columnist for *Working Woman,* shares this confession: "Some women read romance novels. Me, I like to escape into the fantasy world of the personals column. There, browsing through the entreaties of singles—Choose Me! Choose Me!—I look for answers to the age-old question: What do men want?" Jeffrey Shaffer's "Worlds of Love" in *The New Yorker* (1988, p. 25) offers some possibilities: "Slim, attractive male, mid-thirties, crustacean background. Seeking active, aware female counterpart for quality-time relationship"; "Are you a caring female type who combines lust for living with durable high-resilience outer coating?"; "Star Warrior . . . trained for conquest, now intrigued by the pleasures of power-sharing"; or "Cheerful, humor-loving, highly magnetized male has Ursa Major needs for right date mate." Reciprocally, one woman scribed, "Social life needs change of phase. Want responsible, financially secure male friend for possible long-term mix." Two women (actually, two self-described "petite, perky moon maidens") wrote, "Ideal respondents will be generous, electrically neutral, not intimidated by strong feminist outlooks or intense radio-wave bombardment."

Recently, novelist Cynthia Ozick had her panicked-to-marry heroine reading personals in *The New York Review of Books:*[25]

> Fit, handsome, ambitious writer/editor, militant nonsmoker, witty, imaginative, irreverent, seeks lasting relationship with nonsmoking female. Must be brilliant, unpretentious, passionate, creative. Prefer Ph.D. in Milton, Shakespeare, or Beowulf.

> University professor, anthropologist, 50, gentle, intellectual, youthful, author of three volumes on Aleutian Islanders, cherishes the examined life, welcomes marriage or long-term at-

tachment to loyal, accomplished professional woman; well-analyzed (Jung only, no Freud or Reich, please). Sense of humor and love of outdoors a must.

Pulitzer prize-winning columnist Ellen Goodman tried to help her readers cope with post-Persian Gulf War depression: "Miss those long afternoons together? Find yourself looking in the personals column for a burly 56-year-old in fatigues with a 170 IQ and a taste for Pavarotti? Desperately seeking a man who is caring but, well, commanding? If you are among the millions suffering from Schwarzkopf-withdrawal, take heart."

One of my favorite mild personals comes from the (Nashville) *Tennessean*:

LOOKING FOR QUALITY Relationship. More than likely, you are too. Let's start at the beginning with ideas. Here are some ABCs.

A— attractive, active, attentive, appreciative, assertive, amusing
B— basking, bashful, bonding, brave, boldness, belief, best
C— chemistry, comfortable, conversation, competent, creative
D— delightful, demanding, demonstrative, descriptive
E— excellence, entertaining, enjoyable
F— finances, friendship, fun, flowers
G— generous, giggly, gutsy, gusto
H— happy, hair, honesty
I — imaginative . . .

And then too there is the (in)famous "Trader Dick" section of *The Advocate,* which includes sado-masochism and sexual-service advertisements.

Economics of the Personals

Whether they represent an escape into the fantasy world, a symptomatic undercurrent of loneliness in the United States, and/or "the natural outlet of the discreet, the sincere and the sensitive, all seeking kindred spirits for meaningful relationships,"[26] the personals increasingly spell economic success. Although no exact figures were available from the American Newspaper Publishers Association,[27] the personals are a cottage industry that shows continuing

FIGURE 9. Abbreviation Key for Personals Columns

B = Black
B&D = Bondage and discipline
Bi = Bisexual
BW = Black widow
C = Christian
D = Divorced
DTO = Down to Earth
Eng = English (dominance)
F = Female
Fr = French (oral sex)
G = Gay
Gr = Greek (anal sex)
G/S = Golden shower
H = Hispanic
ISO = In Search Of
J = Jewish
L = Lesbian
LA = Los Angeles
M = Male
Ma = Married
MC = Married couple
NS = Nonsmoker
NY = New York
PIX = Requesting a photo
POSSLQ = Persons of opposite sex sharing living quarters
P/P = Photo/phone
Rom = Roman (group sex)
S = Single
SD = Social drinker
SF = San Francisco
S&M = Sado-masochism
SOH = Sense of humor
TV = Transvestite
TX = Transsexual
W = White
W/S = Water sports
W/W = White widow
Y/O = Years old

signs of growth. Self-advertising further has particular promise in the expanding interactive computer field.

Although there is a wide range of content and costs, the over-whelming majority of outlets for classified love advertisements—including print, telephone, and computer dating services—find them extremely lucrative. Consider, for example, that the *New York Post* receives more than 1,000 personals replies per week from a daily circulation of over 900,000. *The Village Voice* forwards some 200,000 letters yearly, reporting that the personals account for about one-twentieth of the newspaper's annual revenue.[28] Listings in various publications might be free, or might cost $5+ per word, $50 for one to five words, or $7+ per line.

Elizabeth C. Hirschman, a professor of marketing at New York University, reported on a "People as Products" (1987) study using the personals as examples of marketing exchange. While location (New York and Washington) didn't appear to make a difference, she found men more frequently seeking physical attractiveness resources from women, offering monetary resources in exchange, while women were the reverse: seeking monetary resources and offering physical attractiveness.

Sociopsychology of the Personals

Calling personal advertising "the quintessential free-market instrument," an offshoot of yuppie pragmatism, Keith D. Mano (1987, p. 52) considers personal advertising "a class phenomenon. Historically the middle and upper middle brokered their passion. Now they have to act as both agent and flack. Blue-collar people have a greater sense of either insecurity or shame." Geoffrey Sheridan (1986, p. 22) talks of how the lonely hearts search breaks traditional barriers of relationship testing: "You *know* that your contact is available (generally speaking). You *have* to be personal, even if you are in the habit of keeping up a front, of image-making . . . . You meet as equals, and the compulsion to be open means that no holds are barred on the questions that can be asked. It can make for an unusual intimacy."

Most academic studies on the personals have come from the fields of sociology or psychology. One of the earliest ones is Harrison and Saeed's 1977 report "Let's Make a Deal: An Analysis of

Revelations and Stipulations in Lonely Hearts Advertisements"
that appeared in the *Journal of Personality and Social Psychology.*
After content-analyzing 800 personals, the authors found women
more likely to offer attractiveness and seek financial security, men
more likely to seek attractiveness and offer financial security.
Another important finding was that classified self-advertisements
can be a useful research source.

Also in 1977 Laner and Kamel performed a content analysis of
359 personal advertisements by male homosexuals, which they
compared to 192 male heterosexuals and 155 female heterosexual
advertisers. Cameron and Sparks (1977), reporting on courtship
styles in *Family Coordinator,* found eight common themes: personality, physical attributes, goals for relationship, recreational and
other interests, appearance, education, occupation, and financial
status. And in 1978 Lumby had an article in the *Journal of Homosexuality* about men advertising for sex. Still, this was all pre-AIDS.

Yet, it wasn't until 1984 that a number of recent studies appeared.
Bolig, Stein, and McKenry came to a paradoxical conclusion from
analyzing the midwestern magazine *Living Single*: neither the men
nor the women who placed profiles in the publication were looking
for those who did likewise, and age continues as a primary factor in
the date/mate selection process.

Deaux and Hanna (1984) looked at influences of gender and
sexual orientation in 800 personals from both straight and gay publications. While finding men generally more concerned with physical characteristics and women stressing psychological ones, homosexuals were found to be more interested in sexuality and
heterosexuals specified a broader range of characteristics. A guide
to the personals for gay men, *Classified Affairs,* by Preston and
Brandt, was published by Alyson in 1984. In 1988, Darden and
Koski read more than 2,000 personals in *The New York Review,* then
interviewed 42 30-to 50-year-olds who had used the service, answering and/or placing ads themselves. They found that most of
their subjects consider playing the personals a "deviant" activity, as
they manifested "embarrassment, reluctance, and secretiveness" in
doing so, and were unwilling to discuss with anyone but close
friends the fact that they had participated.

From a local Columbus, OH magazine's lonely hearts advertisements, Lynn and Shurgot (1984) found most responses were received by "women and individuals providing nonnegative, evaluative self-descriptions than by their counterparts. Also, tall male advertisers and light female advertisers received more responses than their shorter and heavier counterparts. Finally, advertisers with red or salt and pepper hair received more responses than blonde and brunette advertisers." Smith, Waldorf, and Trembath (1990), concerned about sociocultural pressures on women to be physically attractive—especially to be thin—examined 283 male and 231 female personal ads from a singles magazine; as predicted, physical attractiveness was found to be the characteristic most frequently sought by males (56.9 percent), causing the researchers to reappraise the link with current high rates of eating disorder problems with women.

Hirschman's "People as Products" (1987) previously cited study contains a rationale that is worth reproducing:

> Personal advertisements, for which men and women pay to communicate their availability and marketable assets to others, serve as a unique and constructive context from which to examine complex marketing exchanges. First, they are clearly a form of marketing exchange, even in the most traditional economic sense. People may pay to place the advertisements, just as do breakfast cereal companies and automobile manufacturers. Second, like advertisements in a traditional marketing context, personal ads list a set of (presumed) desirable properties (here viewed as resources) that are put forward to attract potential buyers. Third, a price is also stated in the advertisement, which consists of the set of properties/resources sought in return. Thus, in essence, personal advertisements represent the offering of people as products, as a set of marketable resources in search of an appropriate buyer. (p. 101)

Wondering whether personals' usage is a deviant activity, Darden and Koski (1988) read more than 2,000 advertisements from *The New York Review,* then interviewed 42 adult participants between the ages of 30 and 50 years. The authors deduced that the exercise is deviant, saying most subjects manifested embarrassment, reluctance, and secretiveness—searching for fantasy.

Steinfirst and Moran, colleagues at the School of Information and Library Science at the University of North Carolina at Chapel Hill, have made valuable contributions to the study of personals. First (1989), they performed a content analysis of 501 advertisements in *The New York Review of Books* from October 24, 1985 to April 10, 1986, discussing demographics, type of relationship sought (mostly, "to meet"), physical characteristics, and personal interests. Most of their findings were congruent with earlier studies. Next (Moran and Steinfirst, 1990), they decided to find out more about the actual people behind the ads. Choosing 100 persons from *The Spectator,* a free local weekly newspaper, they received permission to interview 19 advertisers: 11 males and eight females primarily in their 30s or 40s, well educated, from a wide range of occupations (blue collar to highly paid professionals). Number of responses received ranged from two to three to between 80 and 90; in most instances, advertisers received many more responses than they had anticipated. No one went out with all their respondents, but one man dated 30 women and three women met 12 men each. They were all very selective. When the participants did meet, it was mostly in public settings, such as restaurants or coffee houses. Physical characteristics seldom matched what was being advertised, women's weight being a particularly sensitive issue. Yet overall, most interviewees found the personals experience to be positive, and said they would repeat it sometime. The process is time consuming, they reported, but worth it to find Mr. or Ms. Right. Thinking they had discovered something of a subculture of personal ad placers, the authors were surprised to learn how hard people work at placing their ads; further, they found an undercurrent of loneliness that they consider might help explain the personals as a means of searching for relationships.

In 1993, Gonzales and Meyers reported in *Personality and Social Psychology Bulletin* on examinations of self-presentation strategies of both heterosexual and homosexual men and women in personals ads, coded for physical descriptors and these characteristics: offers of and appeals for attractiveness, financial security, expressiveness, instrumentality, sincerity, and sexual activities. Finding that the interaction of gender and sexual orientation often was the best predictor of ad contents, they concluded:

a. Gay men emphasized physical characteristics most while lesbians emphasized them least;
b. Heterosexual women mentioned attractiveness more than lesbians did;
c. Women solicited more expressive traits and offered more instrumental traits than men;
d. Gay men mentioned sexuality more than other advertisers; and
e. Heterosexuals were more likely than homosexuals to pursue long-term relationships and to mention sincerity and financial security.

Interested in meanings attached to sexual practices within the gay community, particularly in light of AIDS, Alan G. Davidson (1991) performed three-month block content analyses on personals in *The Village Voice* for the years 1978, 1982, 1985, and 1988. He noted a significant increase in health concerns in the language along with more importance attached to sexual exclusivity. Another contribution to his results was giving credibility to the personals column as a research tool:

> (It is) a potential indicator of sexual meanings both at a given point in time as well as across time. In other words, personals advertisements serve to convey the meanings which people attach to their sexuality both at one point in time and for comparisons over time. Therefore, personals advertisements, though obviously of limited scope and representativeness, are, nonetheless, useful data sources for assessing the meanings people attach to their sexuality, as well as for assessing changes in these meanings over time. (p. 136)

"Content and Changes in Gay Men's Personal Ads, 1975 to the Present" is a work in progress of Hugh Klein,[29] a content analysis of the "personals" and "relationships" ads placed in *The Advocate*—which was selected because it is the only gay publication that has the following criteria: (1) a national audience, (2) consistently published personal ads across time, and (3) has been in existence since well before the AIDS epidemic began. Coding some 250 variables, to date he has analyzed more than 3,000 ads, and we await the results.

On the international scene, Pang Linlin of the Guangxi Institute for Nationalities has compared personals matchmaking in China with the United States (1993, p. 163), finding Chinese advertisers to be marriage-minded and family-oriented, as opposed to their American counterparts. Yet, "Mate-seekers or spouse-seekers in both countries shared the same interest in physical attractiveness, occupation, education, physical height, age, marital status, personal character and place of residence. Besides, the Chinese suitors took interest in health, career-mindedness and loyalty of their potential mates' being intelligent, humorous, athletic and communicative." *The New York Times* (Hedges,1993) has pointed out that personals are flourishing in Algeria, despite Islamic fundamentalist disapproval:

> Personal ads rarely raise eyebrows in liberal Western societies, but they remain taboo in most of the Arab world—except for Algeria and a handful of other countries. First instituted in Algeria in 1989 with the country's democratic opening, personal ads have survived the pervasive censorship imposed since the military coup 16 months ago. But as gun battles between Islamic militants and police have increased, forcing many to stay close to home, as political life has been shut down and as unemployment has climbed to 50 percent among the young, newspapers have been flooded with bags of mail from those searching for a way out. (p. V3)

There are some other undercurrents relative to the personals that are also worth noting. For one thing, there has apparently been an increase in instances of date checking, typically by paid private eyes. Heritage Investigations, for example, reports that its date-check caseload has tripled since 1982. Mostly single females, their clients want to know about prospective dates' finances, sexual pasts, or employment records.[30]

Also, there are privacy concerns. *Editor & Publisher* [31] reports on a homophobic hate group in Chicago who ran the following ad in the *Chicago Reader,* a free "alternative" weekly with wide circulation in the city: "Attractive GWM, 24, shy and U of C Hyde Parker, wishes to meet discreet students and locals only for close friendships." A box number was also included. Those who responded to the ad soon discovered that their action was reported to their employers, landlords, and neighbors. The Great White Brotherhood of the Iron Fist has claimed responsibility for sending out letters stating, "It has come to our attention that your employee is homosexual and a possible carrier of AIDS. Please take whatever steps are necessary to secure yourselves from the threat of AIDS, anywhere from maintaining distance from the employee to firing him." The letters are then signed with only the name of the group and an insignia of a skull and crossbones inside an inverted triangle. At this point, attorneys have said that there is little that can be done for the harassment victims until the perpetrators are found.

More recently, *Fortune*[32] cited a case about a bisexual woman who wanted to place a personal ad in the *Pittsburgh Pennysaver,* it was to become the first test of a city ordinance barring discrimination based on sexual orientation. Melissa Smith, a freshman at the University of Pittsburgh, brought suit when the newspaper refused her ad stating that she was seeking a relationship with a man or a woman.

The Media for Personals

Traditionally printed in cheap tabloids or as the contents of a plain brown wrapper, the personals have come a long, long way.

As has been demonstrated here, more and more mainstream sources are including the personals, even upscale publications like *The Washington Post, Arizona Republic/Phoenix Gazette, New York* magazine, the *Chicago Tribune, Los Angeles Times, The New York Review of Books, National Review, USA Today,* even *The Law Journal* ("Personals for Professionals").[33] Clearly, personals are no longer simply the province of the raincoat trade.

Both stylistically and content-wise, there are wide variations, especially regarding censorship and taboos. Van Wallach (1985, p. 44) states: "Classified ads managers themselves are choosy. They rigorously oversee the propriety of the personal ads—if they run them at all. After all, nobody wants his paper to reflect a sleazy image." *Intro*, for example, demands that personals be in "good taste. Also anonymous." It refuses to run sexually explicit language or code words such as "dominant" or "submissive," won't accept ads from homosexuals or marrieds, and opens and screens all replies; the gist: reviving the art of the handwritten love letter. *The Village Voice* takes precautions to discourage "hookers" from advertising; yet, it has some fascinating "Pen Pals" solicitations from inmates—for instance Derrick at Attica, with 24 months before going home: "I'm a black male, muscle bound & bowlegged, looking for friendship," or the "28-year-old Rasta-Man presently incarcerated. Looking for a sincere woman for relationship. Race, Religion & Age unimportant." *The Springfield Advocate,* an alternative newspaper in my part of New England, refuses massage ads. You might be curious to see some of the personals it does accept:

- Cute and sexy SWF, 26, seeks long-haired rock and roller for spontaneous moments and wild times.
- GWF 20, looking for same up to 25 for first time encounters.
- RINGMASTER. Experienced, thorough, caring, excellent facilities. Strict leather training for frisky colts and fillies.
- HANDSOME male stripper seeks attractive female to have our secret desires fulfilled (No Intercourse).
- DWF, 45, statuesque, Hartford professional, smart, sassy, nonsmoker, loves to laugh. Seeks tall, D/SWM, 40-55, for possible relationship.
- Bi/dude, discreet fun. Satisfaction guaranteed! Macho Spanish and closet "men in uniform" welcome.
- HAPPILY MARRIED Asian man, mid-30s, clean, healthy, no children, willing to be secret surrogate father if you are a happily married WF, 30-40.
- RAPUNZEL SEEKS PRINCE: 34-year-old fiery redhead who's independent, great cook, solid virtues, likes outdoors, spicy food. Seeks secure, stable, and emotionally available S/D male (prefer Jewish) who believes life should be lived to the fullest.
- I saw you at Pride Day Parade. You spoke to me & commented on my bravery. I was wearing blue jeans & white T-shirt. Please call.

- STORM WARNING. Striking BiWF, beautifully built dancer w/intelligence, wit, and hurricane sensuality, seeks sensual, smart, androgynously handsome man for the affair of the century.

A number of adult products are also available via *The Springfield Advocate*; at Rena's Ultra Boutique, for example, you can get adult and domination videos, wrist restraints, old-fashioned Cuban heel stockings, latex rubber, leather, riding crops, inflatable butt plugs, anal beads, ball gags, dominant female collars, studded paddles, leather harnesses, ankle cuffs, adult baby items, blow-up dolls, and a HUGE selection of vibrators. Pale Godiva bills itself as the only firm in the area providing "slender, exceptionally pretty, well-spoken women with a regular income of over $2,000 weekly."

"Ask Isadora" is a syndicated column appearing in a number of newspapers carrying the more liberal personal ads. Isadora Alman, we are told, is a Diplomat of The American Board of Sexology, a licensed relationships counselor practicing in San Francisco, who answers questions concerning douche possibilities, what kind of vegetables are best to masturbate with, "jack-off parties," and the like. She also offers a number of audio tapes on sex and social skills.

Stewart MacLeod (1989, p. 64) has determined that Ottawa has the highest per capita ratio of personal ads, claiming it as the Lonely Hearts capital of the world: "This metropolitan area of 700,000 or so not only has three daily newspapers with let's-get-together ads, it also has a full-blown magazine with 14 pages of absolutely nothing but." Peter J. Ognibene (1984, p. 70) is fascinated with the "Love Letters" section the *Washington Post* runs every Valentine's Day, as is Dorothy H. Roberts (1986); she comments: "The *London Times* published 3,500 of them, *The New York Post* over 1,000, the *Charlotte Observer,* 500. From the small town of Gastonia, North Carolina to Charlotte to Houston to Atlanta to New York to London, England, Valentine's Day messages appear every February 14, their numbers increasing every year" (p. 1). Here are some "Love Lines" featured in the Panama City, FL *News Herald*: "BOO-BOO You are a very special Valentine today, because you are my best friend. Love, Louise"; "xox Melissa xox Thoughts of you are on my mind. BE MINE. Loving you, Muhammad"; "MY CHOC-

OLATE CHIP, Gary. You are always on my mind, you will always be my Valentine. Love, M&M"; "Nurse Geisha, Happy Valentine's Day from the ex-paratrooper. Write me"; and "Chuck—You EXCITE me . . . DELIGHT me . . . IGNITE me! Always, Joann."

Whereas the film magazine *Premiere* features international liasons ("Japanese Women Seek Friendship," "Pen Pals Worldwide," "Young, Attractive Asians," "Scandinavia-Poland-USSR-Worldwide Link"), and *Movieline* offers "Traditional but sophisticated Philippine, Russian, Latin Ladies" or "Intellectual Worldwide Ladies", *Rolling Stone* emphasizes partying ("1/800/283-4FUN," "Fun Party," "Party Connection," "Nationwide Party"). *RS* also has a "Self-Help" section in its classified advertising, such as this one, reproduced in part: "ARE YOU LONELY, TIRED OF BEING BORED? There is a better life! No gimmicks, just self-improvement. Meet more people, do more things. Feel better altogether, it works!!! SASE and $12 gets improvement!!! Step-by- step tapes & guides." It also offers such fare as offical licensed merchandise, for example from "The Simpsons" or Ninja turtles, glow-in-the-dark boxer shorts, information on joining The Children of the Night, for "mature fans of the vampire genre," or new wave/punk tees.

While some classifieds are broken down by Men-Seeking-Women, Women-Seeking-Men, Men-Seeking-Men, Women-Seeking-Women sections, others prefer to begin with demographics ("DWF 30," "SWM, handsome"), while some tend toward openers like "New to area," "Hopeless romantic," "Active in the community," "Your Place, Not Mine," or "Walking in a Winter Wonderland."

The *Chicago Tribune* begins each personal ad with a come-on in caps. Females seeking males, for example, have included SEEKING MILITARY MAN (SBF, 22), BIG AND BEAUTIFUL (SWF, 35, 270 lbs), MINNESOTA FISHERMAN (DWF, 41), CRIMINALLY ACTIVE (DWF, 33, interest in law enforcement and criminal behavior), or DARK AND LOVELY (SBF, 21); males seeking females: ENJOY MY POOL (SWM, 37), VEGETARIAN MALE (34), WIDOWER SEEKS ROMANCE (WW, 52), MODEL EXOTIC DANCER (SWM, 23); "alternative lifestyles" ad possibilities are BI-CURIOUS BLACK MALE (27), RELEASED FROM HIBERNATION (BiBF), and FUN FUN FUN!!! (SBF).

Worcester Magazine GWM ads run an age gamut from "Young, hot 21-yr.-old, college student, very attractive, black hair, brown eyes, 5'8", 140 lbs, great body, love fast fancy cars, dining, movies & pop music, muscles a must!" to "63, 180, 6' brn/bl, poetic, sensitive. Love to cuddle & explore each other all ways. Looking for kindred spirit in need of intimate relation." One women-seeking-women request caught my eye: "WF, looking to meet a caring, feminine but butch Latin woman for intimate, emotional relationship. For friendship first but future possibilities." The *Telegram & Gazette*'s Dateline, whose directions demand that ads be in good taste, have included these: "FIREFIGHTER LOOKING for his last flame to spoil with TLC. Devotion, Pampering & Sharing. Non-smoker"; "DWF, 38, Everything you ever wanted in a lady, but were afraid to ask for, in one neat package. Looking for classy gentleman"; "YOUNG MALE would like to meet older bi-male between ages of 30-50s for friendship & more."

Although it would seem that people are the same the world over, their personals reveal otherwise. Datalink, which bills itself as "Britain's foremost and least expensive national computer dating agency," encourages potential members to fill out a free computer test, consisting, besides demographic information, of data on these items:

1. *Your Personality* (Are you: shy, nervous, affectionate, romantic, intellectual, tolerant, outgoing, self-confident, fun-loving, ambitious, creative, generous).
2. *Your Interests and Activities* (Tick if it pleases you, X if it is a dislike: pop music, pub evenings, dining out, travelling, theatre/cinema, walking/cycling, committee work, watching TV, classical music, dancing, collecting things, spectator sport, poetry/reading, gardening, conversation, museum visits).

The Gazette, Montreal includes under its "personals" column items such as solicitations from a parapsychologist, an immigration lawyer, and a healer, plus information about a weight loss program, a tracing/surveillance service, pregnancy planning, a plea from a "Father seeking birth daughter, born end of May or June, 1975," an anniversary wish, and other diverse items. Here are some "Lonely Hearts" from *In Dublin*: "Ordinary, average male, early 20s, seeks attractive, vivacious, intelligent, witty, wealthy female or failing that, ordinary, average female with a good heart"; "Single country-man, 51, own home, non drinker, enjoys simple things in life: Irish music, C&W, like to meet single lady, widow, 45-55, with view to sharing quiet home, looks not important"; "Wanted: crying, talk-ing, drinking, walking, living doll. I'm scouring the country."

Johannesburg, South Africa's *The Star,* which provides confiden-tial mail boxes for advertisers wanting to remain anonymous, has "The Meeting Place." Here are some examples:

- 5 ft 2, hazel eyes, blonde. I am 45, speak 3 languages, love watching TV, love going out, love going to the theatre, love movies, very updated on all and especially on American poli-tics. I would like to meet somebody with dark hair, tall, at least in the 6 ft category who also has got the same interests. I don't mind smoking it you don't mind the occasional drink.
- Gay graduate, attractive, divorced, young, still looking for that special guy who is decent, honest, sincere, well groomed. Someone romantic who likes sharing life's pleasantries and who is not the normal gay stereotype and into bars and clubs. Someone who knows what they want in life and where they are going and who is ready to settle into a special relationship with the right guy. Please, no effeminate guys, married guys or guys over 38.

The Daily News, from Durban, South Africa, offers a wide range of escort, "Playgirls," and massage services; its "personal" col-umns include astrological, funeral, religious, and income tax advice along with offerings for sex videos, "gay guying live," and offers for companionship. A similar setup is found in *The Natal Mercury,* with offers for cash loans and tanning tips juxtaposed next to "A beautiful angel" (Asian, Coloured, White), "an above average mas-sage to soothe the stress in your life," or the promise that "You'll leave smiling" at Penthouse Spa.

Personals in print publications choose to call themselves by many different names, as can be seen in Figure 10. *Titles of Person-als Columns,* p. 78.

FIGURE 10. Titles of Personals Columns

Astrological Matchmaking
Choice Connections
Christian Singles Outreach
Classic Romance
Classified Love Line
Common Interests
Companions
Datalink
Eligibles
Friends and More
In Search Of
"Ladies" & "Gentlemen"
Let's Be Friends
Living Single
Lunch Dates
Match Maker
Matchmaker, Matchmaker
The Meet Market
Meeting People
One-to-One
People Meeting People
Person-to-Person
Personals
Personal World
Relationships
Rich and Famous
Romance Connection
RSVP
Singles Dance Parties
Singles Scenes
Social Connection
Strictly Personal
Voice Link
Where Singles Meet
Women, Inc.

With the introduction of ever-more sophisticated communications technologies, self-advertisement has now also become a programming source for computers, telephones, and the like. This media will be discussed in Chapter 4.

In addition to other media-related outlets such as broadcasting, comic strips, editorials, press and public relations releases, sound recordings, and billboards, the personals have also been fodder for stand-up comedians, and, as will be discussed in Chapter 5, featured in a number of motion pictures.

The personals, it would appear, are at the same time media messages unto themselves and messages the media is giving us about how to use them.

NOTES

1. Reported in "The Romance of Romance," by Vicki Stifel, in *Worcester Magazine* (October 20, 1993), p. 16.

2. Tania Modelski, *Loving with a Vengeance: Mass-Produced Fantasies for Women* (Hamden, CT: Archon Books, 1982), p. 35.

3. John L'Heureux, "One Man's Sexual Nightmare," *The New York Times Book Review* (May 19, 1991), p. 7.

4. Eric Messinger, "Public Access for the Literate." *The New York Times* (November 17, 1993), p. V8. With my book *Community Television in the United States: A Sourcebook on Public, Educational, and Government Access* (Greenwood Press, 1994), I try to counter negative stereotypes about public access.

5. See my book *Chocolate Fads, Folklore & Fantasies: 1,000+ Chunks of Chocolate Information* (The Haworth Press, Inc., 1994) for lots of examples of kinky uses of chocolate.

6. *Out and About*, 542 Chapel Street, New Haven, CT 06511, Tel. 203/789-8518.

7. *Our World*, 1104 North Nova Road, Suite 251, Daytona Beach, FL 32117, Tel. 904/441-5367.

8. Thanks to Matt LeGrant, Co-Chair of the Bay Area Bisexual Network for encouraging this study to include the bisexual community.

9. Marina Warner, "High-Minded Pursuit of the Exotic: How National Geographic Fashioned the World." *The New York Times Book Review* (September 19, 1993), p. 13.

10. "Desperately seeking. . . " *Entertainment Weekly* (March 26, 1993), p. 9.

11. Illouz mainly focused on all of *Cosmopolitan* and *Woman* from January through June, 1988, as well as articles dealing with romantic relations in *Self, New Woman,* and *Harper's Bazaar.*

12. "Neighborhood Salon: Membership Notes," *Utne Reader* (July/August, 1993), p. 56.

13. Cited with permission from Ed Grossman, Publisher of *Singles Choice,* from the June, 1993 edition, p. 7. It is particularly interesting to note the emphasis on safety.

14. *Singles Connection* (February, 1992), p. 2.

15. "Postings," the *At the Gate* newsletter (July/August, 1993), courtesy of Alan Isaacs, Member Services.

16. Personal correspondence from Robert and Ruth Leach, August 13, 1993.

17. Single Booklovers excerpt list, citing *The Daily News* of January 30, 1992.

18. *Ibid.*, citing *The Wall Street Journal* of January 2, 1991.

19. Correspondence from Bobbi Keppel of the Unitarian Universalist Bisexual Network, July 31, 1993.

20. Correspondence from Laddie Hosler, Editor/Publisher of *The Wishing Well*, July 18, 1993.

21. Dedication to Will, Keith, and Alex in Paul Loukides and Linda K. Fuller (eds.), *Beyond the Stars III: The Material World in American Popular Film* (Bowling Green, OH: Popular Press, 1993), p. iii.

22. Judy Harkison, "'A chorus of groans,' notes Sherlock Holmes," *Smithsonian* (September, 1987), p. 196.

23. Michael Demarest, "Platform for singles," *Time*, vol. 118 (November 16, 1981), p. 103.

24. Van Wallach, "Monitoring the personal touch," *Advertising Age,* vol. 56 (July 25, 1985), p. 44.

25. Cynthia Ozick, "Puttermesser Paired," *The New Yorker* (October 8, 1990), p. 40.

26. "TLC for DWMs and SWFs: Classified love ads are a booming business," *Time* (January 10, 1983), p. 65.

27. Personal correspondence from Yvonne Egertson, ANPA Librarian, June 21, 1991.

28. Carla Marie Rupp, "Promoting personals," *Editor & Publisher* (March 24, 1984), p. 16.

29. Personal correspondence of Hugh Klein, July 17, 1992.

30. "Hot Neurosis: Date Checking," *Rolling Stone* (May 17, 1990), p. 120.

31. Mark Fitzgerald and Debra Gersh, "Misuse of Classifieds," *Editor and Publisher* (April 11,1987), p. 11+.

32. "Only in America," *Fortune* (April 8, 1991), p. 127.

33. See: David Margolick, "At the Bar," "For lawyers seeking another kind of partnership, a staid journal is loosening up with personal ads." *The New York Times* (September 29, 1989), B5.

Chapter 3

Media-Mediated Relationships in the Broadcast Media

Since I have become adept at choosing my experience from 93 channels of tele-sex, I know that I will never be able to have real sex again.

Don Webb, *Future Sex* magazine, 1993

According to media historian Erik Barnouw (1966, p. 7), the age of broadcasting began in 1876 with Alexander Graham Bell's demonstration of the telephone, stirring "astonishing visions of things to come." Yet, as Fred Friendly (1975, p. 15) has pointed out:

New technologies often bring changes unanticipated by their inventors. The day the first horseless carriage puttered down Main Street, no one had considered traffic lights, driver's licenses, the future of the downtown department stores, or the sexual impact of the back seat or the motel. The night KDKA sent a saxophone solo and the results of the Harding-Cox election through its listeners' crystal sets, no one anticipated the need for rules preventing a station in Pittsburgh from drowning out one in Detroit, or an incumbent politician from denying his opponent access to the air, or quiz programs from being rigged. In each such case the invention eventually became the mother of the necessity.

Today, it is amazing to consider the state of broadcasting, still going strong throughout its more than 50 years, in terms of its role for media-mediated relationships. While radio and television are the conduits that will be discussed here, they clearly take unusual forms. There are also numerous outlets; see Appendix 6: *Broadcasting Resources*. Of particular relevance is the notion of broadcasting's talk shows, which Wayne Munson (1993) calls a hybrid genre embracing news/talk "magazine," celebrity chats, sports talk, psychotalk, public affairs forums, talk/service programs, and call-in interview shows. He writes:

> Like the news, the talkshow has become an everyday political instrument as well as advice-giver, ersatz community entertainer, and promoter. Extending the talk-of-the-town tradition that goes back to P. T. Barnum's promotional "humbugs," it has become powerful enough to determine whether or not a newly published book becomes a best-seller. Its range of topics defies classification: from the sensational and bizarre (teenage lesbian daughters and their mothers; *Playboy*'s first transsexual centerfold) to the conventional and the advisory (natural childbirth; preventing the spread of AIDS) to politics and world affairs. (p. 3)

RADIO

Audiences for radio programming have been of critical interest to local and national industry officials, advertisers, and social scientists once it was recognized that real persons existed on the other side of the black box. Beginning with the benchmark Starch Report of 1928 on early radio, those early listenership studies were quasi-qualitative, predominantly based on radio/"crystal set" sales, audience mail and phone calls, responses to promotion, and fan letters. Not until 1941, with the Pulse Reports, did "demographics" become part of the pictures, and Nielsen's Audimeter of 1954 was a major breakthrough. The All Radio Methodology Study (ARMS) of 1965 became a landmark study; focusing on a single city (Philadelphia), spending the largest sum to that point on any audience measurement ($325,000), it represented "a step in the direction of looking for alternative ways of obtaining audience data from smaller, more controlled sample sizes" (Fuller, 1988).

Today, with radio research recognized as an extremely lucrative business, Arbitron, Birch Radio Marketing Research, and Nielsen dominate. And, as television continues to become ever more pervasive and predominant in our culture, radio remains more independent and mobile, more individual (Fuller, 1992a), and more "narrowcasting" in nature—as well as ever more profitable for people involved in the industry. Since FCC's suspension of the Fairness Doctrine in 1987 and the concomitant effects of deregulation, as well as escalating competition for ratings, motivations for challenging public affairs programming have taken some unusual twists. Of particular relevance to this study is the growth of talk radio, best exemplified on a continuum from the conservative Rush Limbaugh to the outrageous Howard Stern, with any number of other personalities in between.

Talk Radio

"Talk" can take many forms, as can "news." As the second-most popular radio format in the Top 75 broadcast markets in the USA, stations might air educational programming, use an agricultural format, have all-news, Black talk, call-ins, shortwave rebroadcasts, all-sports, traffic, weather, participation formats like flea markets and swap shops, and/or a combination of these and many other content types (Marr, 1989). Occurring predominantly on commercial AM radio stations, information formats run the gamut from serious, informed sociopolitical commentary to shock radio.

A longtime media staple, recently receiving renewed attention for its unprecedented growth in popularity,[1] which is why it is being considered here, many people consider talk radio as increasingly influencial to private perceptions and public debates. Labelled "the working people's medium" by consumer activist Ralph Nader,[2] or the "counter-elite media" by political pundits (Smillie, 1992), researchers are beginning to question the role of talk show hosts in influencing opinions. "There exists between the talk show host and his or her audience a relationship which almost defies definition," says Phillip E. Rasak (1993), host on KTBB of Tyler, TX. "The bottom line is this: It really doesn't matter if they agree or disagree. What matters is they listen. They listen to you, and of equal or greater importance, they listen to your sponsors!"

One of the first boosts to wondering about the political clout of talk show hosts can be traced to the 1989 "teabag revolution" incident: members of the National Taxpayers Union (NTU), led by Nader, went on Jerry Williams' WRKO-AM in Boston, MA to urge listeners, opposed to the hefty 51 percent pay increase Congress was proposing itself, to send tea bags (commemorating the 215th anniversary of the Boston Tea Party) to Washington with names, addresses, and protest statements; beyond that, a network of other talk show hosts across the country joined the popular cause. When more than 45,000 tea bags arrived, Congress held off on its raise, if momentarily. Sensing its potential clout from this campaign, the National Association of Radio Talk Show Hosts (NARTSH) was formed as a non-profit organization in 1989 in Boston. Representing more than 2,900 groups, 150 stations, and groups nationally as well as internationally, its stated purpose is to:

1. promote and encourage the exchange of ideas, information, and experiences among people in the field of talk broadcasting;
2. encourage the expansion of activities and improvement of performance and effectiveness in local broadcasting;
3. encourage and assist qualified and dedicated people to enter broadcasting, through work with colleges, universities, and other avenues; and
4. promote the growth of talk radio.[3]

News/talk listenership reached its highest levels yet during the 1991 Persian Gulf War, and although the audience declined slightly afterward, the format was still attracting about 15 percent of all listening time. Then, when Bill Clinton was pushing his administration's health care proposal, he conducted the first-ever briefing by the White House for hosts of the country's radio call-in shows; recognized as the "new" news media, some 200 talk show personalities participated in the media blitz. The New York Times (Kolbert, 1993), citing McLuhan's label of radio as a "hot medium" and the fact that a recent Times-Mirror Center for the People and the Press poll found 42 percent of adults listen to talk radio at least occasionally, 17 percent regularly, reported:

That the medium can also be a powerful—though often unpredictable—political force is something that few in Washington question these days. The consensus is that talk shows, either by galvanizing or simply giving vent to public frustrations, have helped doom several pieces of legislation, including the Congressional pay raise of 1989. More recently, they helped kill Zoe Baird's nomination as Attorney General and convinced many lawmakers to line up against the President's proposal to allow homosexuals in the military.

Considered the "Dean of Talk Show Hosts," Larry King changed the national scene with his midnight-to-dawn *Larry King Show* that was first aired by the 28-station Mutual Broadcasting System network in January, 1978. Recasting forever the state of call-in programs, it was so popular that by 1987 some 310 affiliates were clearing the show—a predecessor of CNN's *Larry King Live*. NBC launched *Talknet*, with hosts such as Bruce Williams, in November, 1981, delivering continuous nighttime programming from 10 p.m. to 3 a.m.; meanwhile, ABC decided to deliver 18 hours of daily talk as of 1982 on its Talkradio network, hosted by the likes of Tom Snyder and Deborah Norville.

Primed to be the next Dr. Ruth Westheimer, the radio and television sex therapist who Buxton (1991, p. 142) calls "a cultural icon," "Dr. Judy" Kuriansky co-hosts Z-100's (New York's WHTZ-AM) *Lovephones*. She is a professional clinical psychologist and visiting professor at New York University with quite a large audience anxious for her advice and counsel. The no-holds-barred program, airing Monday through Thursday from 10 p.m. to midnight, fields a range of questions. "A lot of people call me about things that they see other people doing," she reports. "A guy called in who had walked in on his mother having sex with her best friend. I always encourage them to confront the personal about what they saw."[4]

Trial Talk, a collaboration between Court TV and radio station WABC of New York, debuted in July 1993 with Jay Diamond as host. A prototype for a possible regular syndicated national series, the hour-long live program featured audio highlights of key trial testimony, interviews, and guest commentary along with call-ins from listeners.

Dick Syatt's *Hotline Radio Dating Show*, which he created in 1976, has recently gone national. Originally aired Saturdays between 10 a.m. and 2 p.m. out of Boston's WRKO, callers describe themselves and their dream dates, with the switchboard fielding requests by giving out first names and telephone numbers. While Syatt claims to have launched somewhere in the range of 1,000 marriages, there has been, as Cobb (1990, p. 2) reviews them, the occasional "oddball caller": "Like the woman who wanted to date someone who was legally blind. Or the man who insisted that he would go out only with women named Debbie. Or the guy who called himself Ugly Eddie. Why Ugly Eddie? 'Because I'm homely,' he answered. 'I'm really, *really* homely.'"

Syatt also hosts singles' dances almost nightly, charging between $3 and $7 admission. Many different types show up:

> Dancers come merely to dance, moving from partner to partner as the music shifts gears. Hitters make a connection, enter into a brief relationship, disappear for a few weeks, and return. Cruisers, who are mostly men, seldom make contact at all, preferring instead to roam the room with their hands plunged deeply into their pockets, as if they were touring a high school dance. Nesters, who are mostly women, hover together for protection, occasionally leaving the flock to dance but always returning quickly. Seekers doggedly pursue the kind of long-term walks-on-the-beach relationship that they still believe is right around the corner. Desperados want badly to hook up with someone, for the night or for the weekend, and will stay until the last Donna Summer song in order to do it. Barflies come primarily to drink, blankly watching the action around them as if it were taking place on an oversized screen. (p. 3)

In addition to the dance event, "mixmeister" Syatt also oversees any number of others, such as those for Jewish singles, over-50 singles, bowling singles, various park events, and many more. And so it was big news when his *Hotline Radio Dating Show* went national (see Figure 11, p. 87), running Sunday mornings from 10 a.m. until noon on the Talk America Radio Network. To account for geographics, it runs in regionalized fashion, and has been featured on a number of media, from television shows (e.g., *Donahue, Good Morning America, Real People*) to *Playboy* to *The New York Times*.

Who is the target market for all this talk show programming? *Broadcasting* counters the general impression, declaring that, "The

FIGURE 11

RADIO DATING SHOW

Singles Promotions & Events

Did You Know . . .

- More than 40% of the adult population in the United States is made up of single people.
- Nearly 50% of all households are headed by a single parent.

DICK SYATT CREATED THE HOTLINE RADIO DATING SHOW IN 1976 BASED ON NEEDS AS OLD AS THE HUMAN RACE.

Hotline is for singles of all ages who wish to meet other eligible people. Listeners call in to describe themselves and the type of person they'd like to meet; or to just listen for people that interest them.

- Hotline is not just for singles. Couples listen too because it's entertaining.
- Listeners will meet other singles from the area via your station.
- Dick Syatt's Hotline is available as a weekly 2-hour program live from the Talk America Radio Network or hosted exclusively on your station.

Dick Syatt's Hotline has been featured on:

Donahue, Good Morning America, To Tell the Truth, Real People, Evening Magazine; and in The New York Times, Playboy Magazine, Boston Globe, McCall's Magazine and More.

Dick Syatt has been a professional broadcaster since 1968. Dick has been a talk show host in Miami, Dallas, St. Louis, Providence & Boston (WRKO 1981-1993). Dick lives in Sudbury, Massachusetts with his wife, Andrea and two sons, Lee and Jordan. (Other than a noticeable bald spot, everything else is in great shape).

Post Office Box 302
Sudbury, Massachusetts 01776
(508) 443-0733 ● Fax (508) 443-9578

talk radio listener is not 75 to dead with green hair and a dialysis machine hooked to his kidneys"[5]; Morris (1991, p. 53) claims they are not "mainly kooks, the disenfranchised, the unemployed"; and Roberts (1991, p. 59) describes the talk radio listener as "slightly older—in the 30-to-55-year-old range . . . mid-to-upper-income, and issue-oriented. While Joe Sixpack is still very much a presence of talk's airwaves, anecdotal evidence suggests that many calls now come from corporate executives and others, often using cellular phones in their cars." Yet, "The typical *caller* does not represent the typical *listener* to talk radio except that both tend to be older," Eastman, Head, and Klein (1989, p. 451) remind us:

> Some studies show that callers tend to fall in the lower income groups and be lonelier than radio listeners in general, some forming an unnatural bond with the station and a personality. However, callers represent a very, very small fraction of the audience, and they differ from one another depending on the nature of the program; most important, they are very different from listeners to the same programs. Unlike *callers,* talk *listeners* have higher than average spendable income and saving account balances; they take more than the average number of trips by air, buy more luxury cars and so on. *Callers* do not reveal an accurate profile of listeners, but frequently, station personnel become so focused on calls that they forget about the audience—which should be their prime concern. Switching the emphasis to the listening audience usually makes ratings go up.

While earlier studies of talk radio listeners seem irrelevant due to its more recent exponential popularity (Zoglin, 1989, 1992), it is helpful to review the Avery and Ellis (1979) notion that there are three stages of involvement with talk radio: first, *aroused curiosity,* wherein a listener is introduced to the medium; second, *passive involvement,* when the listener becomes "hooked" on talk radio; and finally, *active participation,* when the listener becomes motivated enough to call the talk show host. Despite the common wisdom that callers constitute only about five percent of the listening audience (Roberts, 1991, p. 59), Armstrong and Rubin (1989, p. 91) found the callers had more affinity with the medium, listening more than noncallers; although they tended to find face-to-face communication less rewarding, and were less mobile, callers' involvement might be affective (through personalities or hosts and other callers), cognitive (through issues and information discussed), and behavioral (by calling the show).

Using a cluster analysis of seven motives for listening to talk radio—relaxation, exciting entertainment, convenience, voyeurism/escape, information utility, pass time/habit, and companionship—and noting that, "Talk radio provides a nonthreatening forum for interaction," Avery and Ellis see talk radio as one of few media that allows spontaneous interaction (p. 92). "As with the telephone, which offers psychological security and anonymity, talk radio's lack of visual contact may contribute to a caller's relaxation and satisfaction. Callers not only listen in on the conversation but also become participants in a mediated, interpersonal encounter, which is freer from threat and embarrassment than face-to-face interaction."

While persons unwilling to communicate might too quickly be written off merely as shy (Buss, 1984), talk show callers to radio psychologist programs have a profile showing them to score lower on measures of psychological health;[6] yet, Levy (1989), who also studied that format, found them to be relatively benign at their worst. From a telephone survey of 354 randomly selected households in Maryland two months after the congressional pay raise issue and during a controversial local bill regarding smokers' being protected from discrimination by their employers, Zerbinos (1993, p. 9) found nearly half of those surveyed listening to radio during morning and/or evening commuting time, only 5 percent to the local all-talk station although some 40 percent of the respondents reported listening to radio talk shows—mainly, "to know why others think as they do," "to be entertained," or "to help obtain useful information about daily life." There were other conclusions:

> The results showed that talk radio listeners were slightly more likely than nonlisteners to have voted; to talk with others about topics in the news; to be aware of the pay raise proposal, the tea bag campaign and the smokers' rights bill; and to be members of a community or neighborhood association. . . . Being issue oriented seems to be a characteristic of the talk radio audience. (p. 13)

While not much of the literature concerns itself with talk radio around the world, three case studies are worth incorporating here. In the early 1970s, Crothers studied "talk-back" radio shows in New Zealand, concluding that they appeared to "exert obvious power only on fairly specific issues which can be anchored in widely held sentiments. The host himself must play an active part in mobilising the opinion, and his campaign must be supported by a substantial majority of his callers, and followed up by citizen action such as letter writing." That critical role played by the host personality was confirmed in Fuller's (1986a) study of Dutch shortwave broadcasting on Radio Nederland, the second-most-listened to Country's offering (after the BBC), whose originator/"compere" of more than four decades was credited with the large audience draw. Jamaican call-in radio was Surlin and Soderlund's (1993) focus, when they studied 132 phone calls made to both the government owned-and-operated radio channel and the privately owned one; here are their overall findings:

1. There are an equal number of male and female callers.
2. Callers are equally likely to speak patois as standard English.
3. There are more middle-age callers than young callers, while older callers are the smallest group (24 percent)—"age" being determined by paralinguistic nonverbal cues.
4. Callers more often offered opinion than information, and were least likely to ask questions (22 percent).
5. One third of all calls dealt with religion/values issues, followed in frequency by issues relating to the Jamaican infrastructure, economics, personal problems, and politics.
6. The average time for all calls is six minutes; about 75 percent of all calls are eight minutes or less, and a little more than one third of all calls are three minutes or less.
7. About seven of every ten calls discuss an original topic and three out of ten rediscuss a previously mentioned topic.
8. Hosts are most apt to discuss the pro and con of a call, about one third of the time the host offers advice or information, and just restating a caller's statement is the least likely host response (22 percent).

9. Hosts are predominantly neutral in response to callers, followed by being supportive, and very rarely displaying outright disagreement.
10. Almost all calls dealt with Jamaican issues (98 percent).

The November 1, 1993 front cover of *Time* carried cartoon images of Rush Limbaugh appropriately on the right, Howard Stern on the left, both screaming into a mutual microphone, the caption above reading "Voice of America?" Quoting Limbaugh's "If the spotted owl can't adjust . . . then screw it" along with Stern's "They didn't beat this idiot [Rodney King] enough," Kurt Andersen writes: "America can pretty much be divided in two: on one side are Rush's people and Howard's people, and on the other the decorous and civilized who tend to be uncomfortable with strong broadcast opinion unless it comes from Bill Moyers, Bill Buckley or, if pressed, Andy Rooney" (1993, p. 61).

Rush Limbaugh

Conservative, controversial Rush Limbaugh, known for equating gayness with persons who are child molesters and necrophiliacs and for telling his audience that he is "the most dangerous man in America," topped the radio talk show ratings by 1992. His radio show can be heard in some 537 markets across the country, boasting 20 million listeners; further, his syndicated television program is available to 200 stations, accounting for 98 percent of the country and drawing a bigger audience than Conan O'Brien or Arsenio Hall. Some 370,000 people subscribe to his 12-page monthly newsletter. And, with the success of his 1992 *The Way Things Ought to Be,* Limbaugh's second book, *See, I Told You So* (Pocket Books, 1993), had a first printing of two million, the largest in American history.

Because of Limbaugh, the (re)issue of the Fairness Doctrine has surfaced with renewed vigor. When it went into effect in 1927, the government saw the doctrine as a policing mechanism necessary for regulating the limited access of the radio; specifically, it placed an obligation on the broadcaster "to operate in the public interest and to afford reasonable opportunity for the discussion of conflicting views on issues of public importance." United States Representative Edward Markey (D) of Massachusetts, a sponsor of the House bill to reintroduce the doctrine, has defended it by saying the Fairness Doctrine "does not allow the government to sit in judgment of the broadcaster's editorial judgment. It makes no requirement upon matters that are private or personal in nature, such as religious or moral views. This is not an onerous burden" (Diamond, 1993). For the most part, talk-show hosts have taken the side of the opponents against the 1993 Fairness in Broadcasting Act. Contending they have public support, they join a number of Washington lobbyists such as David Bartlett, president of the Radio-Television News Directors Association (RTNDA), who fear the ridiculous high costs of complaints and contend that, "The public doesn't want Jesse Helms or Ted Kennedy telling them what they should listen to" (Diamond, 1993).

Limbaugh's major diatribe is against what he calls the Culture War; relentlessly, he assaults the "fuzzy-headed academicians, the sandal-clad theoreticians and the nearsighted pointy-heads," aimed primarily, for the moment, at members of the Clinton administration. Democrats, which he calls "the party that can't wait to fund every abortion in the world," are lambasted along with "feminazis" and environmental "wackos," to name a few targets.

Because he has received so much media attention, it is probably only appropriate to also mention Ken Hamblin, the right-wing talk radio personality of KNUS in Denver who has been called the "black Rush Limbaugh." Writes *The New York Times* (Johnson, 1994): "On his radio show and in his columns, he regularly blasts the welfare system, multicultural education, affirmative action and especially what he calls the 'blame whitey' syndrome."

Howard Stern

The epitome of "shock jocks," "gross-out," and/or "sleaze king," Stern has been called "the most brilliant—and misunderstood—comic artist in America" (Gleiberman, 1993, p. 66):

> He is also the Lenny Bruce of the information age: a kamikaze hipster with a machine-gun brain, a slash-and-burn rock & roll nihilist who, in his hostility and wit, his dazzlingly intuitive observational powers, his savage compulsion to smash every taboo that middle-class society places in his path, is probably

the only professional entertainer in the country who answers to no one but himself. On the air, Stern creates a kind of manic free-associational theater, chain-sawing through the pretensions of celebrities and politicians, of conformists and 'rebels,' and of the entertainment-media culture that binds them all together. What his fans cherish is his blessedly untamed hilarity, the rollicking freedom of his voice.

His listening audience ranges anywhere from Arbitron's estimate of 4 million to the host's of 16 million; but no matter how you look at it, his is still the top-rated show in New York City, Philadelphia, Los Angeles, and Boston. Including something to upset just about every member of the population, his weekday four-hour, in-your-face show features everything from song parodies and scatological sketches (such as "Gay Dial-a-Date") to real and send-up ("self-indulgent, narcissistic, self-important") celebrity interviews to sexual fantasies (e.g., "Lesbianism, let's face it, is a godsend") to satirical news commentary.

Stern's 446-page autobiographical book, *Private Parts* (Simon & Schuster, 1993), vying for top place on the best-seller list with Limbaugh's, is the fastest-selling book in the history of Barnes & Noble; the first week alone, it sold more than a million copies, and some 10,000 people lined up outside the publisher's to get their author-autographed books. Walter Goodman, television critic for *The New York Times,* discusses some of the book's content: "Mr. Stern is heavily devoted to breasts (36D and vicinity), behinds (including his own) and penises (he makes no great claims in that neighborhood), and is drawn to discussions of masturbation, defecation and the expulsion of intestinal gas. His language is more pungent than most newspaper style manuals encourage, which doubtless accounts for some of his appeal."[7] Not to be outdone by Limbaugh, Howard also appears regularly on television—on a one-on-one interview program that runs on the E! cable channel.

Stern has had several run-ins with the FCC—notably over two Christmas programs: in 1988 he featured a "gay choir" singing "I'm dreaming of some light torture," and in 1991, on his short-lived television show, he was included in a sketch giving birth in a manger. His federal fines for "indecency," totaling hundreds of thousands of dollars, to date have all been appealed on First Amendment grounds. Asked why he thinks he has been targeted by the FCC, his response was: "The FCC has decided that what I do is disgusting and horrible for the morality of this country, which I don't agree with. I firmly believe that nothing is offensive. God knows why we're so repressed about sex in this country that if you hear the word *penis* or *vagina* you will somehow grow up to be a bad person."[8]

Some social commentators see the Stern popularity as a symptomatic backlash against political correctness; as Goodman (1993) has pointed out, "He owes a lot to feminists and mainstream multiculturalists, who serve as plump objects for spanking." Imagine that some 260,000 people dialed the 800/52-STERN number, paying $39.45 for his "Butt Bongo Fiesta" videotape, which brought the Stern dynasty more than $10 million. Or, how about 1993's conclusion with "The Miss Howard Stern New Year's Eve Pageant," which was ordered as a pay-per-view program by some 150,000 households nationwide for $39.95. Quite a comment about our times.

The Media of Talk Radio

Talkers: The Newspaper of Talk Media, a monthly based out of Longmeadow, MA, is the only trade publication of talk radio and television. Editor/publisher Michael Harrison[9], the person who coined the term "album-oriented rock" in the late 1960s, was a prime morning DJ on New York's WNEW-FM, then hosted "Harrison's Mike" for a decade, one of the longest running talk shows in the Los Angeles area. Today, he hosts the nationally syndicated *Talk Radio Countdown Show,* a weekly survey of the Top 10 talk radio topics[10] (Martin, 1993). In his "meta-talk-radio role," for which he has been called "the Casey Kasem of talk radio," Harrison not only discusses what is hot where and with whom, but also writes an invaluable editorial column in each issue of *Talkers.* Sample programming for radio station WNNZ/AM-640, his current location, is included in Figure 12. *WNNZ: The Talk Station/AM 640,* p. 96.

The second edition of *Talk Shows & Hosts on Radio,* listing 1,052 shows and their hosts, as well as data on stations by city/state, network/syndicates, and topic/subjects, is available through Whiteford Press. The first annual *Talk Media Directory*, a reference resource detailing talk show hosts, talk radio stations, networks, syndicators, program directors, producers, general managers, a special television section, as well as a listing of publishers, production companies, guests, publicists, organizations, and businesses, was published for the first time in 1994.

TELEVISION

Just as the greatest value of radio is its food for the imagination, television continues to try and exploit us with both titillations and innuendos. While mainstream networks ply us with carefully screened pap, and various cable connections continue to test the limits of the First Amendment (e.g., Showtime's soft-core *Red Shoe Diaries*), as a nation we cannot let go of our romance with the small screen. Witness, for example, the country's fascination with court TV in general, or, as a supplement, CNN's coverage of the O. J. Simpson trial. It still feeds our imagination, long recognized as the human body's single most important sexual organ.

Declaring that the new sexual revolution is mainly about celebrating difference, Walsh (1993, pp. 64-5) draws on one of television's most popular programs:

> For me, the sexiest scenario imaginable is Jerry's apartment on *Seinfeld*—a co-op where neighbors drop by spontaneously, flirt with each other, borrow money and clothes and just . . . hang. It's what everyone is ultimately searching for: human contact and a few laughs. In the fast-paced, fragmented '90s, where neighborhoods and families have become ancient history and/or idealized myth, people have an innate need to connect with each other. And the surest, quickest way to feel good about yourself and your species is by having sex. Real or unreal. Slow or fast, careful or careless.

When the popular television series *thirtysomething* had an episode featuring a brief scene with two gay men talking in bed, anti-gay groups launched a massive boycott of the show's sponsors, costing ABC $1.5 million in lost advertising. It is the rare program,

FIGURE 12. WNNZ:[1] The Talk Station/AM 640

MONDAY-FRIDAY

5:00 am-5:30 am	Jim Bohannon "America in the Morning"
5:30 am-8:00 am	Curt Hahn
8:00 am-9:00 am	"Conversations with Cele"
9:00 am-11:00 am	Dr. Joy Browne
11:00 am-2:00 pm	G. Gordon Liddy
2:00 pm-6:00 pm	Michael Harrison
6:00 pm-8:00 pm	Gene Burns
7-8 pm Monday	Ben Dodge "Race Week"
8:00 pm-9:00 pm	Gil Gross
9:00 pm-11:00 pm	Michael Reagan
11:00 pm-1:00 am	Dr. Joy Browne
1:00 am-3:00 am	Charles Adler
3:00 am-4:00 am	Dr. Paul Schadler
4:00 am-5:00 am	Art Bell

SATURDAY

5:00 am-6:00 am	Art Bell
6:00 am-8:00 am	Michael Harrison's "Talk Radio Countdown"
8:00 am-10:00 am	Tom Goodwin "The 640 Tag Sale"
10:00 am-12:00 pm	Nancy Wojcicki "Nancy's Garden"
12:00 pm-2:00 pm	Melinda Lee "Food For Thought"
2:00 pm-3:00 pm	Dr. David Koffman "Let's Talk Health"
3:00 pm-4:00 pm	Dr. Brian Corwin "Pet Talk"
4:00 pm-5:00 pm	Kent Servis "Outdoors"
5:00 pm-7:00 pm	Steve Crowley "American Scene"
7:00 pm-10:00 pm	Major League Baseball—Game of the Week
10:00 pm-1:00 am	Bob Brinker "Financial Talk"
1:00 am-3:00 am	Melinda Lee "Food for Thought" Encore
3:00 am-5:00 am	Steve Crowley "American Scene" Encore

SUNDAY

5:00 am-6:00 am	Art Bell
6:00 am-9:00 am	Talking Religion with Bill Wildey
9:00 am-10:00 am	Atty. Bill St. James "Call Your Lawyer"
10:00 am-12:00 pm	Gary Thomas "Smart Money"
12:00 pm-1:00 pm	Kathy Duffy "Herbs for Health & Healing"
1:00 pm-3:00 pm	John Dvorak/Leo LaPorte "Dvorok on Compu
3:00 pm-4:00 pm	Mike DeSisto "School Daze"
4:00 pm-6:00 pm	Bob Brinker
6:00 pm-9:00 pm	Barbara Heisler
9:00 pm-10:00 pm	Bruce Dumont "Inside Politics"
10:00 pm-12:00 am	Charles DeRose "The Financial Advisor"
12:00 am-2:00 am	Tom Brown "Nutritional Science Forum"
2:00 am-3:00 am	Talkin' Pets
3:00 am-5:00 am	Michael Harrison's "Talk Radio Countdown"

ROGER LAPLANTE RADAR WEATHER/CBS AND LOCAL NEWS WITH JOHN BAIBAK

[1]Printed with permission from Michael Harrison, WNNZ star personality.

in fact, that incorporates lesbians and gays as "regular" cast characters (Kielwasser and Wolf, 1992). Yet, when Billy Crystal played the role of gay Jodie Dallas on the comedy *Soap* (1977-1981), many viewers were impressed with his decision to not play him as a "limp-wristed, campy kind of guy."

"With few exceptions, American network television has enjoyed a proud 20-year history of dealing 'frankly' with homosexuality without ever depicting its simplest manifestation," wrote *Tales of the City* author Armistead Maupin (1994) about the intolerance for affectionate displays. Tracing the model to the 1972 ABC movie *That Certain Summer*, in which Hal Holbrook and Martin Sheen played lovers who were only permitted a simple squeeze on the shoulder, he claims that the "no-kissing rule" has endured. For women, it seems, there has been a bit of bending—e.g., Amanda Donohoe and Michele Green's same-sex kiss on *L. A. Law*, Holly Marie Combs and Alexondra Lee's on *Picket Fences*, and Roseanne Barr and Mariel Heminway's on *Roseanne*. But think back to 1985's *An Early Frost*, or HBO's rendition of *And the Band Played On*, even the controversial *thirtysomething* episode that had two men in bed, and one would have to agree with him. Countering this blatant homophobia, the organization In the Life has organized to end that stereotypic censorship. Part of the Media Network in New York, it offers a magazine pointing out "movers, shakes and role models" who can help in their efforts, as well as producing its own programming, such as the powerful *Stonewall 25*.

"Television speaks, but it speaks anonymously and indiscriminately," Roger Silverstone (1981, p. 7) reminds us. "Its messages are well defined but abbreviated and ephemeral." Much of television is myth (Marsden, 1980; Breen and Corcoran, 1982; Masterman, 1984; Wober and Gunter, 1988). Much is also ritual; according to cultivation theory, television viewing is largely nonselective by audiences, controlled by the clock rather than by the program. It becomes a regular ritual. Meanwhile, note, other activities are pre-empted—especially activities with other people. While not fully explaining "reality shifts" of heavy television viewers, at least this helps account for how and why some people are influenced by the images they see on the set. Hal Himmelstein's (1984, p. 2) conception is relevant here:

To understand the myth life of our television culture, we must first consider the construction of the television message and the social, political, and economic nature of the processes of construction as they are reflected in the powerful visual and verbal symbols produced and perpetuated by the 'diversified entertainment companies' of advanced capitalism—financial institutions masquerading as culture producers. We must then consider the status of the message receiver—the well-trained viewer—in this process.

Talk Television

The rise of interest in broadcast talk is certainly not limited to radio. A programming component dating to the 1950s, when the radical move was made to extend network television beyond merely Prime Time, it was begun cautiously but greeted enthusiastically. Robert Metz (1977, p. 33), a chronicler of NBC's pioneering early-morning *Today* show, which premiered in 1952, recalls the scenario: "Morning television was available here and there, but watching it was a taboo . . . . It was acceptable to listen to morning radio, but like sex and alcohol, television was deemed proper only after sundown." Still a ratings leader, *Today* ranks with CBS' Sunday evening newsmagazine *60 Minutes,* dating to 1968, for audience loyalty. Numerous imitators of both programs abound, more joining all the time. "Audiences seem to like the combination of chat, comedy, and soul-searching, along with the exploration of relationships and human aberrations, which the talk-show hosts dish up and against which the viewer can measure his or her reaction," notes Hift (1993). "Equally important, in TV terms: Talk is cheap. It's a lot less costly to invite an audience and have a host interview celebrities than to bankroll a sitcom or a drama series. Broadcasters, with an eye to maximizing profits, thrive on that satisfying equation—low-cost programming with obvious audience appeal."

In 1992 Elayne Rapping, crediting the feminist credo that "the personal is political" with helping to fuel interest in television talk shows, cited some currently available fare:

- On *Oprah* today: Women who sleep with their sister's husbands!
- Donahue talks to women married to bisexuals!

- Today—Sally Jessy Raphael talks with black women who have bleached their hair blond! (p. 36)

Since this fairly recent quotation, think of the many other copy-cat talk show hosts who are also appearing on the big screen: Regis and Kathie Lee, Montel Williams, Maury Povich, Geraldo, Joan Rivers, Bertice Berry, Arsenio Hall, Les Brown, Ricki Lake, Jenny Jones as well as the many various "news" interviewers, evening and late night show hosts, sports reporters, comedians, musical monitors, MTV-type youths who speak both with and for their generation, televangelists, and of course all the personnel on the 24-hour CNN, especially Larry King. While Whoopi Goldberg, Chevy Chase, and Vicki Lawrence have already had their brief forays into the genre cancelled, by the time this book goes to press they might be joined by other newcomers, such as Bob Costas, Charlie Rose, Chris Evert, Dennis Miller, Christina, Jenny Jones, Jane Whitney, and many more wannabes. As audience(s), it would appear that we can't get enough of this stuff.

"The insidious thing about television's invasion of the home," contend Goldberg and Phillips (1990, p. 58), "is not the message of its programs, but the audience that is watching." While Phil Donahue was unquestionably the first television talk host to bring credibility and audiences to the genre, today he has slipped in the ratings, and at this writing, Ricki Lake has even passed Oprah Winfrey with a younger population. A construction of intimacy with her audience analyzed by Haag (1993, p. 119) shows how Oprah uses nonverbal aspects as signifier; in the show's opening, for example, "she is shown touching audience member after audience member, grabbing their arms as they ask questions, even resting her chin on one woman's shoulder, virtually cuddling them." That nonverbal intimacy continues: "While she enters the personal, intimate space of her guests and audience, she also makes meaningful, sustained eye contact with them, giving them the sense that she really is interested in what they have to say. And she reacts, no holds barred, laughing, screaming, even crying, at the appropriate times, and allows us to do the same." One of Oprah's shows featured "Women Who Found Their Mates on Billboards." Bringing new meaning to the idea that when you find Mr. or Ms. Right there will be a sign, the program included a Houston woman who responded to an expressway billboard featuring "4 Middle Class White Males, 32-39, Seek Wives"—one of almost 800 respondents to the appeal. For another show, she recreated the *Sleepless in Seattle* scenario, allowing widowers to write about themselves and their searches for another wife—soliciting some 40,000 letters from viewing romantics.

Talk television really got a shot in the arm during the 1992 presidential election, as many media watchers considered Bill Clinton to have extreme broadcasting-savvy. Not only did he appear on both *Arsenio Hall* and MTV, he called for a debate between himself and George Bush (who, in a desperate, last-minute move agreed to be interviewed on Rush Limbaugh's radio show) that would consist of phone-in questions from the electorate. Once elected, Clinton has cannily used C-SPAN and radio, plus an 800 number so that callers would not be discriminated against in terms of payment.

The first academic study of talk shows from the perspective of their participants, *Public Intimacies: Talk Show Participants and Tell All TV* by Patricia J. Priest (Hampton Press, 1995) provides empirical evidence supporting claims that televisual reality represents a valued reality. Labelling the contestants a bunch of outcasts ("evangelicals, moths, plaintiffs, and marketers"), she points out talk television's role in the lives of marginalized grounds wanting to counter cultural stereotypes.

Should you not be able to keep up with all the many talk television offerings available each day, your alternative might be to tune into *Talk Soup*, a half-hour daily distillation on the E! network airing at 6 p.m., 9 p.m., and 11 p.m. Conceived as a modest source of low-cost programming, the show, hosted by Greg Kinnear, tends to feature a roundup of some pretty bizarre segments from 20 or so talk shows.

Soap Operas

Since their debut on radio in 1926[11] as a major dramatic programming fare geared toward women, "the soaps" have remained a strong broadcasting staple up to this day.[12] Many of the primary motivations for listening in those days, while often interrelated, hold for television viewing audiences today:

1. Emotional escape from monotony, personal disappointment, and difficulty;
2. Provision of moral values and guidance in family and interpersonal problems;
3. Bolstering of the female ego;
4. Companionship; and, lastly,
5. Entertainment (Willey, 1961).

Originally conceived as a cost-efficient media vehicle for delivering household products (literally, laundry detergent), soap operas presented a relatively fixed form and formula to their perceived target market until around the mid-1970s (Cantor and Pingree, 1983). Then, with changes in the structure of broadcast networks, the advent of the videocassette recorder, and demands for scripts to keep up with the times, younger characters replaced older ones, scenes shifted from bland interiors to exotic exteriors, and plot lines became bolder.

As early as 1941, social psychologist Herta Herzog interviewed 100 soaps listeners to learn what the "serials" meant to them;[13] to her surprise, a significant portion of the sample—mainly housewives—seemingly accepted many of the stories as real, or at least ones to which they could easily relate. The women provided responses relative to what they learned about child-rearing, medicinal remedies, wifely roles, interpersonal relationships, and other forms of guidance which they actively sought from the radio dramas.

Many of the serials have demonstrated incredible endurance. *Search for Tomorrow,* for example, was launched by CBS in 1951, shifted to NBC in 1982, and held its own for 35 years, until it was cancelled in 1987. *The Guiding Light* has been around since 1952, *As the World Turns,* 1956, *General Hospital,* 1963, *One Life to Live,* 1968, and *All My Children* since 1970, to name a few. Audiences of the soaps have been shown to be exceptionally loyal, many videotaping them for later enjoyment.

Since the appearance of *Peyton Place* on television in 1956, studies of the soaps have been defended by an ever-expanding number of communications scholars with rationales ranging from their value as a perspective on gender perceptions of television fare (Modelski, 1979, 1982; Alexander et al., 1992) to their role in the "cultural production of meaning" (Berchers, 1992) to their psycho-analytic value as narrative subjects (Brown, 1992; Nochimson, 1993) to their role as mediating interpersonal communication (Cathcart, 1986) to the simple endurance of the genre and the ability of the soaps to reflect, rather than shape, societal values (Geraghty, 1991; Frentz, 1992).

"On any weekday afternoon," according to Carveth (1993, p. 21), "between 20 million and 30 million people are glued to their favorite television soap operas. The magazine racks are littered with periodicals devoted to soap operas, ranging from *Soap Opera Digest* to *Soap Opera People*. There's even a computer newsgroup that is devoted to discussing soap operas." Think of it: each weekday between 1 p.m. and 2 p.m., some 14 million television households in the United States are tuning in to *The Young and the Restless, All My Children,* and *Days of Our Lives*. In addition, 950,000 households time-shift *Days of Our Lives* each day from their VCRs, with comparable numbers for *The Young and the Restless* and *All My Children.*

Although *Peyton Place* appeared multiple nights each week during the 1960s, *Dallas,*[14] which premiered on prime time on CBS in the spring of 1978, is considered the first "evening soap opera." Airing at night, the made-for-television sexy series drew a large enough audience so that advertisers and imitators eagerly joined the bandwagon by the next season. In the interim, hooked fans discussed "Who shot J.R.?" so much that the November 21, 1980 program answering the question drew some 80 percent of all television viewers that night.

Communications researchers have approached the subject of soap operas from a number of perspectives. In the early 1980s, as many of the soaps were doubling from their half-hour presentations (only *Loving* and *The Bold and the Beautiful* remained on for 30-minute slots), content analyses indicated a preponderance of sexual activity: pre-marital, marital romances, and extra-marital affairs, rape, prostitution, intercourse, petting, "erotic touching," and other intimacies—mainly heavy titillation in the afternoon, heavier activity at night (Greenberg, Abelman, and Neuendorf, 1981; Lowry, Love, and Kirby, 1981; Greenberg and D'Alessio, 1985; Lowry and Towles, 1989).

Focusing on the intimacy of conversations occurring in the soaps,

Fine (1981) found that, "In terms of relationships, the soap opera community is in a sense a microcosm of the 'real' world. Only a few characters are transients, and this stability may be a prime reason for audience involvement" (p. 99). Yet, there is a contradiction here:

> The preponderance of male-female relationships, particularly intimate ones, is very unlike the world we live in. Men and women appear together on the television screen far more often than they seem to in many people's lives . . . (and) the men and women of soap operas have many friends and intimates of the opposite sex who talk to each other about all things and use intimate conversational style more frequently than do men or women when talking among themselves." (p. 105)

This notion of the soaps as unlike the "real" world, even though they are such a constant communication source for so many people, is relevant here. In his 1974 book *T.V.: The Most Popular Art,* Horace Newcomb suggests that the soaps deserve a place in the aesthetics of television, combining as they do two of the most critical elements of the medium: intimacy and continuity. Four decades after Herzog's interviews, for example, Gerbner et al. (1981), as part of their ongoing content analysis of Prime Time television, found daytime serials to be the largest source of medical advice in the country. Suggesting that the soaps exist as fictionalized representations providing a mirror of the world, Gerbner (1972) claims they demonstrate how power is allocated in society, and how dominance and submission can be idealized. Still, "It is important to recognize that soap opera allays real anxieties, satisfies real needs and desires, even while it may distort them," Modelski (1982, p. 108) reminds us. "The fantasy of community is not only a real desire (as opposed to the 'false' ones mass culture is always accused of trumping up), it is a salutary one."

Considering the soaps simultaneously as "economic product and cultural document," Allen (1987) uses as a case study *The Guiding Light,* a serial that actually began on radio in 1937 and has continued to run to this day on television. Arguing beyond the methodology of content analysis for examining the soaps, he claims: "Creation of meaning and aesthetic pleasure in the soap opera is a much more complex process than is generally recognized . . . what a soap opera means in a social sense is inextricably tied up with how it creates meaning for its viewers" (p. 148). Semiotics, for example, allows a latitude of codes that help make sense of the cultural phenomena, including, but limited to the following:

1. *Video-cinematic codes*—borrowed from Hollywood filmmaking, the complex of visual and auditory representations including "such devices as unobtrusive camera movements, 'invisible' editing, and a naturalistic style of acting, among others—all designed to focus the viewer's attention on the story unfolding on the screen and away from the manner by which that story is being told."
2. *Codes of the soap opera form*—different configurations of time and space, with "multiple, intersecting plot lines" that might continue indefinitely.
3. *Textual codes*—recognizable to the long-time soap viewer.
4. *Intertextual codes*—drawing on networks of other texts, such as occurs when referring to other media, like books, movies, or even other television representations.
5. *Experiential codes*—the viewer relying on his or her own experience of the world. (pp. 151-152)

Relationships on soap operas, according to Allen, primarily take the form of kinship, romance, or social (friend/enemy). It is the idiosyncratic interpretations of these various codes in the soaps that form the basis of this study.

Audiences for the soaps have evolved along with the changing plot lines. While adult women commanded more than 70 percent of viewers in the 1970s, and the genre was found to be most popular with southerners and those in low-income, low-education groups, recently whole new groups are joining those numbers: business people, retirees, professional athletes, pre-teens and teens alike, and, important for purposes of this book, college students. Carveth (1993), who, in an earlier study with Alexander (1985) found five factors representing college students' accounts for soaps viewing— entertainment, character identification, reality exploration, escape from work, and escape from boredom—claims college students are unique as soap opera viewers:

They not only watch if their schedules permit, but often pur-
posely arrange classes so that a favorite show will not be
missed. This had not been possible earlier in their lives, nor
will it be possible once they leave college and enter the job
market. It is not uncommon that community television sets are
tuned to soap operas. Those who are in that particular environment are thus exposed to soaps even when it is not of their own
choosing. For some students . . . viewing is clearly a social
behavior—engaged in, with and because of other people. Further, men or women in a close relationship might introduce
their partners to the programs. (p. 23)

Seeing how all this fits in terms of cultivation analysis, the findings of Lowry, Love, and Kirby (1981) are particularly interesting.
Their most intriguing discovery concerned the ratio of married, as
opposed to unmarried, sexual behavior that was portrayed, the latter
being shown nearly fivefold as frequently. "Soap operas portray
numbers of beautiful, rich, successful (many of them professionals),
and sexy role models engaging in intercourse outside of marriage
twice as often as they engage in intercourse within the bonds of
marriage," the authors contend. "A steady viewing diet of role
models who engage in fornication and adultery may influence or
cultivate viewers' attitudes and values concerning what is 'normal'
and 'proper' in society" (pp. 95-96).

Buerkel-Rothfuss and Mayes (1981), wanting to apply Gerbner's
hypothesis to the nature of soap opera content, collected data from
290 students in an introductory communications course at a large
southern university. They "expected to find a positive monotonic
relationship between viewing soap operas and estimates of real-life
occurrences of infidelity, divorce, illegitimacy, serious illness, nervous breakdown, abortions, and crime . . . (as well as) a similar
relationship between viewing and estimates of real-life professional
occupations: doctors, lawyers, business people, and not working but
well-supported wives" (pp. 109-110). Heavy exposure to the soaps,
it was corroborated, was consistent with similar research on the
influence of mediated electronic means in terms of constructions of
social reality.

Replicating the Buerkel-Rothfuss and Mayes (1981) study, Carveth and Alexander (1985) surveyed 265 college student soap opera
viewers in introductory and intermediate communication courses at
a large northeastern university. Variables considered included exposure to soaps, years of viewing them, and nonserial daily television
viewing. Further, dependent "cultivation effect" measures were
determined by asking respondents to estimate from the U.S. population "out of 100" numbers of females who were doctors, lawyers,
housewives, divorced, and had illegitimate children, as well as
numbers of comparable figures for men. Respondents were also
asked to apply estimates to how many marriages ended in divorce
and how many people have committed a serious crime. While over-
estimations of certain occupational groups and the frequency of
selected behaviors in the "real world" confirmed Buerkel-Rothfuss
and Mayes' findings, other factors differed. Finding that, "The
relationship between motives, exposure, and cultivation revealed an
interactive effect for certain motives," Carveth and Alexander conclude that, "The cultivation effect appears to be strongest when the
motives for viewing are *ritualistic* (enjoyment, boredom) rather
than *instrumental* (reality exploration, character identification).
This suggests that individuals who frequently and ritualistically
select the soap opera genre, and perhaps television viewing in general, as an undemanding activity, may be most vulnerable to television messages" (p. 270).

Limited empirical support to the cultivation hypothesis advanced
by Gerbner and his colleagues was found by Carveth (1993) in his
study of whether soaps opera viewing had an impact on viewers'
perceptions of sexual relationships, or the perceptual creation of a
"promiscuous world," suggesting that concern over their turbulent
and sexual depictions may be unfounded. His study, examining the
potential role of soap opera viewing as a determinant in perceiving
a world marked by romantic turbulence, extended his earlier finding
that it had little or no effect. Yet, Carveth suggests, "It may be that
we are beginning to see a 'mainstreaming' (cf. Gerbner et al., 1986)
effect such that heavy viewers of similar content from disparate
groups develop shared attitudes" (p. 32).

In the summer of 1992, *Swans Crossing,* "a daily, half-hour
syndicated soap aimed at the Clearasil set" (Carter, 1992) appeared,

allowing yet another target niche to participate in "the backbiting, blackmail, and bed hopping that sustain the soap operas." Beginning in November of 1993, E!'s *Pure Soap* television show made its debut, a daily recap broadcast from 4-4:30 p.m. EST, repeated at 7 p.m., 11:30 p.m., 10 a.m., and 12:30 p.m.; hosted by Shelley Taylor Morgan, a former soap star herself, and acerbic *TV Guide* columnist Michael Logan, to date the program has drawn a recognizable following. Overall, though, says Dana Kennedy (1993, p. 37), the soaps are "on the ropes," "taking a bath in the ratings":

> It might be a crisis too messy to be stitched up at *General Hospital,* too complex to be solved by *The Young and the Restless,* too troubling to be soothed by a lot of *Loving* : The daily soap opera is in danger of being washed up. Once the province of TV's raciest stuff, the high-strung, overheated network dramas that have dominated daytime for 30 years are now being outsobbed and outsexed by a glut of syndicated talk shows that are cheaper and easier to produce. In other words, the Bold and the Beautiful are being hung out to dry by the Loud and the Tasteless.

"Relationship" Shows on Television

In addition to talk shows and the soaps, television today features a number of other relevant programs relative to relationships. The 1993 season, for example, introduced *Living Single* ("A new comedy about four single women living under one roof . . . and the two guys trying to move in on them"), and *Fools for Love* ("Relationships: how to start them, keep them, end them—and how to maintain a sense of humor throughout," according to stand-up comedy hosts Jon Brandeis and Caroline Rhea). The front cover of *TV Guide's* Nov. 28, 1993 issue, showing Markie Post and John Ritter of *Hearts Afire,* claims there is a movement toward "Faithful Attraction: Now it's monogamy as sexual sparks fly on TV." Small wonder: married couples can theoretically get more past the censors. *Friends,* which premiered in 1994, has been a network success that has captured the attention of many marketers.

The Real World, MTV's "reality-based soap opera" that features actual goings-on between seven strangers recruited to share rent-free digs has endured several seasons, with a new cast each season; reminiscent of the 1973 PBS series *An American Family,* the dysfunctional Loud clan, it is quite a comment on young people that they are so drawn to viewing others' lives. And not just their generation: consider the ratings popularity of ABC's steamy *NYPD Blue,* created by Steven Bochco, or the enduring global popularity of those scantily clad L.A. lifeguards on *Baywatch,* the third-highest rated syndicated drama in the U.S. (after the two *Star Trek* spin-offs), which Fretts (1993, p. 18) says many people have put in the "guilty-pleasure category":

1. It's among the top-rated U.S. shows in the U.K., France, Germany, Ireland, New Zealand, and Australia.
2. As of (October, 1993), with Rupert Murdoch's Asia satellite broadcast network, Star TV, carrying it, *Baywatch* will begin to reach 72 countries—including Outer Mongolia and Lebanon.
3. The show's producers estimate that 1 billion people will watch it every week, more than have ever viewed any television series since time began. (p. 16)

References to sex on network television has not changed very much in the last 15 years, but Kaplan (1993, p. 12) points out that made-for-TV movies have made inroads dealing with sexual issues such as AIDS, incest, spousal abuse, and date rape. Recognizing their role as part of a "stabilizing, conservative institution charged with keeping order and preserving the status quo—to restrict change," Rapping (1992, p. xii) has studied the *Movie of the Week* to determine its overall place in our collective consciousness; in so doing, she joins a number of us who are trying to find meaning and significance in television texts.

One of my observations, then, is that broadcasting participants are opting for "safe" involvements, using the media to satisfy any number of needs. Think of how many viewers tune into MTV—regular and/or after hours—which Gow (1993) claims works so well because of its production strategy of "pseudo-reflexivity." And then there are all those Court TV addicts, watching first the "dotless" accuser of William Kennedy Smith on rape charges, the Jeffrey Dahmer multiple-murder case, and Rodney King's beating trials, as well as the Menendez murder enticement, and superceded by O. J.'s trial of the century.

Further, I would argue, we have become a country of video vigilantes (Fuller, 1994), fascinated by both sides of the camera— just look at the popularity of programs such as *America's Funniest Home Videos, I Spy Video, I Witness Video,* and the like. *Gay Fairfax,* a television show airing on the Virginia public access channel that is the second most-watched offering (after high school sports), regularly runs its own segment on "The Personals"; profiling the personal, human side of relationships within the gay and lesbian community, it runs weekly in 12 to 14-minute segments.

Spawned by predecessors such as *The Dating Game, The New Dating Game, The All New Dating Game,* and *Love Connection,* a whole new sexier version of the genre has caught on for vicarious viewers. On the Chicago cable system, *Meet Your Match* ("America's Meeting Place") airs for a half-hour mid-weeknights at 9 p.m., Saturdays from 11:30 p.m. until midnight. "Here's a clever new way to humiliate yourself in front of millions of people" (Svetkey, 1991): *Prime-Time Personals (PTP),* a national cable show where interested viewers can call in and hear the advertiser for $2.70 a minute. Billed as the first television personals show, it features ads that are "read aloud as the words are shown on the screen, to the strains of love-theme music or light jazz. As backgrounds, there are romantic settings like fields of flowers, woodsy roads, misty mountains, quaint bridges, sailboats and lots of waterfalls" (R. Alexander, 1991).

PTP soon was joined by the likes of other "gamedies," among them *A Perfect Score, Night Games, That's Amore, Love Struck Live, Meet Your Match, How's Your Love Life, National Dateline,* and *Personals.* "Relationship shows are 'titillating,'" Joel Segal of McCann-Erickson Worldwide is quoted as saying (Magiera, 1992). "There's a certain element of the soap opera in it." Viewers are often encouraged to call in if any of the guests pique their interests. And, while there are hardly any rhetorical taboos, to date none of the shows have had homosexual or interracial contestants. "This is Roman Colosseum television," contends Minsky (1992), "where the viewer is a voyeur and the participants publicly risk dignity, privacy, ego—and, some would argue, even their lives."

While self-descriptions can be great fun (e.g., Christy from California is "unselfish in bed," Monty's grandfather was Captain Cook, and Carrie is a natural blonde who would be happy to prove it), without question the advertisements are the best; ranging from Secret Love records and cassettes to tax help or service announcements about the local rape crisis center, they tend to emphasize escape and fantasy, preying upon our inadequacies. O'Connor (1992) finds a common thread running through all these relationship shows: "Will a connection be made and, stay tuned, will it lead to sex? A veil of coyness is normally drawn over the ultimate revelation, but not before the audience gets the unmistakable message and still another opportunity to squeal with satisfaction." *Marry Me,* a comedy dating show, is perhaps the best of the lot, a clever parody of the flirty-game-show genre (Lawyer, 1992). Marjorie Garber, Director of Harvard's Center for Literary and Cultural Studies, has called these shows "safe sex for the audience. They're clearly an index of loss that people are feeling about post-pill, pre-AIDS society."[15]

And then there is *Studs.* Proudly offered by Fox Broadcasting, the network that unabashedly goes after the outrageous and offensive as audience appeals, the idea is for host Mark deCarlo to make a match from two studs and three studettes who have gone out on dates, then discuss them via lewd double entendres on the air. *Mademoiselle* (Tucker, 1992) says *Studs* provides us with an invaluable service, "giving us a glimpse of a particularly entertaining reel of Hell: a Debasement *Dating Game,* in which single people are encouraged to express their lewdest, most cynical thoughts"; while at its most shallow *Studs* may be the "TV equivalent of going to a Chippendales strip joint," at its deepest also lies "one aspect of what AIDS has done to our libidos: twisted them with anxiety, fear, doubt and rage expressed as mindless silliness." Writing for *The Village Voice,* Mike Rubin (1992, p. 46) cites his personal experience trying out to be a participant (several hundred men and women are interviewed each week); rejected along with dozens of others, he writes, "Our hopes of competing for sexual conquest, or at least of being debased in front of thousands, succumb to an acute case of *studus interruptus.*" He muses (p. 47):

Television lies about and cheats on and trivializes romance only slightly more often than human beings do. It's crass, salacious, and full of shit, but so are we, some of the time. And in spite of its dirty mind, love TV has some moments of genuine sweetness. I particularly cherish the time *Studs* hosted a group of hot-to-trot hopefuls of a certain age, and one of the women reported, "I've fallen in love and I can't get up."

While many of my students claim to be regular *Studs* viewers, my only opportunity to see the show (it airs close to midnight in my area) featured choices between a 24-year-old manicurist, a 22-year-old hair dresser, and a 25-year-old counter clerk, describing their dates in the following ways: "dripping with testosterone," "After two hours he had me bleating like a sheep," "I wanted to tweek his teeny tiny twinkie bum," "He lapped up my flesh like my pores were oozing honey," and "He rubbed me into total arousal." Konigsberg (1992, p. 27) included an amusing expose in *Spy* on how contestants actually are primed for their foul-mouthedness, concluding that it doesn't really hurt us to know how the show meshes: "Now we can love *Studs* because it allows us to wallow in the unashamedly sordid trashiness of low-level Fox segment producers." Small wonder that *Electronic Media* has reported the U.K., Holland, Belgium, Luxembourg, Germany, Spain, Canada, Australia, New Zealand, and Sweden are all preparing their own home-grown versions of *Studs*.[16]

Morrison (1994) has documented *Network Q* a video magazine aimed at the gay and lesbian community. Conceived as an underground alternative communication vehicle in 1992, it provides a welcome monthly programming source and its many supporters hope it will eventually become mainstream.

Most recently, ABC has added the dating show *Street March*, on which willing participants approached on the street are followed on their first dates; hosted by *Another World's* Ricky Paul Goldin, the show aims to hook up people of all ages, sizes, and colors. Also on the line-up are *The Marriage Counselor* (dramatizations simulating what clinical therapists actually see), *Real Personal* (Bob Berkowitz as an intimacy maven), and *Club Connect* (advice for teenagers).

Consider, too, the onslaught of celebrity biomovies, such as ones about Roseanne and Tom Arnold, Princess Diana, Mia Farrow, or Elizabeth Taylor that appeal to our voyeuristic natures.

And how do you explain the popularity of what has been called television's sexiest sitcom, *Friends*? For its debut it was strategically sandwiched on NBC between other popular Thursday fare about New Yorkers, *Mad About You* and *Seinfeld*, and has since attracted a substantial audience all its own. Revolving around "a close-knit sextet of twentysomething singles," (Fretts, 1995, p. 20), the friends themselves are not romantically involved with one another, but monitor and caution the lives of those they care about. It's a far cry from the beach-blanket-bingo crowd.

Television Advertisements

As any critic of the medium will tell you, commercial messages are often the best part of television fare; consider, for example, the popularity of the Cleo awards, the advertisement industry's answer to the Oscars. While in the United States certain standards prevail against prurience, after hours and on certain cable television channels there is a noticeable lessening of those strictures.

Discounting pay-per-view and television channels devoted to eroticism, this section mainly concerns itself with the role of advertisements for phone sex. Predominantly sexist, if not bordering on misogyny, the ads are primarily targeted to heterosexual males. The sex act is a speech act, according to McCarthy (1993, p. 50): "Indeed, the ads clearly mimic the iconography of standard male heterosexual porn: half-naked buxom women, and music that recalls either the sex-aerobics soundtracks of porn's main action or the slinky saxophone solos that accompany the preliminary fictions that serve as the porn narrative's 'front matter.'" She cites *Rhonda's Private Phone Club*:

> Hosted by the amply endowed "Rhonda," (it) offers a clear example of the way phone sex advertisements interpellate the viewer/caller through the ideology of his own personalized sex commodity. The show begins with a man in a living room distractedly flipping through TV channels with his remote control. When he stops at something that attracts his attention,

a female voice-over announces, "Something exciting is about to happen to your television." An animated title card screen zooms out the television set, accompanied by the inducement "you can join in all the fun at home, just by picking up the phone" on the voice track. The "viewer" onscreen picks up the phone, dials, listens, and proceeds to undergo a bodily transformation via special effects—he appears to become a science fictional bolt of energy. The sequence that follows shows the energy bolt traveling along telephone wires outside. A cut reveals the interior of Rhonda's club, full of well-coiffed and scantily clad young women. Rhonda, seated at the bar, picks up the phone when it rings, and the energy bolt streams out of the receiver. It disappears behind the spot occupied by the camera, where it is presumably reconstituted as the "viewer" shown earlier. However, at this point this "viewer" has assumed the gaze of the camera. Rhonda, gasping in amazement, turns to the camera and addresses it/him/us directly. "Well hi there, Mr.-uh-Mr. Guy-Man . . . how are you?" The camera nods up and down, and Rhonda proceeds to take "Mr. Guy-Man" on a tour of the facilities. (p. 51)

The gaze, then, gets turned around in this mise-en-scène. Taking advantage of "the ideological liveness and immediacy of television" (p. 53), phone sex ads openly invite the viewer to engage in fantasies. Unlike the cinematic voyeur, however, s/he might feel more prone to engage in those titillations, particularly due to the fact that the locus of operation is one's private living space. "Like the ads for hair clubs and muscle-toning equipment which surround them," McCarthy argues, "phone sex ads suggest a panic-ridden, anxious insecurity on the part of the male viewer. Yet, as the text of the ad of 1-900-346-GIRL illustrates, the anxiety activated is social as well as sexual" (p. 55).

Also advertised in a number of sources are videos ranging from correspondence resources to erotica (e.g., "Great American Strip Search! Exotic dancers perform their hottest routines!"; "Cross Dressers, TV/TS!"; "Domination! Foot Videos!"; "Bizarre Japanese Adult Videos"; or "Raised Skirt Videos" of the "girls next door"). Ann Cvetkovich (1993) of the University of Texas/Austin has presented a convincing argument regarding cross-over dressing in advertising that is deliberately fabricated to appeal simultaneously to straight and gay populations. Through multi-media examples, she particularly honed in on the work of designer Gianni Versace, who uses nude male bodies in unique combinations.

To go full circle on this topic, it seems appropriate to note the *National Geographic* ad, running two full-color pages in many magazines, that says, "The line between curious and compelling is a fine one."

NOTES

1. Smillie (1992) points out that talk radio stations have gained in audience size from a 3.7 share in Winter, 1991 to a 4.2 share the next year, increasing in numbers from 238 stations in 1987 to 875 in 1992. Martin (1993) writes: "The number of radio stations dubbing themselves either as 'news/talk' or 'talk' has more than quadrupled from fewer than 200 in 1980 to more than 850 in 1993."

2. Cited in Richard Zoglin's "Bugle Boys of the Airwaves," *Time* (May 15, 1989), p. 88.

3. Carol Nashe, "NARTSH Notes," *Talkers* (Late December, 1993), p. 9.

4. "Sex Talk on the Radio with Dr. Judy," *The New York Times* (May 9, 1993), p. V4.

5. "Talk Radio Networks Pursue Role of AM 'White Knight,'" *Broadcasting* (August 27, 1990), p. 41.

6. Bouhoutos, Goodchilds, and Huddy's empirical study of call-in psychology programs found callers tended to be female, unmarried, unemployed, and less educated than noncallers—which fits this profile. See also: Rapping, 1991.

7. Walter Goodman, "Stern's Complaint: Breasts, behinds, insults and a lot of kvetching, from the self-described sweetest radio personality on the planet," *The New York Times Book Review* (October 24, 1993), p. 7.

8. Quoted in Bruce Fretts, "Blow Hard: Is Howard Stern hot stuff—or is he just full of hot air?" *Entertainment Weekly* (October 15, 1993), p. 26.

9. This study owes a great debt of gratitude to Michael Harrison of *Talkers* for his information and input.

10. Cumulatively for 1993, the "Talkers Ten" were: 1. Crime and Violence, 2. Health Care, 3. the Economy, 4. Civil Rights, 5. Education, 6. Natural Disasters, 7. Foreign Affairs, 8. Sex Scandals, 9. Science and Technology, 10. Sports and Entertainment.

11. In her Introduction to *Staying Tuned: Contemporary Soap Operas Criticism* (Popular Press, 1992, p. 1) editor Suzanne Frentz cites this date, but other people have suggested that the first radio "soap" was Irna Phillips' "Painted Dreams," which debuted on WGN in 1929.

12. This section on soap operas owes a debt to Rod Carveth for a careful reading of it in draft form. Alix Kruger also offered invaluable input.

13. Herta Herzog, "On Borrowed Experience," *Studies in Philosophy and Social Science* (1941): 65-91.

14. For a fascinating discussion on global implications, see Liebes and Katz' *The Export of Meaning: Cross-Cultural Readings of Dallas* (NY: Oxford, 1990).

15. Cited in Minsky (1992, pp. H29-H31).

16. Cited in *TV Guide* (June 6, 1992), p. 5.

Chapter 4

Media-Mediated Relationships in Communications Technologies

There now exists a burgeoning cottage industry of highly hygienic flesh options: computer sex (software that produces erotic on-screen images); computer bulletin board sex (in which subscribers trade fantasies through the magic of E-mail); and our old friend phone sex and our new friend virtual reality sex, which have recently been wed on the new "Cyberorgasm" CD.

—Jim Walsh, "The New Sexual Revolution" (1993)

As we enter an era of "high-tech sex," it seems appropriate to consider, as a twist on the Lasswellian mass communication model:[1] who is involved with what kind of communication channel(s), and with what results. The diffusion of communication technology, while varying greatly in intensity among various people, businesses, even countries, can nevertheless be analyzed at three different levels: the enterprise, the user's market, and the market itself (Preissl, 1992). Consider, at this point, the many *Communication Technology Resources for Media-Mediated Relationships* provided in Appendix 7.

Gattiker (1992, p. 1) defines the acquisition of communication technology skills as follows:

Using various means of training, *communication technology skills* are *learned behaviors* needed for achieving desirable performance levels when doing job related tasks, which the content and type of computer skill required for doing a job is in part a *relational phenomenon* (i.e., how many and what type of people have or don't have the necessary skills). Achieving satisfactory performance (during learning and, therefore, on-the-job) hinges *first* upon individual abilities (motor and cognitive process capabilities, e.g., information processing), *second,* the degree of substantive complexity and autonomy-control offered/required by the job and *third,* upon the mix of declarative and procedural knowledge the person has in basic, social, conceptual, technology, technical and task skills *before* training starts as well as the mix acquired during training.

To date, there has been an unprecedented and unpredicted assimilation of communication technology by the general public of the United States; by default, that means many market users—albeit with concerns among many scholars on implications for a technological information gap (e.g., Tichenor, Donohue, and Olien, 1970; Dervin, 1980; Schiller, 1981; Beniger, 1986; Golding and Murdock, 1986; Rogers, 1986; Wasko and Mosco, 1992; Fuller, 1993b; Gandy, 1993). (See Figure 13. *Technology Penetration of Selected Media in U.S. Households,* p. 120.)

While we often lump communication technology into futuristic conceptions, calling it "new" or "emerging," many of its aspects are old media reconceptualized to meet and/or anticipate societal needs. Guided by technological, economic, sociocultural, and public policy forces, telecommunications continues to redefine and reconfigure itself. Ronald E. Rice (1984, p. 34-35), a leading telecommunications expert, reminds us that, "New media—from videotex to personal computer networks, from communication satellites to fiber optics—are blurring distinctions that seemed so clear and useful a generation ago"; he cites some changes:

1. *Technician versus artist.* Computer graphics is a new art form that challenges technical expertise as well as creative genius.
2. *General versus limited access.* The telephone currently provides near-universal access to people in the United States; with regulatory and commercial developments, local telephone usage may in fact become less accessible.
3. *Regulated versus unregulated media.* Commercial network television is heavily regulated; yet the new FCC policies for

direct broadcast satellites are so unrestricted that potential service providers are asking for more guidelines.

4. *Communication versus processing.* This is what the divestiture of AT&T was all about; computerization and communication have nearly completely converged, and both AT&T and IBM are in the "information business."

5. *Time and space.* A public speech delivers a common content to a common set of people at a common time at a common location. Network television delivers a generally common content to a generally common mass. Cable television delivers a (debatably) more diverse content to a generally more diverse set of people. Videotex delivers customized content across varying sets of people, at undetermined times to places potentially unreached by politicians or television.

6. *Active versus passive control.* Early computer-assisted instruction was heralded for letting the student take an active role in learning, but the early systems required nearly mindless passivity from its users, compared to the newest video games.

7. *Transmission versus reception.* A mediated communication exchange now may involve so many transmission transformations that any given medium can be both a transmitter and receiver, both medium and content. For example, filmed content may be transmitted by satellite, delivered by cable, and shown on television.

Called "social computing," the idea is the convergence of a number of communication technologies, such as telephones, computer networks, groupware, cable television, on-line information services, handheld electronic devices, and the like with traditional news media, the entertainment industry, and other aspects of telecommunications. Where it fits into the so-called "Information Highway" remains unknown, but for our purposes the key point is that technology has gone beyond merely the mainframe and has begun to take the user into consideration—along with issues of privacy and security.

FIGURE 13. Technology Penetration of Selected Media in U.S. Households[1]

Technology/service	Penetration percentage
All television	98%
Color television	97
Telephone service	93
VCR	77
Basic cable	61
Answering machine	46
Compact disc player	35
Home computer	33
Video game player	31
Stereo television	31
Camcorder	17
Projection television	8
Backyard satellite dish	3
Cellular telephone	3
Home fax machine	1

[1] John Carey, "Looking Back to the Future: How Communication Technologies Enter American Households," in John V. Pavlik and Everett E. Dennis (eds.) *Demystifying Media Technology: Readings from the Freedom Forum Center* (Mountain View, CA: Mayfield Publishing Company, 1993), p. 36.

"Today's audiences differ demographically and socioeconomically as well as psychologically from those of earlier decades," Brody (1990, p. 8) reminds us. "The occupational traumas of the 1980s are only a part of the societal changes responsible. Single parent households continue to increase in number. Cohabitation has become more or less socially acceptable. By the end of the 1980s, the traditional nuclear family already had become atypical in the United States." Tierney (1994, H1) disagrees: "The erotic technological impulse dates back at least to some of the earliest works of art, the so-called Venus figurines of women with exaggerated breasts and buttocks, which were made by firing clay 27,000 years ago—15 milleniums before ceramics technology was used for anything utilitarian like pots," he argues. "When subsequent artists discovered the medium of cave walls, they produced work like the rock carving that archaeologists have titled 'Nude Woman,' etched more than 12,000 years ago at La Magdelaine Cave in France." Continuing this perspective, Tierney cites that a book of erotic engravings depicting lovemaking positions was published in 1524, that the infamous *Fanny Hill* came out in 1740, a pornographic film industry was thriving by the 1920s, and the lines have become scanter since the recent introduction of cable television and VCRs (p. 41).

This section of *Media-Mediated Relationships* is concerned with the uses of communication technology by the many consumer markets interested in its possibilities. According to McCarthy (1993, p. 50), "The techno-sexual services offered by erotic telecommunication ads fall into four general categories:

1. Phone sex, where a (male) caller engages in sexually explicit conversation with a woman on the other end of the line;
2. Fantasy or confession voice mail systems, where a caller may either call and leave a message—a fantasy or a confession—or retrieve the confessions or fantasies of others;
3. Dating lines, through which callers both leave and retrieve personals; and
4. Chat lines, on which the caller talks with other callers."

These services and more will be the subject of this chapter, which will deal with the role of media-mediated relationships in terms of computers, video, broadcasting/cable technologies, interactive media, and telephony.

COMPUTERS

With a cautionary nod toward technology's drum-beating prophets, we offer an understatement: our creative lives have changed. As happened when the printing press, the telephone, and television were invented, stories and the means by which we tell them will never be the same, not for the people who tell them or for those who take them in. All over the world the gatekeepers are disintegrating as the few who always decided what stories the rest of us would hear are yielding to the millions telling their stories directly to one another. (Jon Katz, 1994)

Computer-mediated communication (CMC) is a topic that has come under investigation by a number of scholars (e.g., Kerr and Hiltz, 1982; Chesebro and Bonsall, 1989; Mosco, 1989; Rapaport, 1991; Gattiker, 1992; Lea, 1992; Perse et al, 1992). How computer networks operate is yet another important avenue for discussion, especially in terms of interpersonal communication (e.g., Dutton, Rogers, and Jun, 1987; Rice and Love, 1987; Forester, 1989; Brooks, 1992; Walther and Burgoon, 1992; Joe, 1993). Considering estimates that telecommunications media and the computer have expanded at annual rates in excess of 25 percent per year, in terms of cost-performance ratios, for at least the past two decades,[2] their interface becomes critical in terms of their usage.

Sherry Turkle (1993), a professor of sociology in the Program in Science, Technology, and Society at the Massachusetts Institute of Technology (MIT), discusses personal implications of what she calls "Computational Seductions": "My computer writing environment is as seductive to me as are the screens of videogames to two generations of children who can testify to their almost hypnotic fascination. My computer environment is as seductive to me as are programming languages to the hackers who spend as much time as they can in the company of their machines" (p. 18). Focusing on the psychology of computer-human interactions, she argues beyond the metaphor of addiction:

> First, the computer's hold relates not to its nature as an analytical engine but to its second nature as an evocative object, an object that provokes self-reflection. . . . Second, computers offer experiences in which thought is externalized and embodied. As in the story of Narcissus and his reflection, people fall in love with the artificial worlds they have created or that have been built for them by others. Computers offer an experience of minds extending, meeting and merging, a new and compel-

ling source of technological holding power. Third, these machines offer diversity to the many different kinds of people who come to them. (p. 19)

In 1983, when I was working at MIT's Research Program in Communications Policy, under Ithiel de Sola Poole, we embarked on a major study of videotex, trying to establish and/or embellish data bases that could be used for interactive technology. Our results: the overall market simply was neither ready nor responsive at that time to this offering. A decade later, a subset of the population is finding very creative uses for the technology. Still, there are a number of hurdles yet to overcome—to wit:

> Regulatory (the Government has to determine whether the pathways are public or private, and who gets the bandwidth), legal (in the form of copyrights), financial (how is the cost of the new services to be shared?), cultural (if you can't program your VCR, why would you buy insurance over a wireless Newton Message Pad?), and, of course technical (Apple won't even let me touch a Message Pad until I've flown to California for a few hours of indoctrination, which is hardly a good sign for something that is supposed to be a consumer product). (Lewis, 1993)

Lovebytes

Sex-on-line, made possible through computers, is a business that is growing, if you will pardon the pun, by leaps and bounds.[3] Equally available from mainstream and alternative sources, it might include anything from CompuServe's special offering of an advisory service on sexuality information, staffed by professionals, to Echo's LOVE conference, which is open to anyone, or its SEX conference, which requires access permission.

"As increasing numbers of Americans, searching for intimacy in the age of AIDS, turn to computer keyboards to aid their fantasies," Markoff (1992) notes, "computerized sex play is becoming a growing issue for the companies that sell on-line information services." Pointing out the possibility of increased law-enforcement surveillance and other restrictions, he cites a case of the 42-year-old

California man who posed as a 13-year-old homosexual boy over a nationwide computer network who was approached by a 50-year-old New Yorker who wanted to arrange a meeting. With hidden identities, role changes need to be taken into account for what becomes called "lots of heavy clicking out there":

> While computer video games with sexually explicit cartoon-like animations have been available and routinely exchanged over networks for a decade, these incidents arose from a newer phenomenon—an emerging form of interactive computer sex play. Like telephone encounters, in which people dial 900 numbers to listen to fantasies described by an anonymous sexual surrogate, computer bulletin boards and conferencing systems permit individuals who don't know each other to "meet" and exchange intimacies by typing messages back and forth.

Called "computer graffiti" by some sources, sexually oriented electronic bulletin boards provide an outlet for a number of fantasies. Wright (1993) says Internet, which is considered the "network of networks," is "the promised land for amateur anthropologists. Never has there been a way to observe people and groups so accurately and unobtrusively. As a place to eavesdrop, cyberspace is without peer in all of human history." Jon Katz (1993, p. 35) describes digital news as, "the purest journalistic medium since smoke signals." Chew on this from a 26-year-old student and mother of two from the Atlanta area who is a frequent contributor to a bondage-discussion group on Internet: "I have a nontraditional lifestyle. I'm polyamorous, I'm a pagan, I'm into S&M" (Kantrowitz, 1993, p. 45). *New Media* (Stefanac, 1993, p. 38) claims:

> It was bound to happen: libidinous exchanges heating up bulletin board services; raunchy ads in the back pages of major computer magazines touting digitized scans and striptease Quick Time movies; risque demos at computer trade shows attracting hordes of oglers; experts at communications conferences seriously debating whether 976 dial-a-porn services will be videoconferencing's killer application. In short, multimedia sleeze has arrived.

Futuristic erogenous zones are clearly being explored by "cyber-swingers linked together by networks of adult-oriented bulletin boards with names like KinkNet and ThrobNet," according to Kantrowitz (1994, p. 62). "Loaded with libraries of X-rated pictures and interactive adult games (like 'Pin the Tail on Your Wife'), these on-line services draw users to the computer the same way porno videos attracted consumers to VCRs a decade ago. Subscribers download pictures and chat with others of their ilk in steamy electronic forums." Yet sadly, as linguist Deborah Tannen (1994, p. 53) has discovered, there are gender inequities and sexist language in cybersex; still, a number of men seem to feel freer to express themselves on E-mail: "It's a combination of the technology (which they enjoy) and the obliqueness of the written word, just as many men will reveal feelings in dribs and drabs while riding in the car or doing something, which they'd never talk about sitting face to face. It's too intense, too bearing-down on them, and once you start you have to keep going. With a computer in between it's safer."

On-line computational exchanges take many different forms, some punctuated by what John A. Barry has termed "flame wars"[4]—vitriolic electronic diatribes that can be publicly observed on general bulletin boards or privately received via E-mail (electronic mail, although some people think it should stand for "erotic mail") in one's personal mailbox. Yet, no matter how squishy or hardened they may appear, these messages lack nonverbal cues, or "paralanguage," as sociolinguist Peter Farb[5] calls expressive vocal phenomena such as volume, pitch, stress, tempo, and intensity. To help express themselves better, some hackers use "emoticons," or hieroglyphics, to indicate various emotional states, such as those found in Figure 14. *Computer Hacker "Emoticons," p. 126.*

Gareth Branwyn (1993, p. 780), editor of the magazine *bOING-bOING,* is fascinated by the interative and sexually explicit storytelling that abounds in on-line computer sex, which he labels "Erotica for Cybernauts": "Compu-sex enthusiasts say it's the ultimate safe sex for the 1990s, with no exchange of bodily fluids, no loud smoke-filled clubs, and no morning after. Of course, there's no physical contact either. Compu-sex brings new meaning to the phrase 'mental masturbation.'" A bizarre blending of computer dating, phone sex, and high-tech voyeurism, computer sex offers a

FIGURE 14. Computer Hacker "Emoticons"*

<u>Examples</u>

:—)	=	smiley face
:—}	=	grin
;—)	=	wink
:—(	=	sad face
[ ]	=	hugs
:*	=	kisses
:—	=	male
>—	=	female
8—)	=	wide eyed
:—X	=	closed mouthed
:—0	=	Oh No!

* Note: Read sideways!

dizzying variety of sexual orientations, especially through its "private" offerings. Its most commonly reported forms include these:

1. Compu-sex where participants describe and embellish real-world circumstances: how they look, what they're wearing, what they're doing; such as "I'm taking my shirt off. I'm touching myself now."
2. Interaction creating a pure fantasy scenario, like "We're in a health club doing our workouts, only we're both totally nude."
3. "Tele-operated compu-sex," performed by the remote control of a robot or computer, where one party might give lovemaking instructions over the computer to another party, like "Jim, I want you to slowly undress Carol." (Branwyn, p. 786-787)

Calling us the "first nation in cyberspace," Elmer-DeWitt (1993, p. 62) discusses the sudden immense popularity of Internet, drawing discussion groups where any of the 20 million users can participate with anyone "from lawyers to physicists to sadomasochists." Howard Rheingold (1994), editor of *Whole Earth Review* (which operates Whole Earth 'Lectronic Link, or WELL) and author of the definitive *Virtual Reality* (Summit, 1991), claims that computer networks have created a whole new form of human social life, which he calls "virtual communities," and which he considers an important step toward realizing a true decentralized democracy.

With the number of bulletin boards having skyrocketed to more than 60,000 nationwide, "they're transforming American life, uniting—via electrons—individuals with like interests and concerns" (Davidson, 1993). Many are simply on-line orgies. *Boardwatch* magazine reports from a members' poll that three of its top ten computer bulletin boards were explicit "adult" systems, such as Pleasure Dome's ThrobNet, SwingNet, StudNet, and KinkNet (Elmer-Dewitt, 1993). Netsex is the ultimate in safety—if distant, as in this:

> By 11 p.m. the scene has begun to heat up. A man named Norm is nuzzling a young woman who calls herself Tricia. Tricia, in turn, is gently biting Brit's neck, while Annabeth flirts in the corner with Chaz. Then Suzi breaks in and asks Norm if he's looking for some real action. As if to test the waters, Norm gives Suzi a passionate kiss. Suzi kisses Norm back hard. With no further preamble, Norm takes off Suzi's shirt. You can almost feel the temperature in the room start to rise.

Except that there is no room, no shirt and, for all we know, no woman named Suzi. These events, and their steamy denouement, exist only as text messages scrolling by on a computer screen and as libidinous images in the mind's eye—in this case, the imagination of the three dozen men and women who have chosen this particular moment and this computer locale (the "sex" channel on the Internet) to exchange pseudonymous X-rated fantasies. Participants simply type in their best pickup lines and indicate what physical actions they are taking—such as kissing or undressing.

Computer Connections

Database compilation and retrieval services made possible through computer technology have greatly facilitated the work of the dating industry. Great Expectations, for example, reported an increase in sales of 25 percent once it integrated its membership on an

Arcnet-based network (Wexler, 1992). SF Net in San Francisco, based on a system of terminals fixed to tables in a dozen cafes, has computerized blind dates whereby customers pay to log on and find like-minded persons ("Lovebytes," 1991). Kantrowitz (1993, p. 44) relates an actual story from SF Net:

> Her nom de net was Jungle Goddess. His was Bill-Winkle Moose. After promising electronic interaction on SF Net, a San Francisco-based bulletin board, they finally met and started dating. Alas, computer- generated romances can turn as sour as conventional love affairs. They broke up, but Jungle Goddess, a.k.a. Edith Alderette, isn't bitter. "It's not the net's fault," she says. "It's ours." Alderette, a 26-year-old graduate student, says the net is the center of her social life. She likes the privacy: "You can sit with Cheez Whiz in your hair and chili running down your face . . . and in the most un-P.C. terms you can get things out."

America Online offers a number of "rooms" for meeting, for example, "Naughty Girls," "Romance Connection," or the "Gay Room"; using "handles" as names, interested loggers-on can visit where and with whom they choose. It also services SeniorNet On-line, featuring local and national news, movie and book reviews, games and play, public-domain software, travel information, airline reservations, shopping, and much more (Shannon, 1993). Event Horizons, the largest of the private bulletin boards specializing in adult chat areas and graphics exchange, boasts 64 lines and a clientele of 35,000 customers internationally—accounting for annual sales of $3 million.[6]

With 1.7 million people on-line via Prodigy, parties interested in getting to know one another better can communicate via electronic mail (E-mail); said one subscriber, "It's kind of like having a computer pen pal" (Pauly, 1992, p. 24). Thinking this was a "refreshing and less expensive alternative to dating," where he had found relationships could become too emotional, he continued: "Getting too close too fast can sometimes tear you apart. I've had my share of relationships that I felt could have gone further but minimal misunderstandings got way out of hand because of intense emotions." Talk about safety valves.

Estimating around 100 million messages being delivered each day via E-mail, about four million of which are for personal correspondence, according to the Electronic Mail Association, one unforeseen byproduct of all this electronic exchange has been "a modest renaissance of the written word" (Emerson, 1992, p. L-1).[7] Here is an actual romantic scenario:

> Last year, Kennesaw, Ga. native Tommy Williams, a sometime country singer, sat down at this computer and wrote to his new love. Though they'd never met, they'd exchanged scores of cathode-ray letters, hers signed "Judith of the Valley," his signed "The Seeker."
>
> "If you are as serious as I about our love and life, may I have your typing hand please? And a paper clip?" he tapped on his keyboard.
>
> A world away, near Sacramento, California, Judy Lewis lifted her hand, and followed her suitor's instructions: "Now modify the paper clip . . . and pretend I am putting it on your finger."
>
> Suddenly their three-day, on-line dalliance had become serious. They dropped the pen names. Then, after a few days and much more electronic mail, Williams popped the question. "When our day does finally arrive," he typed, "will you marry me? I am so serious."
>
> The waiting was excruciating. Five hours later, her one-word answer flashed on his screen:
>
> "Yes."
>
> Ah, hard-disk romance.

Yet, don't discount the capability of computers for simply a sought-for companionship. Or advocacy. SeniorNet, initiated thanks to funding from the Markle Foundation in March of 1986 at the University of San Francisco, was initially established at five senior centers throughout the United States; today, the number of SeniorNet sites has grown to more than 42, with a membership of 15,000 people. Dispelling the myth that older adults are technology-phobic, SeniorNet services an active exchange on its many databases, encouraging "forums," exchanges of helpful hints, opinions, community-service project participations, even security. It has been a godsend to people in nursing homes, linking them with the world; "some members trade bawdy limericks; others are group-writing a novel. There are also nightly 'cocktail' parties for group chatter and jokes" (Beck, 1992). Mary Furlong (1989, p. 147), who started the nonprofit group as a research project at college, explains that there are four network features that enable members to find and communicate with one another: the Member Directory, Mail, the Forum, and Conferencing. The creation of an "electronic community" for older adults, providing an information access system as well as an emotional support system, has even spawned romance:

> JoAnn Oakes first "met" Mayer Solen, a 76-year-old widower from Carson City, Nev., during an on-line discussion about the problems of widowhood. "I liked what he said, and he liked what I said," says Oakes. They began talking on screen every night from 8 p.m. to midnight. Solen leaves love poems for her in her private electronic mailbox. They've met several times, and plan to travel to Chicago this month. Says Oakes, "He touched my soul, on line" (Beck, 1992).

VIDEO

With the preponderance of video and videogames available, this technology continues to dominate the field of technoeroticism. "Technological changes have played a major role in the development of the adult films business," Macero (1994, p. 6) reminds us. "The days of big screen porn theaters were all but doomed when the VCR was introduced. And watch-at-home sex film loops that once were the rage at stag parties." We are truly in the midst of a video revolution.

Video Cameras

With the price of camcorders within the price range of so many consumers, a whole new industry of amateur sex videos has been spawned. Claiming that our appetite for televised images began some 30 years ago when we witnessed the live murder of accused assassin Lee Harvey Oswald by Jack Ruby, Frank Rich (1993) updates it today with, "All the world's a Zapruder film that can be endlessly re-examined frame by frame on a VCR."

Videodating Services

Replacing more traditional sources of relationship formation, including the neighborhood, the church, schools, and even bars, dating services continue to gain favor as a monitoring device. Woll and Cozby (1987) have pointed out how this high-tech alternative to traditional approaches to relationship initiation provide a "real-world laboratory" for scholars interested in investigating early stages of interpersonal attraction.

In 1984 *The New York Times* cited the large matchmaking firm of Gentlepeople's claiming a 30 percent marriage rate (Butterfield, p. 8), while *Business Journal* reported on a profitable entrepreneur claiming that 40 percent of her first-time matches have resulted in committed relationships (Lindquist, 1987). Great Expectations, which boasts being the nation's largest franchise for video dating, aggressively advertised its more than 4,000 marriages from a membership of around 45,000 (Larson, 1987).

For their 1991 study of loneliness and communication competence in the dating marketplace, Bell and Roloff had their subjects pretend they would be video taping themselves, and asked them to write an accompanying script; their finding on self-disclosure: "When given the task of 'strutting their stuff' in a video-dating exercise, the subjects in the present study chose to focus on superficial demographic features to a greater extent than nonlonely people, and gave less attention to social aspects of their personalities" (p. 70).

Focusing on strategies subscribers to videodating services employ, Woll (1986) found age and attractiveness by far the most frequently mentioned factors in decision making, a result that held regardless of gender, age, and length of membership in the organization. Shaw (1992, p. 12) thinks the phenomenon recalls an earlier era—parlor life and the sentimental culture of the nineteenth century, where rules and behaviors ensured certain "safe," "clean" social skills; drawing on K. Halttunen's *Confidence Men and Painted Women: A Study of Middle-Class Culture in America, 1830-1870* (Yale, 1982), she writes: "Nineteenth-century society developed its sentimental code as a means to protect its genteel members from societal dangers in the forms of the confidence man and painted woman. In a like manner, twentieth-century society has created its own 'cultural condom' in the form of video dating."

While it might seem that the value of videodating would be the opportunity to save time and effort (plus face!) in the singles scene, Woll and Young (1989) found that 74 percent of their sample involved in the self-presentation process did so to prescreen potential dates. A smaller portion (20 percent) reported undertaking the search to consider the number and variety of eligible partners. Adelman and Ahuvia (1991, p. 285) cite their own studies, where respondents "reported being so tired of bad dates that they told the matchmaker not to introduce them to anyone else unless she was sure they would like the person." In an interview on dating services for *Chicago* magazine (Jannot, 1993), Aaron C. Ahuvia, a marketing professor at the University of Michigan, reported how, "People in the dating service were found to be less shy and have higher self-esteem than in the comparison group (and) also tended to have significantly higher standards in what they were looking for." Their conclusions about subscribers to dating services: "They're not there because they're not good enough for anybody else, but because they can't find anyone who's good enough for them. They're choosers, not losers" (Adelman and Ahuvia, 1991).

Video, which has traditionally been used as a powerful grassroots advocacy tool by a number of progressive individuals and groups, has recently come under something of a backlash, having been discovered by the Religious Right. Ouellette (1993, p. 18) tells about their amateur camcorder-produced documentary "The Gay Agenda" that opens with footage of gay men gyrating in G-strings and features bare-breasted lesbians dancing in front of children; it comes with this warning: "The gay rights movement is waging an aggressive nationwide offensive to force approval of their lifestyle." In response, the Gay and Lesbian Emergency Media Campaign (GLEMC) was formed, quickly producing a counter video called "Hate, Lies, and Videotape," followed later with "Sacred Lives, Civil Truths"; yet, to date the damaging homophobic images have unfortunately prevailed in terms of distribution and negatively mediated images.

And then too is the Better Sex Video Series, produced by the Learning Corporation of Pompano Beach, FL, sexual aids with names such as "Making Sex Fun" and "You Can Last Longer" that sell for $29.95. Ordered anonymously by mail, their appeal is the presentation of sex as nonthreatening and nonidealized. "Better sex is relentlessly ordinary," reports Swartz (1992). "People who aren't model-perfect go at it indoors, outdoors, in hot tubs, and solo—but in an excruciatingly ordinary way," showing people under stress, people not in the mood, even people who don't have erections. As explosive sales of these tapes have demonstrated, media-mediated sex doesn't even have to be extraordinary.

INTERACTIVE MEDIA

With possibilities such as *Penthouse* subscribers being offered the bonus of ordering free computer software enabling them to "talk" electronically to the "Pet of the Month," the interactivity business is booming. Predicated as long ago as 1909 in E.M. Forster's sci-fi story *The Machine Stops*—where humans were isolated from one another, forced to communicate through a two-way television device—interactivity today is considered a computer smorgasbord. Allowing an information exchange between the viewer and the programmer, enabling viewers to respond immediately to programming, it's technology that covers a wide range of services.

Two-Way Connections

California software publisher Sierra On-Line has initiated a commercial network that allows subscribers to control animated graphic interactive simulations that are versions of its computer games. One is slated to transform the company's best-selling adult software program, "Leisure Suit Larry," changed to "Larry Land": "Restricted to people who sign a statement that they are 18 or older, users will be able to configure the appearance of their own characters and engage in a variety of adventures with cartoon characters controlled by other users. When sex takes place, only faces will be visible on the screen" (Markoff, 1992).

Games, according to Reveaux (1994, p. 48) are big business; we are currently spending more on computer video games than on tickets to the movies, and "The U.S. Department of Commerce reports that spending on in-home entertainment climbed from $135.96 billion in 1985 to $223.3 billion in 1992." *New Media*[8] reports on one such addition to our technoculture:

> Lynn Hershman's computer-based installation *Room of One's Own* casts viewers in the role of peep-showvoyeurs. From the moment you step onto the mat in front of the kiosk and look through its rectangular slit, the installation's audio sensors know you are there. By peering through a small opening at a miniature bedroom scene, the viewer triggers video and computer action. As you peek in, a voice with a heavy German accent invites, "Look at your own eye. It's a television." A digitized video image of your own eye peers back at you from the screen of a tiny television set in the room, making you a "virtual" presence in the *Room of One's Own.*
>
> As you look at the tiny bed, telephone, table and television, your eye movements are tracked by a tiny video camera. As each object is seen, the location information is relayed to a computer, which in turn projects predetermined segments from a videodisc on the back wall of the bedroom. Hershman's San Francisco-based Hotwire Productions, which has created several provocative computer- and video-disc-based interactive installations, has recently finished production on a film entitled *Virtual Love.*

"The prevailing world view embedded in the games is one of extreme caution, even paranoia," concludes Gailey (1993, p. 89) about the mediated messages embedded in home video games, a content analysis presenting "a grim, even Hobbesian, picture of life, replete with sexism, racism, class hierarchy, competitive exclusion and other Social Darwinist notions" (p. 91). And yet, sales and rentals continue at ever-escalating rates.

BROADCASTING/CABLECASTING TECHNOLOGIES

Even though radio has been around for nearly a century and is still the most pervasive and ubiquitous telecommunications medium in the world, researchers and consumers alike tend to think of the power and presence of television when it comes to broadcasting. Those of us who monitor the field note a drastic move just within this last decade, however, from the notion of mass communication to that of "narrowcasting," targeting specific, specialized, self-selected viewing niches.

Probably nowhere is this trend more evident than in the service of pay-per-view (PPV). It may come as a surprise to you that this technology is not a new one, as it actually dates to early experiments conducted by the Zenith Radio Corporation's "Phonevision" back in 1947, when a just-developing television signal was offered unscrambled to a reluctant paying public. Typically offering sports and movies as principal venues, PPV's *The Miss Howard Stern New Year's Eve Pageant* of 1993, grossing some $16 million, became the best-selling entertainment pay-per-view special of all time.

Even though it is again becoming popular to publicly rail against violence on television, its global influence has hardly ever been questioned. As Michael J. O'Neill, former editor of *The Daily News,* recounts in *The Roar of the Crowd: How Television and People Power Are Changing the World* (Random House, 1993), the instant information flooding out into our oral-visual society, along with other communications technologies, demonstrate how difficult it is to grasp implications of such constantly flowing data sources. Economically, politically, and socioculturally, we need to maintain constant vigil over the mass of messages that pour forth into our homes each day, being particularly cognizant of their hidden meaning for the many viewers who use/need them for relationship purposes. Ken Auletta (1993, p. 68) sums it up best:

> While it is true that rap music that refers to women as "bitches," and Arnold Schwarzenegger movies in which people are casually killed ("*Hasta la vista, baby*"), and video games that invite players to gain points by slaying an opponent, and made-for-TV Amy Fisher movies, and tabloid-TV and blood-and-guts print journalism have less impact on vio-

lent behavior than poverty, drugs, guns and broken homes, as Hollywood claims, it is also beyond doubt that media images can affect the way people act.

VIRTUAL REALITY

A recent development in fully immersive, three-dimensional, computer-generated environments, "virtual reality" (VR) combines sight, sound, and touch; further, it is billed as the ultimate in compu-sex. "To enter virtual reality," according to Branwyn (1993, p. 789), "the user dons a head-mounted computer display and a pair of position-sensing gloves. As the user's hands move in real space, an analogous computer-generated pair of hands is seen moving in the head-mounted display. Eventually, full-body 'data suits' will be added which can read the shape and position of a user's body and display that information in the helmet."

For novelist Marc Laidlaw (1993, p. 648), virtual reality functions mainly as "a wonderful *plot device,* one that allows surreal effects without recourse to dreams or hallucinations. VR is a fine way of exploring, within the context of technology-oriented science fiction, the nature of reality." Susie Bright (1992b, p. 62) quotes a co-founder of Telepresence Research as distinguishing gender differences in the individual approach to VR: "Men see virtual reality as a clever way to avoid dealing with women, sex, and their own bodies. By contrast, women . . . speak of taking the body and all its wonderful sense organs with them into another world—not leaving it slumped over a keyboard when the brain zips off down some network."

Sexual prosthesis in virtual reality can be dealt with via "teledildonics" (Branwyn, 1993, pp. 789-790):

> Instead of a penis penetrating a vagina, the real-world penis is "invaginated" by the computer through means of a data-sensing "condom" or the vagina is penetrated by a dildo-like input/out device that reads and responds to the vagina. Sensors and responders ("tactile effectors") would work in tandem to simulate intercourse. The user's partner (or partners), also dressed in VR sex gear and connected via phone, would appear in the

head-mounted display as they wanted to be seen. Participants would construct desirable data forms for their partners to interact with.[9]

"Interactive sleaze began in 1986 when Mike Saenz designed his well-endowed, if cartoonish, Maxie MacPlaymate to respond to the user's mouse clicks," Stefanac (1993, p. 40) informs us. It was soon followed by the infamous floppy "Virtual Valerie," to date the best-selling CD-ROM title in the genre's brief history; Valerie has captured about 25 percent of the erotic sector, having sold about 25,000 a year, for a total of 100,000 units. Soon, we can anticipate the release of a "director's cut" of Valerie, as well as a more explicit and complex "DonnaMatrix." Also, Star Ware Publishing of Deerfield Beach, FL recently introduced "Wicked," starring a former Playboy Playmate, a suspense movie playing on Apple's QuickTime which it bills as "the first adult photo CD." The idea of photo CD technology is that it can store ultra high resolution images, each file containing 24-bit color (16.7 million colors) along with five different resolutions. Some of the company's interactive CD-ROMs include "Penthouse Interactive," "The Adult Movie Almanac," "Scissors-n-Stones," "Digital Dancing," and "Carnal Escapes," to name a few. Part of the Not-for-Cable-TV-Bundle-number-four is "GBL" (gay, bi, lesbian), which Star Ware calls the first CD solely devoted to "Alternative Lifestyles"; containing 347 megabytes in 2,494 files, it lists more than 300 bulletin boards and 155 erotic stories.

Penthouse offers "The Virtual Photo Shoot," where you position Dominique, Julie, and Natalie to "go through their video paces"; you "shoot" while the actors preen and poke, lick and look. And when you are done, editor Bob Guccione critiques your photographic prowess. From PC CompoNet in La Mirada, CA you can order titles such as "Visual Fantasies," "My Private Collection," "XXXtasy," and various "Hot Pix."

Not to be outdone, "NightWatch," by Interotica, allows the voyeur/player the ability to snoop around a plush singles resort; for example, "Dream Machine" provides an on-screen female guide and "Digital Dancing" is a striptease CD-ROM inviting the children's game 'paper, rock, scissors', and "Deep Contact: The Incomplete

Sexual Fantasy Disk" features a guide named Marion who lures the viewer into her computer world, encouraging communication throughout. What possibly can be next?

"Electronic Orgasms, Love Games of the 90's You Should Know About"[10] aired on *Donahue* in May of 1993. Using as an example the intererotica video "The Interactive Adventures of Seymour Butts," about a theoretical man who has found a video camera on Hollywood Boulevard and who uses it for a series of sexual adventures, Phil (as guinea pig) got to try out a number of options. After a few attempts, one of his callers commented, "I just wanted to say, you got it before I did. That's a great alternative for safe sex in the future." His guest, Andy Halliday, who was billed as a virtual reality expert and who is president of Edison Brother Entertainment, claims that the technology will continue to improve: "You have a fearless opportunity in cyberspace to practice social interaction. You are not encumbered by your physical appearance (and) you have control over your appearance. You could be a woman, for example, if you chose to be." R. U. Sirius, editor of the cyberpunk magazine *Mondo 2000,* added this about the social consequences of virtual reality: "It's an ambiguous gift that we have here. Obviously, human beings in general live fairly isolated lives, and it's a tremendous opportunity for people to reach out to thousands of people, people who generally just live at home, just interact with family and friends, to suddenly be on a network with thousands and thousands of people."

While all this is going on line, there is also a concurrent discussion ongoing about issues such as censorship, sexual harassment, pornography and obscenity, corporate responsibility, privacy, ethics of the media, protecting children, potential causal links to aggression and crime, differing "community standards," and the like. As the technology keeps reinventing itself, the dialogue needs to be brought forth to a wider public.

Predicting that cybersex will soon be a ubiquitously accepted legitimate entertainment, as well as recognized for educational and therapeutic purposes, Saenz claims: "Just as a flight simulator is used to train pilots before they climb into a real plane, I think sex simulation could be used to prevent unwanted pregnancies and warn about sexually transmitted diseases."[11] Technoeroticism, whether to relieve anxieties, prevent AIDS, and/or to stimulate the sexual palette, continues to redefine itself.

TELEPHONY

"While phone sex has existed as part of the sex industry for several decades (one used to pay for it the 'old-fashioned' way: with a credit card)," according to McCarthy (1993, p. 51), "the 'telerotic' 900 number is a recent phenomenon, a result of the simultaneous deregulation of telecommunications and broadcast and cable television during the Republican administration of the last decade." Goldstein (1991) has called it "The dial-ectic of desire." As Sarch (1993) has documented, the telephone has long been an important medium for personal relationships, especially for women, who she concluded use it as a means of exerting power and control with their dates. Understandably with the growth of pre-paid phone card use in Europe and Japan, we can expect a great deal of debit dialogue.

Phone Sex

No technology, according to Clark (1991, p. 984), has created more trouble for policy makers than "dial-a-porn":

> Prompted by the impending deregulation of the telephone industry in 1982, dozens of telephone entrepreneurs entered government lotteries to win the right to market telephone sex services that include both live encounters (known as "junk sex") with audio-prostitutes and recorded conversations that offer users the sounds of sex in all its variety in the privacy of their own receivers. The obvious problem with such services, which began as prefix 976 numbers but now also use 900, is that minors have easy access to them.

Harper's (Dec. 1990) has included a funny training manual for "Becoming a Dream Girl" on a live sex service mediated by telephone. On Valentine's Day of 1993 *Maury Povich* aired a program about workers in the erotic phone sex service. Marlene, an overweight 54-year-old woman with two children, reframes herself on the line as slim, sexy "Dorothy," whose specialty is that of a matrix; many of her regular customers, she claims, report having improved their sex lives. Her daughter "Amanda" has also recently begun working for the same company—it's an easy way to make extra money ($30 to $40 per hour), part-time, and from her own home. "Laura" likes working with couples—usually five or more at a time on a conference-type call line. A lesbian, "Joan," enjoys talking her clients through masturbations. While the workers are told not to meet their callers, some in fact confessed to breaking the rules—with mixed results. Overall, they describe their typical callers as white men, middle class and married, who are lonely enough to be willing to pay $50 for 20 minutes of conversation. One of their regulars spends about $500 per month; he's perfectly content, saying that it's still a lot cheaper than dates.

In the 1993 movie *Distinguished Gentleman,* Eddie Murphy is first seen around the Girls of Many Nations party line (800/PHONE SEX), where an operator is saying to a client, "You told me you wanted me to tie you up and. . . . " Once engaged in the service, the caller is told to push button number one for a "hot-blooded Italian," two for "perky American cheerleaders," or three for "a busty Swedish love goddess." When everyone else is busy, we laugh when Murphy himself answers that last line, feigning the proper accent to state, "I am Inga and I'm here from Sweden and I'm lonely."

Worcester Magazine (Valle, 1993) interviewed "Ernestine," co-owner of a fantasy phone service. Pointing out how regulated the 900 numbers are (no children, saying or pretending you're under 18, animals and things, incest, and the like), her company uses an 800 direct call-back system that clients can charge to Visa, MasterCard, AMEX, or charge to their home phone. Playing any number of characters, depending on what is requested, she exclaims how important it is to meet the $2.99 a minute contract: "A common misconception is that the women who work these lines are just real dumb or whores or something. But one of the most important things, like when I'm hiring a girl, is that she has to be intelligent." They can also draw the line as to how far they'll go—for example, mistress calls, ghost fantasies, devil desires, other women, whatever. Callers represent a wide range, including law students and celebrities amongst them: "A lot of people get very hooked, very quick, if you're personal with them, if you use their name a lot. There are a lot of ways to get them hooked very quickly." Men, Ernestine shares, "tend to want things that are really raw and raunchy, everything they don't have with their women. . . . They hang up just thinking they're stud of the month." Lesbians, she says, are very easy: "You just talk to them, you give them a bubble bath, a back rub and a little champagne, and you're all set." One person talked all night—the whole eight-hour shift; add it up: that's $1,435.20.

Through the *Springfield Advocate,* phone services are available ranging from cross-dresser guides to golf tips to soap opera updates; Date Lines has Gay Voice Personals, Sexy Singles, 24-Hour Easy Romance, HOT Gay Men; and Talk Lines offer Horny Housewives ("Oral Orgy with wet lip ladies"), uncensored Everything Goes, English Victoria's Pleasure Dome, Lip Service, "Live Nasty Nymphos In Heat," or Girls Talk Hot. The *Arizona Republic's* conversation classifieds have Babes Live 1 on 1 Talk, Exotic Live Talk, Explicit Group Action, Foxy Girls, Hot Forbidden Pleasures, Secret Desires, and Talk Any Way You Want It!

Almost from the moment that the Bell companies were dismantled, according to Tierney (1994, p. H18), "the purveyors of phone sex have been the leading innovators in the marketing and technology of pay-per-call services. They are already anticipating videophone sex, perhaps within two years." Many media watchers ("Stations hanging up on party lines," 1990; Rubens, 1990; Coy and Galen, 1991; Califia, 1992) are wondering just how far phone sex will go.

Voice Introduction Personals

Voice Introduction Personals are a fairly new phenomenon that appears to have great potential for the personals field. Whether local, national, or international, its usage for telephone researchers bears notice. Voice Mail typically is available on a 24 hours/day basis, which many participants prefer over the more traditional (and oftentimes agonizing) method of writing a response.

Writing in the *New Statesman,* Richard Walker (1990, p. 12) reports on one ad that he responded to:

> Hi, I'm Danielle. I'm 29 years of age, a vivacious redhead, five feet eight inches tall, medium build, and busty. I love to wear slinky clothes and underwear. I love the smell of leather. Frankly, I'm told I'm oversexed, extremely naughty, and need to mend my bad ways. In fact, I'm probably in need of a jolly good spanking by a tall, good-looking, well-endowed master who's slim, up to about 38 years of age, and who will certainly have his work cut out for him.

Forbes (Meeks, 1991) has documented a number of financial success stories made possible through voice mail—the *LA Weekly* reported an average of 9,000 calls per issue, as compared with five letters under its old system; the *Tucson Weekly* quadrupled personal ad revenues to around $60,000; even *The Village Voice* expanded its personals columns from two to six or more pages.

Moreover, just as the *Boston Globe* classifieds encourage you to meet that "someone special" through an organization called Rich and Famous, or the *Advocate* classifieds help you "Learn the Art of French Domination" or connect with Male-to-Male Hardbodies or the S&M Connection, there are many such services; see Appendix 8: *Telephone Resources for Media-Mediated Relationships.*

Other Types of Telephony

Whether by using fiber optics, radio waves, and/or the Integrated Services Digital Network (ISDN), there is no question that telephony is at the heart of the telecommunications revolution. While radio-based technologies, such as cellular telephones, personal communication networks, or mobile satellite services, predominate, or whether voice mail, videophones, or enhanced facsimile machines prevail, there is no doubt that marketers will find ways to reach relationship seekers. Influenced by Everett M. Rogers' groundbreaking work in *Diffusion of Innovations* (3rd ed., 1983), those of us who monitor media will continue not only to observe but also to consider implications and ramifications of communications technologies. At the same time, we keep a vigilant eye on Washington, questioning and advocating for access in the current re-regulatory climate.

Closer to interpersonal networks, Roan (1992) has documented the role of telephones as a burgeoning aspect of therapeutic counseling. Lasting less than 30 minutes, at about $80 per session, 900-number psychological phone lines offer quick, convenient, cost-effective suggestions—hopefully properly diagnosed.

"Tomorrow's media will be shaped not only by technology but by their audiences," claims George Comstock (1988, p. 324), "and much can be learned about the future of the media from what we know about today's audiences." He offers some propositions:

1. Public opinion and behavior in regard to the media are marked by incongruities.
2. The mass media are accorded a place in social life very much on their own terms; liking them or disliking them has little to do with whether they are used, how they are used, or even how much they are used.
3. Evaluation of the mass media is aligned with other fundamental attitudes and dispositions but behavior in regard to the media is to a large degree independent on such attitudes and dispositions.
4. Opinions about the media, and particularly evaluation of them, have far less to do with media use than do the time available and the prevailing norms.
5. The performance of the mass media does not rank high among the concerns of the public.
6. What the public says in regard to television news and what it does are incongruent; television is the symbol but not the agent or regular news delivery.
7. There is no newly emerging public disenchantment with the news media.
8. The news media cannot avoid audiences perceiving them as biased, and having an informed public will not eliminate the perception of bias.
9. The public has a poor understanding of the First Amendment as the constitutional basis of mass media policy in the United States.

10. The public assigns more importance to the responsibilities than to the rights of the mass media. (pp. 324-338)

"The mass media will occupy an increasingly prominent place in everyday life," Rice predicts (p. 153), saying that development of technologies will only further usage trends. "Whatever our view of the media may be, we can expect that they will be with us and we with them increasingly." Depending on what media resources we have, and have access to, our utilization of the information inherent in that data bespeaks volumes about us as individuals and as members of a wider society. Even though information, intangible as it may seem, has traditionally been ignored by neoclassical economists, Gandy (1993, p. 92) has argued that, "Personal information is a vital component of the technology of economic, social, and political management in the current stage of late capitalism. Its transformation into a commodity whose production, distribution, and use is governed by a complex of laws, customs, and technological constraints generates a host of practical and theoretical problems." Trying to make sense of the dizzying array of technologies entering our consumer marketplace, and wondering where they fit into combining multiculturalism with multimedia, Gallimore and Fuller (forthcoming) caution us to keep questioning sociocultural considerations about the information rich and the information poor.

NOTES

1. Harold Lasswell was an early theorist of mass communication who developed a simple narrative model posing four questions: *Who says what? In which channel? To whom? With what effect?*

2. Book review of Martin Lea's *Contexts of Computer-Mediated Communication* in *Communication Research Trends*, Volume 13, No. 3 (1993), p. 2.

3. See, for example, Stein (1991), Dolan (1993), Valeriano (1993).

4. John A. Barry, *Technobabble* (Cambridge, MA, 1991), p. 243. Cited in Mark Dery's "Flame Wars," *South Atlantic Quarterly*, 92, No. 4 (Fall, 1993), p. 559. See also Martin Lea, Tim O'Shea, Pat Fund, and Russell Spears' "'Flaming' in computer-mediated communication" in Lea (1992), p. 89-112.

5. Peter Farb, *Word Play* (NY: Alfred A. Knopf, 1973), p. 69. He writes, "Within each speech community, the language spoken mirrors human life—the personalities of the speakers, their attitudes and beliefs, their styles of thought and expression, their interactions with one another" (pp. 366-367).

6. Cited in Stefanac (1993, p. 39).

7. Judith Berck (1992) also points out that while estimates are that the bulletin board industry is worth $500 million, there are also some 60,000 public access facilities in the U.S.

8. Gay Graves, "Room of One's Own," *New Media* (January, 1994), p. 126.

9. Branwyn reports that, "An on-line orgasm looks like something out of a comic book, with drawn-out ohhhhh's, ahhhhhhhhhh's, WOW!!!'s, and the obligatory 'I'mmmm commmmmmmmminnnggggggggg!!!!!!' "

10. "Electronic Orgasms, Love Games of the 90's You Should Know About," *Donahue* transcript #3746 (May 25, 1993).

11. Cited in Stefanac (1993, p. 41).

Chapter 5

Media-Mediated Relationships
in Motion Pictures, Music, and More

In past years Hollywood has brought us such high notes of sexual delirium as Marlon Brando buttering up Maria Schneider without taking his own clothes off, William Hurt breaking hard-to-replace windows to go after Kathleen Turner's little red skirt in the foyer of her Florida mansion, Art Garfunkel having a final session with the post-suicidal body of his troubled, beloved Theresa Russell, and, more recently, Sharon Stone masturbating with extraordinary sincerity in her bathtub and, ho-hum, Jaye Davidson turning out to have a penis, and even more recently, the way-too-nude Harvey Keitel going native with Holly Hunter's amazingly heart-shaped butt. What will they think of next?

—Campbell and Rebello, "Futuresex" (*Movieline,* 1994)[1]

As has already been documented here, the entertainment industries are laden with case studies supporting the notion of media-mediated relationships. What follows here are yet more instances—in film, sound recordings, and other venues.

MOTION PICTURES

In their book *The Classical Hollywood Cinema: Film Style & Mode of Production to 1960* (Routledge & Kegan Paul, 1985), film historians David Bordwell, Janet Staiger, and Kristin Thompson make the following argument: "The historical and aesthetic impor-

147

tance of the classical Hollywood cinema lies in the fact that to go beyond it we must go through it." I have been developing a theory regarding an instrumental approach to "going through" film studies through investigating some of its sub-contextual elements. Coining the term "intracinematology," (Fuller, working paper) thanks to my sources at the (Springfield, MA-based) G. & C. Merriam Company, I envision it as a means of penetrating into the deepest aspects of motion pictures, uncovering the many aspects and layers of film that can provide clues to our better understanding both its manifest and latent content.

"Movies did not last much more than a few minutes in the 1890s and an embrace was almost all they had time for. Later, the motion picture camera learned to peer through keyholes, which may be why the nickelodeons appealed to those who liked the peepshows on the seaside promenades," writes David Shipman (1985, p. 7). "Romantic love had long been a preoccupation of the stage but the cinema added a prurient note, leaving audiences to speculate on what exactly occurred between the cuddling couple in the railway carriage as their train went through a tunnel; or what thoughts passed through the mind of the shoe store assistant when his customer raised her skirt a little higher than necessary." Arguing that contemporary action cinema "inflects and redefines already existing cinematic and cultural discourses of race, class and sexuality," Yvonne Tasker (1993) supports the notion that scholars need to consider not just the pleasures but also the political significance of films.

Going beyond aesthetic and personal responses to consider connections between social phenomena and social reality, intracinematology will be put to the test here in terms of media-mediated relationships. The *Filmography* in Appendix 9, as well as *Film/Video Resources* in Appendix 10, give some indication of the many relevant motion pictures and industries that will be discussed here. First, the environmental aspects will be considered in terms of psychosociological angst as demonstrated in film, followed by examples of dating/mating and then specific media mediations.

Psycho-Sociological Angst

As this book goes to press, Hollywood has been enjoying an unpredicted heyday both at the box office and in after-markets such as video rental stores and abroad. Also unprecedented is the success of nonformulaic films, which break tradition with standard action-adventure fare (e.g., Arnold Schwarzenegger's *Last Action Hero* of 1993 lost some $40 million), sequels of nearly anything that once made money, and traditional views of romance. The simple stories of *Forrest Gump* and *The Lion King* as well as nostalgic reconstructions such as *The Flintstones, Little Women,* and *The Brady Bunch Movie* have garnered enormous box office attention.

Love in the movies nowadays, for example, oftentimes is obsessive and downright sad. Bob Hoskins performs brilliantly as the repressed chauffeur to an elegantly ensnaring prostitute in Neil Jordan's *Mona Lisa* (1986). Obsessive love is also the theme of *A Short Film About Love* (1988), *A Flame in My Heart* (1990), and *Damage* (1992). Love in the movies doesn't come easily. Consider the demented characters in Norman Mailer's *Tough Guys Don't Dance* (1987), or the thirtysomething Peter Pan types of *Slaves of New York* (1989) or *Watch It* (1993) who fear commitment to the opposite sex, and just want to remain party animals.

We have lots of compulsions to worry about, it would seem. In 1991, two films aired about the social disease of the era—eating disorders—in Henry Jaglom's *Eating* and Katherine Gilday's *The Famine Within*; through these, we hear examples of women talking about preferring a well-prepared potato to sex. *I Don't Buy Kisses Anymore* (1992) stars Jason Alexander as a shy, overweight shoe salesman who feeds his loneliness with Baci chocolates; the plot progresses when his food obsession becomes the subject of Nia Peebles' masters thesis and she becomes the subject of his attentions. Will food become the ultimate sex substitute? The movies *Betrayal* (1983), *Cousins* (1989), *Consenting Adults* (1992), *Damage* (1992), *Indecent Proposal* (1993), and *Married People, Single Sex* (1993) assure us that philandering is out. We wonder: what *is* safe?

It is quite a statement that some of the hottest movie scenes recently have hardly involved contact at all. Consider, for example, these scenes from 1993 fare: when, in *Age of Innocence*, Daniel Day-Lewis unbuttons Michelle Pfeiffer's glove; Emma Thompson backs Anthony Hopkins into a corner in *The Remains of the Day*; Jodie Foster nicks Richard Gere during a shave in *Sommersby*; Harvey Keitel fingers Holly Hunter's leg through a tiny hole in her stocking in *The Piano*; an entrée is foreplay in *Like Water for Chocolate*; and Meg Ryan at last gets to see Tom Hanks in *Sleepless in Seattle*. If television's *Seinfeld* is supposed to be the trend-setter in today's entertainment in which "nothing is happening," perhaps it is all for a purpose.

Despite the continual climb in sales and rentals of porn movies, mainstream movies often give quite different messages. Pornography itself even comes under attack in recent films. Consider, for example, Canadian director Bonnie Sherr Klein's 1981 *Not a Love Story*, where the perspective is that porn is not culturally determined, but instead is inherent in man's latent misogyny. Or another feminist response in Betty Gordon's *Variety* (1993), where a woman who works as a ticket vendor at a porn cinema finds herself being slowly drawn to both the ambience on the screen and one of the older clients. *Kamikaze Hearts* (1986) examines the porn industry as a whole, especially the women in it, focusing in particular on star Sharon Mitchell.

Deception as a plot convention abounds. While nothing can compare to the public surprise at Neil Jordan's *The Crying Game* (1992), ten years earlier *Cafe Flesh* (1982) was projecting a post-apocalyptic future where 99 percent of the remaining inhabitants were Sex Negative, unable to indulge in intimacy without becoming nauseous. Consider closely the comedic premise of *Made in America* (1993), where Afrocentric Whoopi Goldberg's daughter finds out that her father was (white) sperm-bank donor Ted Danson ("He was only three inches tall, and came in a tube," protests the mother). The sex in 1994's *Exit to Eden*, based on an Anne Rice novel, is S&M, "Fantasy Island" style.

Blame it on our urban context. A couple of documentaries set the stage. *Rate It X* (1985) included interviews with men involved in the "consumer zone," unearthing ugly layers of sexism that continue to permeate our society. Benz' 1988 *Heavy Petting* asked celebrities Sarah Bernhard, David Byrne, Spalding Gray, and others about their sexual initiations, providing yet another view of how sexual codes of conduct have shifted. On the big screen, Sharon Stone starred in a little-seen 1990 psychological thriller called *Scissors* portraying a woman living alone in the big city who thwarts an assailant with scissors, but then lives in fear of his vow to return.

Three box office hits in 1992 pounded harder on this theme: John Schlesinger's *Pacific Heights*, about the landlord from hell; a twist on depending on the police in *Unlawful Entry*; and Ellen Barkin as a woman who decides she needs an attack dog in *Man Trouble*—a canine trained by Jack Nicholson. The main message: it's a scary world out there.

It's especially frightening if one is alone. Dating back to Richard Brooks' 1977 *Looking for Mr. Goodbar*, starring Diane Keaton as a sad single woman cruising bars for Mr. Right in a thriller based on the Judith Rossner novel, the filmic lesson to be learned is that there are a lot of psychos out there. E. Ann Kaplan (Metheun, 1983, p. 75) sees *Goodbar* in the genre of post-utopian idealism of the 1960s of films featuring "the desperate search in the singles bars for drugs and the sexual 'fix' that would mask the loneliness of alienated lives, spawned by increased mobility, the new industrial patterns of the computer age, and the further breakdown of community in the large urban centers." Soon we got *Lonely Lady* (1982), Harold Robbins' sleazy story of a Hollywood ingenue; *The Lonely Guy* (1984), a comedy with Steve Martin about loneliness among the not-so-swinging singles set; and *The Game of Love* (1987), where the lonely lost and found gather at Henry's bar to quench their various thirsts.

Foreign films also reflected the theme, as in the Australian *Lonely Hearts* (1983), about two losers who meet and mangle romantic visions through a dating service; Maggie Smith's brilliant performance as a middle-aged Irish spinster in *The Lonely Passion of Judith Hearne* (1987); and the 1990 Soviet film *Lonely Woman Seeks Life Companion,* a statement about the bleak life of all singles. That same year brought the Indian immigrant hero of *Lonely in America* (1990) to the big screen, focusing on adjustments that any unattached person needs to make. Our young, reluctant hero gets sucked in by a television advertisement for The Learning Annex, which promises to help you become popular, and get dates; when he enrolls, the advice is that you can't just wait for the perfect guy or gal, however,—you need to go out there, make yourself interesting, emit a glow saying that you're fun and available.

John Candy plays a 38-year-old policeman who still lives with his mother (Maureen O'Hara) in *Only the Lonely* (1991). *Lonely Hearts* (1991), starring Beverly D'Angelo as the pawn to smooth-talking con man Eric Roberts, reeks with warnings about compulsive, desperate behavior, while *Are You Lonesome Tonight?* (1992) carries a caution about getting involved with phone sex.

Voyeurism, formally known as "scoptophilia," or the morbid desire to watch, began its development as a film genre with Alfred Hitchcock's *Rear Window* of 1954, where James Stewart, immobilized because of a broken leg, begins checking out his fellow apartment dwellers, first with binoculars and then with a camera; by limiting the film's camera to Stewart's point of view, murder mixes with black humor in this meta-filmmaking classic. That same year also saw Richard Quine's *Pushover*; Hitchcock's *Psycho* (1960) continued an appeal to our prurient needs. *Peeping Tom* (1960) brought the story of a Brit's obsessions; Antonioni's *Blow Up* (1966) allows the audience to view things along with the photographer; and *Extreme Close-Up* (1972) takes a legal stance on privacy.

In 1980 Burt Lancaster ogles Susan Sarandon in *Atlantic City* as she is bathing her breasts at the sink, while *Private Lessons* concerns itself with a case of teen-oriented voyeurism. After a romantic trauma, Joseph Bottoms loses his sight and has a computer embedded in his brain in *Blind Date* (1984)—a preview of many man/machine films that were to follow. *Lady Beware* (1987) concerns Diane Lane as a talented store window dresser who is pursued by a psychotic who watches her every move. The evil of it all is further revealed in *Cheap Shots* (1988), *Monsieur Hire* (1989), and *Over Exposed* (1990), where women become psycho-bait victims.

The repressed 1990s have embraced voyeurism with a vengeance. While topless dancing clubs, X-rated cable channels, and virtual reality continue to be considered hot activities, the trend is also apparent in the motion pictures. Madonna, the stellar star of our voyeuristic age, commissioned her own documentary: *Truth or Dare* (1991). The camera, usually one with a telephoto lens, tries to tell all. *Blind Vision* (1992) features a murderous Peeping Tom; *Dance with Death* (1992) concerns the killings of a number of topless dancers, as *Sunset Strip* (1992) stars Michelle Foreman, a Los Angeles stripteaser. *Basic Instinct* (1992) preys on our perverse fascination with the fact that Sharon Stone is panty-less during an investigation; *Animal Instincts* (1992), supposedly based on a true story, concerns a husband/cop who can only get aroused by viewing his wife on video with other men; and *Fade to Black* (1993) centers around a voyeuristic professor who finds himself in the thick of a murderous blackmail plot after he inadvertently captures a murder on his video camcorder.

Sliver (1993), starring Sharon Stone, unabashedly promoted its tacky thriller theme of voyeurism, when actually it was meta-voyeurism; while it didn't do well at the box office—many people boycotted it—its video history has kept it alive. *Entertainment Weekly* (O'Toole, 1993, p. 72) made an astute observation:

> Every decade gets the blond icon it deserves. Depression audiences found posh refuge in the ultraglamour of Marlene Dietrich. The repressed '50s sought the luscious dizziness of Marilyn Monroe. The silly '70s had the big hair and bland smile of Farrah Fawcett-Majors. The over-the-top '80s ate up Madonna. And the '90s have Sharon Stone.
>
> Why? There's the obvious: As the sexually ambiguous Catherine Tramell in 1992's *Basic Instinct*, Stone exemplified a certain type of '90s woman, a sexual maverick with a great body and Amazonian attitude—a woman in complete control. A phenomenon, though not necessarily a star, was born.

Other media too have picked up on the idea of considering the consumer as spectator. For one thing, it has begun to receive some academic interest (e.g., Denzin, 1995; Dixon, 1995). Advertisers, too, have taken note at the "gender bender" possibilities of the wildly successful Diet Coke ad where women leer at a hunk construction worker who takes off his shirt while downing his soda. The book *Shot in the Heart*, the story of executed killer Gary Gilmore, is told by his father from the vantage point of the voyeur, complete with photographs and an intimate view of the family. And Garcia (1994, H17) has even noted how men and women find eroticism quite differently in various cinematic scenes.

Dating/Mating

First, there were matchmakers—literally, Thorton Wilder's *The Matchmaker* (1958) and its sequel-of-sorts, *Hello Dolly* (1969). Following on its Broadway success, the musical *Fiddler on the*

Roof came to the big screen in 1971; directed by Norman Jewison, it recounts the story of a poor dairy farmer who, at the turn of the century, is trying to marry off his three daughters. *Mail Order Bride* (1963) is a twist on the western, telling about a bride who has been chosen in the hopes that she would be "woman enough to tame" a wild young cattle rancher. In 1982 Valerie Bertinelli starred as a magazine writer assigned to run an advertisement for a husband in *I Was a Mail Order Bride*. More currently, videodating services have preempted the matchmaker role.

Supplementally, "the oldest profession" has frequently been featured in film—if with variations since the uptight 1980s. While *Prostitute* (1980) provided a British perspective on harassment by police and the courts, treating sex for sale as a job like any other, *Best Little Whorehouse in Texas* (1982) came off as a raucous, raunchy musical on the subject starring Burt Reynolds, Dolly Parton, and Dom DeLuise. *Scarred* (1983) showed the scary, sleazy side of the issue; Kathleen Turner divided her time between being a serious career woman by day and ultra-hooker China Blue after hours, acting out male fantasies, in *Crimes of Passion* (1984); and director Lizzie Borden focused on prostitution as an economic alternative for some women in *Working Girls* (1986).

Several semi-biographies also appeared around this time—notably, Bob Fosse's *Star 80* (1983), about *Playboy* pinup Dorothy Stratten's life prior to her being murdered by her husband; *Personal Services* (1987), based on the true-life story of British madam Christine Painter; and Candice Bergen as the debutante Sydney Biddle Barrows, who was known as the *Mayflower Madam* (1987). *Elliot Fauman, PhD* (1990) had as its creative premise the idea of a psychology professor (Randy Dreyfuss) who was studying call girls—a far cry from Julia Roberts' vivacious Vivian in *Pretty Woman* (1990). And most recently, *Secret Games: The Escort* (1993) brings us full circle to the kinds of trouble dealing with call girls can bring.

Single life as profiled in Helen Gurley Brown's *Sex and the Single Girl* of 1964 today looks just as anachronistic as *For Singles Only* (1968), the latter about a group of California "swingles"—big-breasted women and beefcake men, living together in an apartment complex. *The Rachel Papers* (1989), based on the Martin Amis novel, tells the tale of an Oxford youth who plots the seduction of a beautiful American girl via his computer. Fast forward to Cameron Crowe's *Singles* of 1992 to see twentysomethings going through the paces in contemporary Seattle and the anomie and anxiety shine through. One of my favorite scenes is when a group sits around critiquing Sheila Kelley's video for self-advertisement; titled "Expect the Best," it begins with her in the shower with *Psycho* music in the background, zooming in to her eyes, then having her fly on an oriental rug like Superwoman, giving a statement about craving respectability, having serenity as a goal, along with knowing men who can understand her. "No druggies" gets inserted before the sexy ending that she delivers after taking a big drag on a cigarette: "Come to where the flavor is—Debby country!"

Looking for Mr. Goodbar (1977), cited earlier, still stands as the defining film about the price one pays in our alienating urban centers. The Richard Brooks thriller, starring Diane Keaton, reveals that she has come from a dysfunctional family, but strongly includes heavy doses of morality embedded throughout the erotic overlay. *The Personals* (1982) adds yet another perspective on the singles scene in the early 1980s. *Single Bars, Single Women* (1984) is a comedy-drama about relationships, as is *The Game of Love* (1987), which takes places at a trendy Los Angeles club. Dating is definitely different for aforementioned *Singles* (1992) Campbell Scott, Kyra Sedgwick, Bridget Fonda, Matt Dillon, and Sheila Kelley.

Further, "In the current cinema, gay men are portrayed as sexual obsessives or simpering invalids," bemoans *Details* (Weir, 1994, p. 131). "Why can't anyone get it right?" Arguing that homosexuals in contemporary film are mainly depicted as a social problem, Weir writes: "Movie homos lately come in two varieties. They are either part of the acceptable mainstream fantasy, thankfully scrubbed clean of sexuality and regrettably dying, or they are living on the faggot fringe, tortured to a sadomasochistic frenzy (see Demme's *The Silence of the Lambs*) or suicidal despair by their unmanageable sexual desire" (p. 132). Richard Dyer (1990) blames it on our hetero-obsessed society. Its history in film, according to Fejes and Petrich (1993), dates to Thomas Edison's 1895 short *The Gay Brothers*, showing two men dancing together, that shocked audiences way back then; a century later, it could be argued, we certainly have not made much progress. Consider, for example,

John Malkovich as a repressed homosexual in *Queen's Logic* (1991); Damon Wayans' take-off on gays in his jewelry store romp for *Mo' Money* (1992); the gay teacher who tries to blackmail a student into having sex with him in *Stephen King's Sleepwalkers* (1992); the revival for our memories of vitriolic, anti-Communist, and homophobic crusader Roy Cohn in *Citizen Cohn* (1992); the young murderers Loeb and Leopold in *Swoon* (1992); or the demented homophobic fag-bashing skinhead in *Falling Down* (1993), whose diatribe was devised for comic relief.

Claiming that lesbian images have been virtually invisible in Hollywood cinema, which tends instead to deal mainly with heterosexual romance, Weiss (1992, p. 1) has written: "Each lesbian image that has managed to surface—the lesbian vampire, the sadistic or neurotic repressed woman, the pre-Oedipal 'mother/daughter' lesbian relationship, the lesbian as sexual challenge or titillation to men—has helped determine the boundaries of possible representation, and has insured the invisibility of many other kinds of lesbian images." Later, she comments on the role of the spectator in this process: "The few lesbian images offered by the cinema were created for heterosexual male viewers, to appeal to male voyeurism about lesbians and to articulate and soothe male anxieties about female autonomy or independence from men" (p. 4).

Only recently have inroads been made in scholarship on gays and lesbians in film—notably Dyer (1984, 1990); Weiss (1986, 1992); Russo (1987); Bad Object Choices (1991); Hadleigh (1991); Kauffman (1992); Rich (1992); Doty (1993); Fejes and Petrich (1993); Stewart (1993); and Tyler (1993). Following the success of Harvey Feirstein's *Torch Song Trilogy* (1988), which Matthew Broderick helped bring straight audiences to, drag life as depicted in Jennie Livingston's documentary *Paris Is Burning* (1991) is much more raw;[2] the latter, while it received good critical review, brought little empathy or box office revenue from a distinctly removed public.

If death is coming to the voguing movement, the onslaught and fear of AIDS is also taking its toll on a number of transvestites. *Fun Down There* (1988), another movie made after a popular theatrical production, began a series showing gays as regular people, a trend which many people wish would continue. Instead, *My Own Private Idaho* (1991) portrayed pitiful loneliness; *No Skin Off My Ass*

(1991), a joint Canadian/German release, observed obsessive behavior of homosexual punks; and *The Lost Language of Cranes* (1992), produced by the BBC, concerned the torment of a gay married man leading a double life, whose son has the courage of his convictions to come out. More encouraging is the appearance of gay symbols consciously embedded in film, such as the T-shirt with "SILENCE = DEATH"[3] along with the inverted pink triangle worn by Whoopi Goldberg's co-worker at "The African Queen" boutique where they work in *Made in America* (1992).

Of particular interest to me, in my ongoing study of the role of communication in the AIDS pandemic, is how the disease is played out and perceived in motion pictures (Roth and Fuller, forthcoming).[4] While it is beyond the scope of this book to detail Hollywood's slow progress toward dealing with the issue, it should be pointed out that a few feature films—notably, Arthur J. Bressan, Jr.'s *Buddies* (1985), *Longtime Companion* (1990), and most recently Jonathan Demme's highly publicized *Philadelphia* (1994)—have conspicuously aimed at presenting gays as "regular" folks. The "just-happens-to-be-gay" next-door neighbor character is beginning to appear in film, such as in *Prince of Tides* (1991), *Frankie & Johnny* (1991), *This Is My Life* (1992), and *Single White Female* (1992). Yet, what is really disturbing, in contrast, is gay backlash, hurting or even hiding gay characters, such as has been recently happening in films such as *Silence of the Lambs* (1991), *Fried Green Tomatoes* (1991), and *Basic Instinct* (1992).

Together Alone (1992), which was a hit on the gay/lesbian film festival circuit, centers around a conversation between two strangers who meet at a Los Angeles nightclub, have unprotected sex, and talk about many of the issues concerning them. A hopeful sign also is the recently released *Sex Is. . .* (1993), Marc Huestis' documentary celebrating gay intimacy. *The Wedding Banquet*, an Oscar nominee for Best Foreign Film of 1993, brought cross-audiences not only in terms of sexual orientation but also of varying cultures. And Mary Louise Parker's performance as a hetero with AIDS in Herbert Ross's *Boys on the Side* (1995) was well regarded by both critics and audiences. Perhaps the answer lies in outing movie homoeroticism along with our cultural homophobia.

Regardless of our opinions about individual films, stars, producers, directors, genres, and/or individual plot conventions, there is no question about the power of pictures in advancing contemporary mythologies. As film producers see growing box office receipts for date movies (Berkman, 1993), it is the business of those of us who teach in this field to point out critical skills for examining both wider and specifically embedded themes that can be extrapolated from Hollywood fare.

MEDIA MEDIATIONS IN THE MOVIES

The motion pictures have a number of media-relevant themes. The telephone, for example, figures in *Don't Answer the Phone* (1980), which had a perverted photographer stalking patients of a psychological talk-show hostess, as well as in 1988's *Call Me* and *Smooth Talker* (1990). More prominently, however, are the roles of the personals, phone sex, radio relationships, and video and its variations.

The Personals in Film

Regarding the print media, "the personals" have been featured in a number of recent motion pictures.[5] Movie critic Caryn James (1989, p. C19) has pointed out how a number of the words used in personal advertisements also reflect the movies. Whereas *Desperately Seeking Susan* stole from the personals, advertisers frequently use expressions and names: Indiana Jones, Vicki Vale, Peter Pan, Valmont, The Bear, Woody Allen, Harry wanting to meet Sally, or someone wanting to cross Delancey, join a Dead Poets Society, or get *The Little Mermaid*.

The earliest self-advertisement recorded in the motion pictures dates to the silent era. Consider this comedy, produced in black and white nearly a quarter of a century before the introduction of sound, as delineated by film historian Robert Sklar (1994, p. 29): "When Biograph made a funny film, *Personal* (1904), about a Frenchman who advertised in the paper for a wife and then was chased around Grant's Tomb and through Riverside Park by more than a dozen husband-seeking women, the Edison company made its own version, same story, same location, and called it *How a French Nobleman Got a Wife Through the New York Herald Personal Column.* Another manufacturer simply copies the Biograph print and sold it as its own."

Although they undoubtedly appeared in many movies prior to Leonard Kastle's *The Honeymoon Killers* (1970), that feature marked the first filmic convention in which the personals figured prominently in a plot. Based on a 1947 true crime story about two lovers who became known as the "Lonely Hearts Killers," who met through the personals, they are described as "victims of romantic delusion—self-styled star-crossed lovers driven to hideous extremes to preserve their passion—without excusing the viciousness of their crimes."[6]

The 1980s have witnessed a rash of personals-related movies. First, there was Moshe Mizrahi's *I Sent a Letter to My Love* (1981)—Simone Signoret as an aging spinster who, faced with the prospect of loneliness should she lose her paralyzed brother, places a personal advertisement in the local newspaper; unbeknownst to either of them, the brother in fact is the one who responds to the ad, and the two begin a romantic correspondence. In 1982 came *Eating Raoul*, a low budget, funny film noir that has become something of a cult classic. Paul and Mary Bland decide to make money by collapsing their morals, instead advertising kinky sex through the personals. "We do anything . . . whatever your fantasy," their appeal reads—for cash. Their first victim begs to be disciplined by a mommy, while another dresses like a Nazi and wants to be tied up. The Blands link up reluctantly with Raoul, who owns a lock service, but when he makes too many demands (he gets cash for bodies at Doggie King, a burger joint), they murder him too. The couple then decides to grind him up for a special Mexican dish, gloating, "It's amazing what you can do with a cheap piece of meat."

Sex was also the theme of 1983's teen comedy sensation *Risky Business*. Friends of clean-cut Joel (Tom Cruise) whose parents are off on vacation respond to an ad that reads, "For a good time in the privacy of your home, call Jackie," and have a hooker sent over to him. "She" is a black transvestite who relinquishes duties to a young woman ends up having one wild night with Joel and his friends. *The Personals* (1983) is a light comedy following a Woody Allen-type recent divorcee (Bill Schoppert) who is trying to get back into the dating game. Agatha Christie used the sedate personals column of Chipping Cleghorn's *N. Benham Gazette* in *A Murder Is Announced* (1984), where in fact a death occurred as announced in the classifieds; needless to say, Joan Hickson as Miss Marple found the killer.

By mid-decade, things get more complicated. As the personals began to gain in both actual popularity and presence, their content changes—reflective of just the time when the media was discovering AIDS as a valuable news story. *Desperately Seeking Susan* (1985) is the ultimate personals film, and the clearest one from which to examine the tenor of the times. For the first time, the personals were treated not for sex, but as a means for finding excitement, companionship, acceptance of self. Directed from a feminist perspective by Susan Siedelman, its plot concerns a bored housewife (Rosanna Arquette as Roberta) who wants to add some excitement to her life, and so follows the personal love columns. Via a number of unlikely plot convolutions involving mobsters, hit men, Madonna, and identity crises, we are all drawn in as voyeurs.

The next year, we became engrossed in Michael Mann's thriller *Manhunter*, where the jailed psychopathic psychiatrist Dr. Hannibal ("The Cannibal") Leckter and a man being hunted are in contact—through the personals. Their codes need to be deciphered for the case to be solved. *Classified Love* (1986) focuses on three co-workers who decide to improve their social lives by placing ads in a magazine's personals column. The comedy *Perfect Match* (1987) centers on a couple who get their due from falsifying claims about themselves in the personals, while in the oddball *Tough Guys Don't Dance* (1987) one of the characters places an ad in *Screw Magazine* reading: "Young white Christian couple seeks outlet weekend with other couple."

Lately, the main message in the print personals, as discussed in Chapter 2, has been the suggestion of their use for finding romance, commonality, nest-building, a blending of similar interests without the prerequisite sexual involvement. Recent films reflect this trend, demonstrating that the traditional use of self-advertising columns could, in fact, get you in trouble—even, as the contemporary books dealing with the personals imply, murdered. Witness, for example, the 1989 hit *Sea of Love*, where Al Pacino plays the role of a NYPD detective in search of a serial killer whose male victims have all played the personals seeking members of the opposite sex. Or, consider Woody Allen's *Crimes and Misdemeanors* (1990), where his sister is tied up and defecated on by a man she met through the personal columns. That notion of retribution also appears in the 1990 made-for-cable *Personals* starring Jennifer O'Neill as a librarian who develops fatal attractions for the men she meets in the classified columns, as well as in *Bad Influence* (1990), where bad boy Rob Lowe gets his.

Perhaps nowhere is the theme of urban angst better reflected than in 1992's *Single White Female*, starring Bridget Fonda as a young woman who opts for the safety of a roommate; in answer to her "SWF" advertisement, however, she gets seemingly sweet but soon patently psychotic Jennifer Jason Leigh. Labelled by director Barbet Schroeder as a "Hitchcockian relationship of codependency," *SWF* was interpreted by some viewers as yet another example of what happens to strong women wielding power. That same year also brought the comedy *Lana in Love* (1992), about a lonely woman placing an ad to find Mr. Right; in *Animal Instincts* (1992), cited earlier, a nymphomaniacal wife of a cop places a personal that runs indefinitely, saying, "Beautiful young woman seeks discrete interludes"; and *Deadbolt* (1992)—*SWF* in reverse—has Justine Bateman advertising for and taking in a male roommate.

Dying to Love You (1993), originally titled *Lethal White Female*, stars Tracy Pollan, in what was billed as being based on a true story from FBI files, as an attractive con who uses her wiles to manipulate and ensnare men. Her means: running ads in *Washington Magazine*, saying "Dreams come true for us with patience." Lonely, divorced Tim Matheson bites and his first time responding to the personals soon becomes his initiation into a deadly obsession. The motion pictures, it would seem, lead us to think that personal ads are an invitation at best not necessarily to relationships, but instead to some form of psychotic behavior.

Phone Sex

Telephones have been factors in film since their introduction, today even locating when and where a movie takes place according to their configurations, including such concepts as telegraphic receivers, rotary phones, switchboard operators, phone booths, videophones, cellular phones, answering machines, even allowances for fiber optics and the Integrated Services Digital Network (ISDN). As was pointed out in the last chapter, telephones have featured heavily in relationships; in film, they have mainly figured around the topic of digital dialing for sexual satisfactions.

Although there were a number of earlier instances, for our purposes this section begins with discussion of Edward Yang's *The Terroriser* (1986); known by its Chinese name, "Kongbufenzi," the title character refers to a girl delinquent whose prank phone calls spark off crises in the lives of a diverse number of characters. The prank theme draws on the 1965 *I Saw What You Did*, which was wonderfully frightening with Joan Crawford and John Ireland, far less so in its 1988 remake.

Call Me (1987) represents the beginning of the plot convention of being drawn into the telephone; in it, Patricia Charbonneau as Anna starts receiving and responding to intriguing phone calls that suck her into contact with an organized crime syndicate. In *Out of Order* (1987), some British layabouts run a pirate radio station, with one of them a phone fetishist who needs to develop a way to telepathically tap into the network. A brother and sister trap dates, then kill them, through the *Party Line* (1988). Twists on the 976 phone sex number also figure in *976-Evil* (1989) and *976-Evil 2* (1992) and *Smooth Talker* (1992), where a policeman searches for the "976 Killer."

Since its appearance after deregulation, obsession with phone sex is being reflected in film. In *Family Viewing* (1987), for example, a father's phone penchant causes his wife to leave him; later, his son happens upon a woman who works for this same phone-sex business. Employees of the Suite Nothings phone-sex business, presided over by Karen Black, appear in the 1988 slasher pic *Out of the Dark*. In *Intimate Stranger* (1991), a murderer lines up a phone-sex operator as his next victim. *The Phone Call* (1991) perpetuates a perverse stereotype: a psychotic ex-con who talks dirty to gay men over a male phone-sex hotline.

One of the more interesting telephone treatments is Bashar Shbib's *Julia Has Two Lovers* (1991); although hers is a wrong number, Julia (Daphna Kastner) ends up talking to the caller (David Duchovny) for hours, sharing her deepest concerns about an impending marriage to her live-in boyfriend. Once so discouraged, she ends up meeting him, they sleep together, and then she finds out that it is a pattern of his to call strange women, meet them, but never follow through on relationships because he fears getting involved. Between her second thoughts and his fears about letting people getting to know him too well, this is as close to *cinema verite* as anything we have seen lately.

Are You Lonesome Tonight? (1992) stars Jane Seymour as a wealthy socialite who hires a private detective (Parker Stevenson) to find out about her husband's mysterious disappearance; as it turns out, he was having an affair with a phone-sex operator. It is becoming rather a common occupation, it would seem—Jennifer Jason Leigh plays a mother selling phone sex in Robert Altman's acclaimed *Short Cuts* (1993), and Miami private eyes search for a killer of phone sex operators (1-900-MIAMI) in *South Beach* (1993). No matter how you dial it, we certainly have come a long way since *Pillow Talk* (1959), when Doris Day and Rock Hudson shared a party line.

Radio Relationships

While radio has figured in a number of musicals, Jonathan Demme's *Citizens Band* of 1977 becomes a critical starting point for the discussion of this medium, as the CB craze here is a symbolic metaphor for lack of human communication. The medium became a common plot device in the late 1980s. Most have a twist. While 1984's *Choose Me* featured a radio sex therapist who draws the sad and lonely, *City in Panic* (1986) uses a radio talk show host to help catch a psychotic mass murderer of gays, and the plot line of *Freeway* (1988), which was based on the Los Angeles freeway shootings, centers around a murder who contracts a radio psychiatrist from his car phone.

Oliver Stone's *Talk Radio* (1988), based on the story of controversial DJ Alan Berg, who was assassinated by white supremacists, shows only the tip of the iceberg about audiences for this kind of broadcasting. The aforementioned *976-Evil* (1989), while actually a telephone "horror-scope," deals with a lonely teenager who directdials demons from hell.

A young man who works at one of the video rental stores I frequent, happily recommended *Pump Up the Volume* (1990), starring Christian Slater as "Hard Harry," an out-of-it angst-ridden teenager who secretly operates a pirate ham radio station from his home. Providing audacious sexual actions along with advice and forbidden music, he attracts a huge following from his classmates—but no one knows who he is, and he resists exposure. While many of his fellow students giggle openly at Hard Harry's masturbatory antics, privately they are glad that someone is expressing some of their anxieties. The ending brings everything full circle.

In 1992 came *Night Rhythms,* the story of a late-night radio talk show host catering to lonely, frustrated women both on and off the air; *Sexual Response,* an erotic thriller in which radio hostess Shannon Tweed fields questions about relationships but doesn't practice her own advice within her own marriage; and *Straight Talk,* starring Dolly Parton, who accidentally becomes the popular "Dr. Shirlee," a radio psychologist who actually can relate to people.

And then there is *Sleepless in Seattle* (1993), the runaway box office hit directed by Nora Ephron. Influenced by *An Affair to Remember* (1957), which starred Cary Grant and Deborah Kerr as shipboard lovers forced to leave one another but who promise to meet six months later on top of the Empire State Building, the modern movie concerns Meg Ryan as a Baltimore reporter about to marry a bore—until she hears the voice of sensitive Seattle widower Tom Hanks responding to a radio shrink's questions about Hanks' son who has called the show, worried about his father. It is quite a statement on our times that this phenomenally popular movie, which is billed as a romance, never has the two leads meet until the very end—and they certainly don't end up in bed before our eyes, either.

Although there are also a number of films dealing with television, most of them are industry specific. A few exceptions stand out. *Love Machine* (1971) is not a sex aid, but instead is a ruthless, sadistic newscaster, played by John Phillip Law. *Delirious* (1991) refers to John Candy as a soap writer who literally becomes enmeshed in the ridiculous ongoing plots. And, "Living in a situation in which everything depends upon one's attachment to, or rejection of, certain images" is the theme of Atom Egoyan's 1989 *Speaking Parts.* One character wants to turn her dead brother's life into a made-for-TV movie; another obsessively uses her television to watch videos of the man she loves who plays an extra in movies (significantly, he has yet to land a "speaking" part); and a man links up his television to a video telephone link as a sexual aid. Rather than advance communication, however, the television mainly acts as a deterrent to it.

Video and Its Variations

Linkages have been made between *Speaking Parts* and Steven Soderbergh's *sex, lies, and videotape* (1989), the latter a minimalist movie that actually centers more on conversations about relationships than physically showing them. When the camera turns on the various self-centered actors, they realize how they have been shirking from taking responsibility for their lives. Semeiks (1992, p. 147) has called *sex, lies, and videotape* "a long paean to the video camera. . . . It creates erotic desire, it alleviates and even cures sexual dysfunction, it heals a divided self, it creates honesty and intimacy and reforms human relationships. In short, though a mere machine, the camera is a sexually- and emotionally-liberating device, capable of generating powerful erotic experiences and emotional responses."

Video and video-surveillance as plot conventions expand in film as the technology penetrates more into our society. *Death Watch* (1980), a futuristic thriller, revolves around a video camera that has been implanted in Harvey Keitel's brain. David Cronenberg's *Videodrome* (1983) stars a sleazy James Woods programming sick satellite porno until he himself begins hallucinating because of it.

Videodating is the theme of Robert Altman's 1979 *A Perfect Couple*, where lovers meet through a service in Los Angeles; the story is extended in *Beyond Therapy* (1986), this time for Lonely Hearts subscribers and New York neurotica. In *Dangerous Love* (1988) an innocent computer nerd decides to join a videodating club, and soon becomes a key suspect when a manic killer with a camera begins murdering members of the club.

Night Eyes (1990) lures a surveillance expert (Andrew Stevens) into an assignment where he has been hired to videotape everything a soon-to-be fiancée (Tonya Roberts) is doing. "Watching's dangerous. Touching's deadly" is the opener for the equally sordid sequel, *Night Eyes 2* (1991), where this time the triangle is completed by sexy Shannon Tweed. Both are classic cases of metaviewing.

A camera for the blind is introduced in Wim Wenders' *Until the End of the World* (1991), a kind of virtual reality that extends and explores much more than the action introduced in the Stephen King sci-fi story *The Lawnmower Man* (1992). Lizzie Borden's *Love Crimes* (1992), which was inspired by real events, revolves around a man who poses as a top fashion photographer so women will come home with him to be shot—if not literally, at least psychologically, as he positions them in humiliating stances, seduces, and robs them; doubly victimized, most of the women remain reluctant to press charges.

The trouble begins in *Secret Games: The Escort* (1993) when an unhappily married woman joins the "Afternoon Demitasse," an exclusive brothel, and gets involved with a man who pushes her too far by videotaping his wildest fantasies. And, as has been discussed earlier, the video-surveillance plot of *Sliver* can be interpreted as yet one more warning on the potential for self-destruction in our technocratic culture.

Pointing out how far photojournalism has come since the days of Civil War pioneer Mathew Brady, forever transformed by George Holliday's invaluable videotape of the Rodney King assault in Los Angeles, Armond White (1993, p. 58) talks about its relevance: "Like the little boy holding up his hands at the Nazi concentration camp, the Vietnamese youth having his brains blown out, the JFK motorcade, the napalmed Vietnamese girls, and the Kent State coed screaming with her arms outstretched, the Holliday video crystallizes an era." Slices of life dealing with actual or would-be relationships in motion pictures make a similarly strong impression on us.

MUSIC

Not so much concerned with music[7] for its power as an advocacy tool but rather as a reflection of current concerns that people might be having or feeling, it is instrumental to examine some rhetorical themes that have been emerging in sound recordings lately. In his introduction to *Popular Music and Communication,* Lull (1987, p. 12) states two important fundamental theoretical assumptions:

> First, *participants in human communication that involves popular music, and in all forms of symbolic interaction for that matter, act willingly and imaginatively in nearly every instance of*

its occurrence. The encoding and decoding of music are intentional human activities that serve a wide range of purposes.

Second, *the potential for exercising these communicative capacities is indeed influenced by the structural circumstances that surround their existence.* Music, like other forms of communication, is constrained and given direction by the relations that people have with each other. . . . Technology plays a roll in all of this, at once providing a resource for the creative construction, consumption and use of music by its makers and audiences, and at the same time providing a mechanism through which corporate profits are realized and social relations are affected.

As can be seen in Appendix 11: *Songs about Media-Mediated Relationships,* some relevant themes have been around for a long time, owing a particular debt to the blues, some country fare,[8] a version of gospel, and rock and roll. While it might be tempting to classify the content as dealing with loneliness, strains of alienation and anomie would actually go further than, say, a Marxist might interpret them; instead, a pervasive component here seems to be an ever optimistic notion of angst that could/would be solved by finding that "someone special"—even if the search is scary, or unsafe, or unsettling for whatever reason. Garcia (1994, p. H31) would argue that the search is for a higher sense of spirituality; citing the rebirth of religious themes in popular music, he ponders why faith is so fashionable again: "Part of the answer seems to lie in the increasingly ephemeral nature of modern life. In an age when cultural fads are gobbled up and dispensed within nanoseconds, the timeless versions of good and evil speak with new authority." Consider, for example, a band such as ZZ Top that has been around since the 1970s, now strumming a safe-sex song in their album *Antenna* (1994) imploring, "Say baby I want'cha/I'm hurtin' so big/take out some insurance/and cover your rig."

Up until now there has been a paucity of literature in mainstream media on relationships between gays and lesbians and music. In 1979 Avicolli published "Images of gays in rock music" in *Lavender Culture*; in 1982 Grillo's "Gay moments in straight music" appeared in *Gay Books Bulletin*; *The Journal of Homosexuality*[9] contained a review of Eric A. Gordon's 1989 *Mark the Music,* a biography of (gay) composer Marc Blitzstein, by Lawrence D. Mass, a physician, writer, and associate editor of *Opera Monthly*; and R. Brian Attig had an important article on "The Gay Voice in Popular Music" in Wolf and Kielwasser's *Gay People, Sex, and the Media* (1991), in which he talked about its potential to create "positive social change regarding societal values about homosexuality." Interpreting earlier celebrities (e.g., Little Richard as "the self-proclaimed Georgia Peach . . . an apparition in a zoot suit") and songs (e.g., Elvis Presley's "Jailhouse Rock" talking about "the cutest jailbird I ever did see") from a gay perspective, he particularly focuses in on the Communards' video "Don't Leave Me This Way": "The opposing values that the video addresses are society's repression of gay people versus gay people's struggle for acceptance from society and with themselves. The video's symbolic conflict between these opposing value systems is manifested on three levels: (a) narrative content, (b) use of symbols in the narrative, and (c) lyrical content" (p. 194).

The 1990s have seen homophobic barriers somewhat lessened in the music world, particularly as audiences have welcomed out performers such as k.d. lang, the late Freddie Mercury, Melissa Etheridge, teasers such as Madonna, and cross-overs such as Elton John and Peter Townsend. And just recently Teldec has become the first major recording company to aim specifically at the gay market; its *Sensual Classics, Too* (1995) features two men embracing on the cover, Tchaikovsky (who was gay) leads off the list, and the back cover lists an AIDS-hot line number. Regardless of sexual orientation, it would seem, those privileged enough to have music in their lives—both performers and audiences—are reflecting angst over relationships.

AND MORE

In addition to the media outlined in this book—print, electronic, technological, and filmic—know also that advertising plays a role, that "news" inevitably deals with relationships, and that dozens of public relationships campaigns are waged to entice the very people who are subjects here.

Games and Simulations

Board games are available such as "How to Host a Romantic Evening" (an event for two that comes complete with "more than 50 suggestions for awakening romance"), or "Life Stories: A fun game of telling tales and sharing smiles with family and friends," that encourages the generations to share their stories and goals. Imagine purchasing a game just to stimulate conversation. *Reader's Digest* puts out a book called *Family Traditions: Celebrations for Holidays and Everyday*, by Elizabeth Berg, that encourages people to record their long-cherished traditions and rituals so that future family members will be able to perpetuate them.

Relationship Surrogates

Just as *Made in America* (1992) centered around complications from artificial insemination, so too are other artifacts replacing many of our other customs. A brief review of this book shows, for example, print media going from allowing to actually encouraging previously taboo material; talk show hosts serving as our opinion leaders; movies moving from sordid to sappy; "virtual" reality stimulating us more than "real" reality.

Still, our bodies continue to crave nourishment for basic functioning. Eating, for example, is back in vogue. The chocoholic in *I Don't Buy Kisses Anymore* (1992) is a character type I described in my first book for The Haworth Press, Inc., *Chocolate Fads, Folklore & Fantasies*[10] (1994), which divulges our chocolate binge— including the following:

> chocolate boutiques, chocolate cruises, chocolate tours, Chocolate-of-the-Month clubs, chocolate-scented perfume, chocolate binge weekends at participating hotels, chocolate fairs and festivals, chocolate sweepstakes, chocolate fund raising, chocolate-decorated clothing, chocolate FAXes, 24-hour emergency chocolate services, chocolate novelties like pacifiers, tobacco, pills, and lip gloss, chocolate games, *Chocolatier* magazine, chocolate sniff-and-scratch labels, and any number of chocolate orgy combinations.

The main point is that chocolate clearly is filling a need, which can be physical and/or psychological. Substitute coffee, alcohol, frozen yogurt, tobacco, junk food, even "health store" items, and the resulting phenomenon remains the same: we appear to be looking for whatever it takes to feed our needs, even if they are relationship surrogates.

NOTES

1. Virginia Campbell and Stephen Rebello, "A selective preview of 1994's onscreen Futuresex displays of physical affection." *Movieline* (Jan/Feb., 1994), p. 65.

2. See: Jesse Green, "Paris Has Burned," *The New York Times* (April 18, 1993), V1+.

3. *Silence = Death* is the name of a 1990 documentary co-directed by Rosa von Praunheim and Phil Zwickler about New York City's artistic community's response to AIDS; *The Guardian* called it, "The best AIDS film to date . . . a minifestival of activism."

4. In "AIDS as (Filmic) Entertainment," a paper presented to the Eastern Communication Association in New Haven, CT in Spring of 1993, I argued how foolish they have been to still consider it a gay disease, saying: "In a period where the epidemic has been kept at bay by an informed, communicative gay population and yet is spreading exponentially into the less informed and less communicative populations of minorities and IV-drug users, this oversight from the film community is remarkable."

5. See: Linda K. Fuller, "Desperately Seeking Meaning: 'Personals' in American Popular Film," in Paul Loukides and Linda K. Fuller (eds.), *Beyond the Stars III: The Material World.* (Bowling Green, OH: Popular Press, 1993): 89-96.

6. Maitland McDonagh, "All About Evil: Capturing Killers on Film," *Entertainment Weekly* (March 29, 1991), pp. 22-3.

7. This section on sound recordings owes a debt to Alex Fuller, Alix Kruger, and Michael Schmidt. Robb Carty was particularly helpful for the section on gays and lesbians in the sound recording world, as well as pointing out particular songs to include in Appendix II.

8. George Lipsitz calls country music and the blues "working people's music" in an article he wrote for *Cultural Correspondence* (August, 1976), saying it is possible to see how they "have been used as an escape, how they reinforce bourgeois values, and how they prefigure more liberated forms."

9. Book review by Lawrence D. Mass of *Mark the Music*, by Eric A. Gordon (NY: St. Martin's Press, 1989, 605 pp.) in the *Journal of Homosexuality*, Volume 21, No. 3 (1991): 131-139.

10. Subtitled *1,000+ Chunks of Chocolate Information*, it traces the "chocolate phenomenon" characterized by our going from buying 25-cent chocolate candy bars to spending more than $25 per pound for gourmet/designer chocolates.

Chapter 6

Concluding Comments About Media-Mediated Relationships

When an individual enters the presence of others, they commonly seek to acquire information about him or to bring into play information about him already possessed. They will be interested in his general socio-economic status, his conception of self, his attitude towards them, his competence, his trustworthiness, etc. Although some of this information seems to be sought almost as an end in itself, there are usually quite practical reasons for acquiring it. Information about the individual helps to define the situation, enabling others to know in advance what he will expect of them and what they may expect of him. Informed in these ways, the others will know how best to act in order to call forth a desired response from him.

—Erving Goffman, *The Presentation of Self in Everyday Life*[1]

When all is said and done, a looming question posits itself: can the topic of *Media-Mediated Relationships* be reduced to the concept of loneliness in contemporary society? In a way there is a binary opposition: caring and a desire for connectedness on the one end of the spectrum, anomie and alienation on the other. Yet, like many other events that are occurring so pervasively around us without our conscious attention, the many instances cited here—ranging from personals and private introduction services to talk shows and 900 numbers and on-line computer services—amount to something of a cultural hegemony whereby our social realities are constructed commodities.

Maybe it's the millennium. "Ending a century is ominous enough, especially at a point at which rock-and-roll will be 50 years old, television channels will number in the hundreds and personal computers will be as common as toasters," declares David Browne (1994, p. H30), music critic for *Entertainment Weekly*. He makes a prediction about entertainment in the year 2000: "Media analysts and artists envision a world in which your television will program whatever you want, when you want it; albums will be piped into your home with the press of a button, and telephone and media companies will merge." No question about it: we continue to become more and more enculturated by media. But what about our relationships with other people? Will they go the way of face-to-face communication that many businesses have replaced with teleconferencing? Will they be on-demand, like our other pleasure needs? Will we spend more time searching for them and fantasizing about them than actually engaging in them?

The shared information environment fostered by media usage doesn't necessarily, according to Meyrowitz (1985), determine identifiable attitudes and behavior among its individual consumers; to the contrary:

> It does lead, however, to a common awareness and greater sharing of *options*. The choice of dress, hair style, speech patterns, profession, and general style of life is no longer as strongly linked as it once was to traditional group ties. Another outcome of the homogenization of information networks, therefore, is the development of many new, more superficial, and temporary groupings that form against the now relatively unified backdrop of common information. People traditionally divided into groups that corresponded primarily to social class, ethnicity, race, religion, occupation, and neighborhood, but current groupings also develop on the basis of wearing similar clothes, participating in similar sports, owning the same type of computer, appreciating the same type of music, or attending the same class. Many sub-groups are now formed through the exercising of similar options. (p. 134)

Media usage, as cultivation analysis reminds us, involves an intricate intermixing of various gratifications and probable effects. Communications, as we keep reminding our students, involves media working in symbiotic relationships within, between, and amongst themselves—often including, it should certainly be noted, a mingling also of interpersonal as well as intrapersonal communication. Think of the many examples in this book: the television program *Pure Soap*, that updates the audience on serials; the movies *Talk Radio*, a biography about controversial DJ Alan Berg, or *Desperately Seeking Susan*, on the personals; the book *Vox*, about interactive phone sex; newspapers advertising personals and magazines advertising software for virtual reality; interactive video games based on Hollywood movies; best-selling books by radio talk show hosts Rush Limbaugh and Howard Stern that have been featured on practically all the media, as well as the book *All Talk*, about talk shows; and many more.

MEDIA-MEDIATED RELATIONSHIPS: A SURVEY

In an effort to put a face to the theory of cultivation analysis applied to relationship mediation in terms of various media, it was determined that a survey should be performed. Although no previous surveys along these lines can be cited and therefore compared, what follows is baseline data on information from a specific target population at a particular time and place.

Methodology

In late 1993, the survey instrument displayed in Appendix 12: *Media-Mediated Relationships: A Survey*, was administered to 214 students enrolled in communications courses at a New England state college. Participation was strictly voluntary and, although no incentive was offered, none of the students refused. It is relevant to discuss this target population a bit more in depth.

There was a fairly even *gender* split among the survey participants: 104 men (48 percent), 111 women (52 percent). In terms of *gender orientation*, only 5, or just over 2 percent, declared themselves as other than heterosexual: 2 "gay," 1 "queer" (a woman), and 2 "homosexual."

Age breakdowns, which are listed in Table 1, show that many of the participants were of typical college student age, some 84 percent represented ranged between late teens to early thirties.

The wide majority of this sample (80 percent) was white, many of that number labelling themselves Caucasian, others listing "W," or "C," one writing down "American white," another "white lady." Table 2 lists specific racial categories. "Black" included three respondents who listed themselves as "African American," and "Other" included one each of these self-selected descriptions: Mexican American, Hispanic, Irish-French, Filipino, Native American, 1/2 American Indian, Irish-American, and Indian. While the majority of these respondents listed their occupation as "student," Table 3 delineates a number of others.

It is important to stress that state college students typically do not have a great deal of discretionary income—a factor, for example, in

TABLE 1. Ages of Survey Participants

Age ranges	Frequency	Percentage
11-20	60	28%
21-35	120	56
36-50	17	8
51-65	2	1
66+	3	1
No reply	12	6
Total	214	

TABLE 2. Ethnicity of Survey Participants

Race	Frequency	Percentage
Asian	1	0.5%
Black	8	4
White	172	0
Other	17	8
No reply	16	8
Total	214	

TABLE 3. Occupations of Survey Participants

Occupation	Frequency	Percentage
Student	98	46%
White collar	26	12
Blue/pink collar	47	22
Other	1	0.5
Unemployed or retired	7	3
Don't know or N/A	1	0.5
No reply	<u>34</u>	16
Total	214	

both the dating scene and in terms of telecommunications usage, like spending money on self-advertising or videodating services. Income levels are listed in Table 4.

Findings

1. *The personals.* In answer to the first question, as to whether or not they had ever placed a "personals" ad, only ten, or 5 percent of the sample replied affirmatively: five "only once," three "2-3 times," and one each "4-24 times" and "100+ times"—all in newspapers. Here are some of their experiences:

21. (F24)[2] Nightmare date from Hell.
29. (F36) Worth it, but you need to be very careful.
36. (M42) Not very good.
40. (F/Retired) Responses have been very exciting.
72. (F32) I have thought about answering one of those ads but I was fearful of what type of person was writing those ads. Some sounded very interesting, but friends pointed out that they might be looking for women to hurt or whatever. It just feels scary.
88. (F28) One of my male friends answered an ad out of the paper. She was a nurse and they went out to dinner and had a

nice time, but there was no spark there. Although they both felt the same way, it was not right.

106. They are fine. They are a fun way of meeting new people.
120. A good laugh.
123. Personals, as in "partner wanted"? No (never needed it.) Either way, I wouldn't. Too dangerous nowadays—world's full of psychopaths.
153. (M28) Eventually married one of the respondents.
161. (M) The experiences I gained were self-confidence and motivation.
171. (GM35) Found it interesting.

About the same number of survey participants had ever responded to a "personals" ad: 11, or just over 5 percent. While fewer wrote comments about their experiences, a 20-year-old woman wrote, "I feel that the personals are a convenient way to locate someone, as long as I was positive he or she is reading them"; a man the same age said they gave him "ideas that were lacking in my repertoire"; and a gay respondent added, "They never really tend to be who they say they are."

While five persons indicated they had joined reading groups, only a few added comments: a 23-year-old male said it was a good service, another disclosed "It gave me an open mind by learning from people new skills that I did not have from reading," and another wryly indicated that, "My grandmother joined me up."

2. *Radio.* While 138 (64 percent) of the sample indicated being familiar with radio call-in shows, only about 15 percent were very frequent listeners—see Table 5.

TABLE 4. Income Levels of Survey Participants

Income	Frequency	Percentage
Less than $30,000/year	164	76%
$30,000/year	12	6
More than $30,000/year	21	10
No reply	17	8
Total	214	

TABLE 5. Radio Listenership of Survey Participants

Listenership	Frequency	Percent
Only once	9	4%
Seldom	56	26
Not very often	41	19
Often	32	15
Not applicable	72	34
No reply	4	2
Total	214	

Rush Limbaugh won the popularity poll as the most listened to radio talk show host, named specifically by 14 respondents; Howard Stern was named by 12, followed by sports radio with 10. Four persons each mentioned listening to Larry King and Dr. Ruth, and about two dozen other programs and personalities were also cited.[3]

Only 16, or 13 percent, indicated having ever called into a station's show: a male who reported calling about privatizing, another several times ("On issues I'm interested in and have had experience with—i.e., welfare, jobs, etc."), and a 20-year-old woman added, "I called about the exposé on the real reason that Rush hates the Democrats—namely the Kennedys. He has charisma-envy. But they wouldn't let me on." Seven of the respondents added that they feel like calling often, but haven't done it yet.

3. *Television dating shows.* In answer to the question, "What are your experiences with, and opinions of, television shows like *Love Connection, The Dating Game, Prime Time Personals, Studs, Infatuation,* etc.?" 182, or 85 percent of the respondents added comments, a small portion of which are included in Appendix 13: *Survey Comments on Television Dating Shows.*

Love Connection was the most frequently cited show (18), especially its host Chuck Woolery, one person saying he watches it every day; further, *Studs* was mentioned by 12 persons, *Dating Game* by seven, *Infatuation* by two, and by only one, *Prime Time Personals.* The widest overall impression was that these television dating shows are fun/funny, entertaining, and "good for a laugh" (51 comments), although about 15 had quite negative responses (e.g., garbage, pointless, serve no purpose, dull, pretty stupid, wasteful, shallow), and about the same number indicated simply not being interested. A few found them degrading, one saying they are sexist, and another declaring they should be banned. While two persons specifically said these shows are unrealistic, a number of the other comments negate that opinion as individuals seemingly get involved with the shows' participants. Still, nine respondents mentioned they would never go on any of the programs.

Of particular interest to me was the number of media-related comments included here. Several, for example, said these television dating shows were "a waste of airwaves," "bandwidth," or "media space"; a 20-year-old man wrote, "All these TV shows are made up. The writers make it look more glamorous than it really is." Another said, "My opinion is that they only choose the best couples—i.e., argumentative, sappy, etc., for the network because of ratings"; and a few referred to the shows as big business. One 22-year-old in the survey had been rejected on *The Dating Game,* and he now thinks, "They're all lame!" A young woman had a friend on *Love Connection* who didn't get along with her date, "So they gave a script to both of them"; in parentheses she adds, "I never knew that." It makes those of us who teach courses in Media Criticism excited to see such assertions.

4. *Relationship movies.* Even though about a half-dozen respondents said they rarely go to the movies, comments here show these students to be quite motion picture literate. Just over three-quarters of the sample (76 percent), or 163 persons, added comments, a portion of which are listed in Appendix 14: *Survey Comments on Relationship Movies.* In accordance with the question asking about experiences with, and opinions of, various relationship movies, see Table 6.

Specifically, one respondent referred to *Sea of Love* as a "Very interesting relationship between detective and female suspect formed through personal ad—trust lacking to a high degree." A number mentioned *SWF* as scary, *Sliver* as just a bad movie (e.g., "Worst movie of the year"), *Singles* as fun (a few mentioned especially liking the sound track), and many commented on loving

TABLE 6. Citations of Various Relationship Movies

Movie	Number of Times Cited
Desperately Seeking Susan	17
Sea of Love	18
Paris Is Burning	1
Single White Female	30
Consenting Adults	11
Sliver	8
My Own Private Idaho	7
Singles	23
Together Alone	1
Sleepless in Seattle	8

Sleepless in Seattle (e.g., "It was refreshing because the relationship was not based on sex but love"; "Favorite—great ending"; "Liked it the best—the most realistic and fun").

As with the television dating shows, the most frequent comments had to do with enjoyment/entertainment (47), fun/funny (7), interesting/realistic (11), as opposed to eight that labeled them unrealistic and the seven or so who lambasted them in general (e.g., weak, stupid, boring). Again, there were a number of media-related comments, such as movies being an art form, how Hollywood endings are so unrealistic, that movies are too violent for today's young adults, helping people get together, formulated/predictable, the role of directors and casts, and keeping movies in perspective. In retrospect, it might have been helpful to see how many of these students had taken our courses on film history, aesthetics, and/or special topics about various genres.

5. *900 Telephone numbers.* "Rip off" was the most common reaction (12 or so) to the issue of opinions about sex phones. They also drew the most number of comments—from 124, or 58 percent of the sample. As can be gleaned from some of the opinions listed in Appendix 15: *Survey Comments on 900 Telephone Numbers,* general reaction here was predominantly negative (e.g., waste of time,

waste of money, ridiculous, trash, expensive, sleazy, tacky, scam, useless, stupid, weak, not socially acceptable). Still, a surprising number of students backed off, saying they didn't want to judge those who used the services (e.g., "I guess it gets some people off"; "If adults want to use them, it's their own business"; "They may be OK for some people who want to connect with this"; "Don't use but let them be"). And a fair number cut to the bottom line, seeing 900 numbers as a big business (e.g., "Someone is making a good deal of money"; "They only want money"; "Great money-making concept"). A 21-year-old coed said it best: "Safest sex you can have."

6. *Electronic mail.* They liked E-mail. As can be seen from selected excerpts in Appendix 16: *Survey Comments on Electronic Mail,* for the most part reaction was very positive; 15 students called it useful, six a "good idea," many others interesting, easy, fun, fast. One person pointed out its use for the handicapped and hearing impaired. Nearly half the sample (46 percent, or 99 individuals) commented that they are already using this technology at school, work, or both. Several commented on meeting new friends through it, connecting with others (e.g., "You can 'write' to people all over the world"), even deliciously annoying some through this means. There were a few negative responses, too—that E-mail is expensive, impersonal, confusing, and brings too much junk mail. One woman wrote, "I hate it and love it."

Two students referred to the fact that E-mail is an excellent communication pathway; several called it an "interesting form of communication"; others note that it simplifies communication, and some students made predictions about it being the wave of the future.

7. *Videodating.* This medium drew comments from 35 percent of the sample, and had reactions from those 74 survey participants that were all over the place. Appendix 17: *Survey Comments on Videodating* shows a selection of those responses, which range from stupid/ridiculous, dumb/crappy to curious to nonjudgmental. Along the theme of "desperate," some said videodating is for sociopaths or people who can't make it in society, who are "nuts," "weird," and who should know that it could be dangerous. "To each his/her own," "Whatever floats your boat," and "I guess it's okay if it works, why not?" were indicative of students who had not necessarily used videodating services but thought they could be perfectly fine for

others. The wide majority had never actually done it, and hardly any mentioned knowing people who had. One older male student wrote, "Could be fun, wouldn't do it myself—possibly safer than meeting someone in a bar."

8. *Virtual reality.* This fascinated these respondents, although only 64 (30 percent) made specific comments. Some put question marks next to it, a few asked "What?", and others very openly said they wanted to find out more about it. A few wanted to show their knowledge, citing having seen the Stephen King movie *The Lawn-mower Man*, which has a virtual reality gimmick in it, or having seen demonstrations of the technology. Appendix 18: *Survey Comments on Virtual Reality,* while limited, gives the overall impression: high interest, mostly positive (e.g., love it, it's cool, excellent). As with E-mail, a fair number of students predicted that virtual reality bespeaks the future (e.g., "That's a *true* step into the future!"; "The next 'craze' in entertainment"; "Video game of the future"). A nurse observed, "Sometimes too 'real' is too 'scary.'"

Discussion

Encouraged to add further comments on the survey and its theme, one 22-year-old male student wrote, "Unbelievable and awesome, the amount of information at our fingertips. I use it for good things. Lots of bad people could take advantage of people more easily." His statement seems to sum up how these students felt: for the most part, they had quite strong feelings about their media usage and how others should behave also. Their respect for new technologies also came through, along with their cautions.

CRITICAL APPRAISAL

Shortcomings of This Study

Unquestionably, the survey mentioned just above is severely limited in terms of demographics; it cries out for comparisons with other target markets.

Also, critics might understandably begin an analysis of this book by checking out the references, and be appalled by a nearly equal weighing of academic and trade publications—particularly evident in Appendixes 4 and 5. Yet, that inclusion—where a professional journal in the communications field might be cited in juxtaposition with something from *TV Guide* or another entertainment industry source—has been necessary to get at the essence of media-mediated relationships, as they cover such a wide range.

While an effort was made to incorporate as many international examples as possible, that area is also lacking. Most of the examples of self-advertisement were gleaned from my own travels, and I can only hope that readers of this book will send me more, from disparate sources.

Methodologically, the idea was to use print and electronic media, along with other miscellaneous media sources. While much of my background is here, along with extensive research in and publication on film studies and emerging communications technology, my weakness is clearly in the field of sound recording. Although I have been a faithful reader of *Rolling Stone* since my college years, my own musical preferences preclude my keeping up with the many groups and genres that mark the field. At least here I was fortunate enough to have several young people as reliable resources.

Both the best and the most tenuous part of this study relates to its timeliness. As an attempt to document a phenomenon, it hopefully will get to press as soon as possible—but even then, it undoubtedly will seem dated.

Contributions of This Study

As a descriptive case study, *Media-Mediated Relationships* has evolved as a barometer for better understanding the many singles and others searching for meaning in the sociocultural milieu of the 1990s. As such, it has unabashedly discussed mass communication that involves masses of people, ranging from romance and Gothic novels to soap operas to various broadcast offerings. In terms of the high culture-low culture argument, this book has been indiscriminate. Richard Dyer (1981, p. 177), pointing out aspects of utopian sensibility most commonly found in mass culture—energy, abundance, intensity, transparency, and community—envisions mass art as escapist, offering as it does the image of "something better" or "something we want deeply that our day-to-day lives don't provide." Re-read some of the appeals in various personals, review voyeurism in the movies, and re-run a few relevant television programs that have been cited here.

For marketers, valuable insights abound into specific target niches, especially how they are and can be approached and ensnared. From the many resources cited here, business people and consumers alike can take note.

For media scholars, the argument has been raised to consider the personal advertisement columns as a pivotal resource—not only to monitor content change, but also to consider rhetorical choices over time, and similarities and differences of self-description between and among persons of various sexual orientations. The language of media-mediated relationships contains its own codes, with recurrent themes like finding someone special, looking forward to hearing the many messages on one's voice mail machine, looking at the positive side, fulfilling fantasies, and, most of all, "being protected" (anonymous, secure) for the ultimate safe sex.

The incorporation here of a wide range of media sources—print, broadcasting, emerging communication technologies, motion pictures, and more—is meant to provide an holistic frame from which to consider a phenomenon; overall, the goal has been to use that approach as a model. Using a version of contextualism (Perry, 1992), which concerns itself with a synthesized whole not just the individual parts of an event or events, and with interactions between the knower and the known, this book has concerned itself with media-related effects. Throughout runs the theoretical argument for considering cultivation analysis; or, as George Gerbner has said:

> The message systems of a culture not only inform but form common images. They not only entertain but create publics. They not only satisfy but shape a range of attitudes, tastes, and preferences. They provide the boundary conditions and overall patterns within which the processes of personal and group-mediated selection, interpretation, and image-formation go on.[4]

For scholars in general, especially social scientists, the argument posited here for incorporating bisexual, gay, and lesbian populations into research hopefully will encourage much more of this inclusion in their work. On a wider note, this examination of a phenomenon from a systemic approach calls for considerations of the whole picture, rather than unconnected fragments or biased perspectives. Including not only the history and background, but also the economic, political, psychological, narrative, and sociocultural concerns in a description make it, by default, more critical.

And finally, *Media-Mediated Relationships* is meant to stand as yet one more contribution to the field of popular culture, hopefully encouraging more research documenting the pervasiveness of media, and the overwhelming value of communication, in our lives.

IMPLICATIONS

Bearing in mind that this book is being written in the mid-1990s, it is important to consider that a number of psycho-societal phenomena are simultaneously at play. As symbolized in the broadcast media by the popularity of both conservative Rush Limbaugh and wild Howard Stern, probably never before have such disparate forces been vying for our attention.

When a mainstream television network can bring us *NYPD Blue,* how can we be so righteous about *Beavis and Butthead*? Bruce Fierstein (1994, p. 23), a writer for television and the movies, states his objection: "Television is under siege from every side these days. Attorney General Janet Reno condemns violence, Rev. Donald Wildmon complains about language and sex. Personally, I'm appalled by gratuitous violence: shoot-'em-ups with no redeeming value, sordid little women-in-jeopardy films, grotesque 'based on a true story' murders of the week."

David Nasaw, in his book *Going Out* (1994), has documented the rise and fall of a sense of community in the United States afforded by our public amusements arguing that the mass market no long exists. Instead of crowds going to palatial movie theaters anymore, we tend instead to entertain ourselves individually, watching videos on our VCRs. Instead of attending headlining musical events, we plug in our portable audio machines or turn on the car radio and listen alone. Instead of talking to intimates on the telephone, we tend to leave messages on their machines or call up anonymous numbers; whatever the transmission(s), we are paying dearly—both money-wise and in loss of concern for others and our own esteem. Woll and Cozby (1987, pp. 71-73) delineate five barriers to the initiation of a relationship: shyness, lack of access, lack of time, stigmata, and special needs. The better issue is whether, indeed, people today want to initiate relationships, or whether they are satisfied with alternatives.

In 1983 Andrea Dworkin and Catharine MacKinnon wrote a legal definition for pornography:

> Pornography is the graphic, sexually explicit subordination of women that includes one of a series of scenarios, from women being dehumanized—turned into objects and commodities—through women showing pleasure in being raped, through the dismemberment of women in a way that makes the dismemberment sexual. If men, children, or transsexuals are used in place of women, the material is still pornography.[5]

Walter Kendrick, professor of English at Fordham University and the author of *The Secret Museum: Pornography in Modern Culture* (1987), has observed that, "Pornographers are excluded from the mainstream channels, so they look around for something new, and the audience has a desire to try any innovation that gives them greater realism or immediacy."[6] It has been clearly demonstrated by numerous examples in this book that both mainstream and alternative media channels are responding to audiences clamoring for their utilization in relationship seeking/monitoring.

Meanwhile, the popular culturist in me takes note of the *Newsweek* (Woodward, 1993, p. 53) feature article on the resurgence of interest in angels in our society: "Driven by book sales approaching a heavenly 5 million copies, the angel subculture is off on more than a wing and a prayer. . . . The AngelWatch Network in Mountainside, NJ, monitors angelic comings and goings through its bimonthly journal, which has 1,800 subscribers," and the Angel Collectors Club of America has some 1,600 members. Consider also the continuing growth of evangelicalism in the United States, and there is no doubt about our spiritual searches.

Testing his theory of sociocultural mediations as a new approach to notions of audience reception and popular culture, Martin-Barbero (1993, p. 38) is interested in the evolution of various media genres within contexts of different national cultures. Appropriately applicable to this study, he writes: "'Popular' presents a double challenge to the critics: the need to include in popular culture not only what is produced by the masses but also what is consumed, what feeds them; and the need to conceive of popular culture not as limited to the past, a rural past, but linked to modernization, racial integration and the complexity of the city."

And, as the refrain of "safe sex" has permeated these pages, it is also well worth noting a move toward chastity in certain circles. Mostly being introduced by sex educators in the bellwether state of California, the idea is to emphasize abstinence, rather than contraception for teens (and pre-teens). While spearheaded by religious groups, such as the Baptists' "True Love Waits" campaign, or Christian rap artists, the movement really has less to do with values than sheer pragmatism, with more than one in nine teenage women, more than one million a year, becoming pregnant. "There is no preaching here, no explicit references to chastity, but rather some practical reasons for abstaining: Because one can get herpes, genital warts or crabs while using a condom," writes Jane Gross (1994, p. 19) about one such effort in San Diego. "Because once a girl has sex, she is likely to be labeled the neighborhood 'hoochie.' Because a boy cannot support a baby on lunch money. Because there are better ways to be a real man or a real woman."

And so, for very real reasons, relationships at many levels are being mediated—typically, increasingly by the media.

NOTES

1. Erving Goffmann, Introduction to *The Presentation of Self in Everyday Life*. (New York: Doubleday Anchor,1959), p. 14.

2. The number refers to their designation as a survey participant—for example, this was respondent #24, while in parentheses are gender, age, and (where relevant and available) information on sexual orientation and race.

3. Some of the shows mentioned were *Talknet, Talk of the Nation*, rockumentaries, and "anything as long as it's talk"; radio stations included WRKO, WTAG, NPR, WBZ, WURI, WNNZ, WBCN, WEEI, KISS, WCUW, WAAF, KGO, AM-1030; and specific radio hosts cited were: Tom Hykus, Jerry Williams, Upton Bell, Dr. Dean Eckel, Norm Nathan, Bob Rally, Marjorie Claprood, Eddy Andelman, Greg Hill, Liz Wild, Paul Rogers, Bruce Williams, and Dr. Harvey Rubin.

4. George Gerbner, "Cultural Indicators: The Third Voice." In George Gerbner, Larry Gross, and William H. Melody (eds.), *Communications Technology and Social Policy: Understanding the New "Cultural Revolution,"* (New York: John Wiley, 1973), p. 567.

5. "Where Do We Stand On Pornography?" *Ms.* (January/February, 1994), p. 34.

6. Cited in Tierney (1994), p. H18.

Appendix 1

Correspondence/Introduction Resources
for Media-Mediated Relationships
(A Partial Listing)

American/Latin Introductions
Tel. 305/534-8586

Amour and More–2 locations in the Chicago area
Tel. 708/988-7333,708/832-0236

The Asian Experience
PO Box 1214TA
Novato, CA 94948
Tel. 415/897-2742

Artistic Connections
PO Box 116
Chatham, NJ 07928
Topic: for singles who enjoy the arts

At the Gate
PO Box 09506
Columbus, OH 43209
Topics: ecology, peace, personal growth, spirituality

Australian Singles
Pen-Mates
PO Box 1796
Ft. Lauderdale, FL 33302

Beautiful Oriental Ladies
Japan, Box 30323
Sun Valley, NV 89533

Catholic Dating Connection
PO Box 4286
Arlington Heights, IL 60006
   Tel. 708/520-2193

Cherry Blossoms
190PM Rainbow Ridge
Kapaau, HI 96755
   Tel. 808/961-2114

Club Prima
13164 Memorial Drive, #240FB
Houston, TX 77079-7225
   Tel. 713/973-1515
   Specialty: "Beautiful international women!"

Club Thai
Box 4417 (f)
Miami, FL 33114

Concerned Singles Newsletter
Box 555-U
Stockbridge, MA 01262
   Topics: environment, peace, social justice, gender equity,
   personal growth

Cupid's Choice
Dateline for New England and New York
900/835-5700

Currents
PO Box 525
Homecrest Station
Brooklyn, NY 11229
   Specialty: National/international letter exchanges

Dateline
3712 N. Broadway, #552
Chicago, IL 60613

Dateline
414 Main Street
Melrose, MA 02176

DateMaker, Inc.
1150 Wehrle Drive
Williamsville, NY 14221
Tel. 900/786-1175

"Double Happiness" Correspondence Service
POB 2347-SPB
Melbourne, FL 32902
Specialty: "Lovely Oriental ladies seeking romance/marriage"

The Dr. Kate Relationship Center
875 North Dearborn Street, #400
Chicago, IL 60610

Family International
1608 N. Cahuenga Blvd, #4
Los Angeles, CA 90028
Tel. 213/467-2334
Specialty: "Meet truly beautiful Russian women by mail"

First-Class Connections
POB 3022-DP
Fort Lee, NJ 07024
Specialty: "Asian ladies"

Firstdates, Etc.
PO Box 371, Dept. SE
Wayland, MA 01778
Tel. 800/833-DATE

Foreign Exchange
Box 904
DeKalb, IL 60115
    Specialty: "Single men/women from USSR, eastern Europe"

Friend Finder
PO Box 8013
Piscataway, NJ 08855

Friends and More Dating Services
171 Park Street
West Springfield, MA 01089
    Tel. 413/746-3283

Fusion Box
3275-P
Everett, WA 98203

Golden Threads
Box 60475
Northampton, MA 01060
    Topic: Lesbians over 50 (and younger)

Great Expectations–national organization with 40+ centers
    Tel. 800/432-9200

Harmony
Box 82295VW
Phoenix, AZ 85071

Hermes
Box 110660/R
Berlin 11, Germany

International Connections
Box 5828
Bellingham, WA 98227
    Tel. 206/734-5254

International Contact Bureau
7811 SE 27th, #106
Mercer Island, WA 98040-2979
   Specialty: "Single women in the Baltics"

International Friends
444 Brickell, #51-140
Miami, FL 33131
   Specialty: "Sweet Latinas seek lifemates"

International Introductions
POB 992
Twin Falls, Idaho 83303

International Neighbors
Box 310
Lindsborg, KS 67456

International Society of Introduction Services
San Francisco, CA
   Tel 415/777-9769

Interracial Singles International
   Tel. 708/612-5667

Intro Magazine
PO Box INTRO
Studio City, CA 91604
   Tel. 213/384-6876

It's just Lunch
101 W. Grand Avenue, #212
Chicago, IL 60610
   Tel. 312/644-9999

Jewish Single Line
Bethesda, MD
   Tel. 301/654-5397

Jewish Singles Connection
Tel. 708/818-1400

Latin Ladies
Latin Introductions
Box 26750
Ft. Lauderdale, FL 33320
Tel. 305/486-1373

"Latins"
Box 1716-sp
Chula Vista, CA 91912
Tel. 800/992-0625

Liasons France-Amerique
PO Box 2054
Los Angeles, CA 90028

Life-Mates
PO Box 5953
Phoenix, AZ 85079
Tel. 602/973-9676
Specialty: "Lovely Oriental Ladies"

Matchmaker International
2505 Hillsboro Road
Nashville, TN 37219
Tel. 615/269-4500

Meet Thai Ladies
PO Box 11495
Honolulu, HI 96828
Tel. 808/734-0099

Midwest Adventures International
PO Box 11238
Milwaukee, WI 53211

Moscow Connection
Box 700
Clayton, CA 94517-0700
  Tel. 510/672-1512

The Movie Lovers Club
Box 2035R
Bala, PA 19004

National Singles Register
PO Box 567
Norwalk, CA 90650
  Tel. 213/864-2742

Natural Connections
Box 655-W
Pomona, NY 10970

Nudism Without Sex
  Tel. 708/676-2183, 9-11 p.m.

OK Letters International
Box 4321-wa
Huntington Beach, CA 92605

The Pacific Century Club
110 Pacific #208
San Francisco, CA 94111
  Tel. 816/942-1668

Pacific Island Connection
PO Box 461873
Los Angeles, CA 90046
  Tel. 213/650-1994

Pearls of the Orient
PSL
Blanca, CO 81123-1750
  Tel. 719/379-3228

Penfriends England
Box 525-SY
Brooklyn, NY 11229

Penfriends-England-USA
Harmony
Box 82295
Phoenix, AZ 85071

Penfriends–England, USA, Worldwide
Currents
Box 525
Brooklyn, NY 11229

Person-to-Person
Box 165
Laurel, MD 20707
Tel. 301/953-1144

Personal
In Dublin
129 Lr. Baggott Street, D2
Dublin, Ireland

Personal Interactions
1315 Butterfield Road
Downers Grove, IL
Tel. 708/963-8833

Personal Profiles
10 East Ontario Street
Chicago, IL 60611
Specialty: professionals (minimum salary of $35,000/yr)

Personal Introductions Dating Agency
49 Welles Street
Glastonbury, CT 06033
Tel. 800/662-3311

Plump Partners
PO Box 11-047
Newington, CT 06131-0047
Tel. 800/34-PLUMP

Rural Network
6236 Borden Road
Boscobel, WI 53805
Topic: friendships among the country-oriented

Scanna International
Box 4
Pittsford, NY 94534
Tel. 800/677-3170

Science Connection
PO Box 188
Youngstown, NY 14174
Topic: science/nature enthusiasts

Selective Search
858 West Armitage Avenue, #220
Chicago, IL 60614-4329

Single Again
1552 Hertel Avenue, #961
Buffalo, NY 14216
Tel. 416/944-2375
Specialty: Monthly newsletter

Single Booklovers
Box 117
Gradyville, PA 19039
Tel. 215/358-5049
Topic: get unattached people acquainted

The Single Gourmet
133 East 58th Street
New York, NY 10022
Tel. 212/980-8788

Single Life
PO Box 728
Bloomfield, CT 06002
   Tel. 203/243-1514

Singles Adventure Travel Club
   Tel. 312/935-0959

Singles Directory
8391 Beverly Blvd, #126
Los Angeles, CA 90048

Singles Network
Dept F, Box 181
Mentor, OH 44061-0181

Singles Travel
14715 Clifton Blvd.
Lakewood, OH 44107

Sober Only Singles
PO Box 88207-C
Carol Stream, IL 60188-0207
   Tel. 800/439-3773 (24 hours)

Sunshine International Penpals
Box 5500-XE
Kailua-Kona, HI 96745
   Tel. 808/325-7707

Sweet 'n' Sexy Seniors
5580 La Jolla Blvd., #423
La Jolla, CA 92037

Thai Asian Worldwide Ladies
Box 937 (SC)
Kailua-Kona, HI 96745
   Tel. 808/329-5559

Thai Women Waiting
Thai, Box 4417
Miami, FL 33114

Together
310 N. Main Street
East Longmeadow, MA 01028
 Tel. 413/732-2775

Together Development Corporation
The Meadows
161 Worcester Road
Framingham, MA 01701
 Tel. 509/620-1115

Transatlantic Penfriends
Box 2176-P
San Pedro, CA 90731

TV Guide Classified Mart
100 East Ohio Street, #632
Chicago, IL 60611

Unitarian Universalist Bisexual Network
PO Box 10818
Portland, ME 04104

Venus Club (Polish-American)
 Tel. 312/237-5937

The Wishing Well
Box 713090
Santee, CA 92072-3090
 Tel. 619/443-4818
 Specialty: women-loving-women

Appendix 2

Business/Agency Resources for Media-Mediated Relationships
(A Partial Listing)

Advertising Council
261 Madison Avenue
New York, NY 10016
Tel. 212/922-1500

American Association of Retired Persons (AARP)
601 E Street, NW
Washington, DC 20049
Tel. 202/728-4752

American Civil Liberties Union (ACLU)
122 Maryland Avenue, NE
Washington, DC 20002
Tel. 202/544-1681

American Council for the Arts
1 East 53rd Street
New York, NY 10022
Tel. 212/223-2787

American Library Association (ALA)
Office for Intellectual Freedom
50 East Huron Street
Chicago, IL 60611

Anti-Defamation League
823 United Nations Plaza
New York, NY 10017
 Tel. 212/490-2525

Association of Gay and Lesbian Psychologists
210 5th Avenue
New York, NY 10010

The Benton Foundation
1710 Rhode Island Avenue NW, 4th floor
Washington, DC 20036
 Tel. 202/857-7829

Center for Constitutional Rights
666 Broadway, 7th floor
New York, NY 10012
 Tel. 212/473-3400

The Center for Democratic Renewal
PO Box 50469
Atlanta, GA 30302-0469

Center for Media & Values
1952 Shenandoah
Los Angeles, CA 90034
 Tel. 213/559-2944

Citizens Communications Center
Georgetown University Law Center
600 New Jersey Avenue, NW
Washington, DC 20001
 Tel. 202/662-9535

Communication for Change
147 West 22nd Street
New York, NY

Consumer Federation of America
1424 16th Street NW, #604
Washington, DC 20036
  Tel. 202/387-6121

Creative Coalition
1100 Avenue of the Americas, 15th floor
New York, NY 10036
  Tel. 212/512-5515

Cultural Environment Movement (CEM)
PO Box 31847
Philadelphia, PA 19104

Electronic Arts Intermix
536 Broadway, 9th floor
New York, NY 10012

FAIR (Fairness & Accuracy In Reporting)
130 West 25th Street
New York, NY 10001

Funding Exchange
666 Broadway
New York, NY 10027

Gay and Lesbian Alliance Against Defamation (GLAAD)
150 West 26th Street, #503
New York, NY 10001
  Tel. 212/807-1700

Gay Men's Health Crisis Center
129 West 20th Street
New York, NY 10011
  Tel. 212/807-7035

Global Information Network
777 United Nations Plaza
New York, NY 10017

The Institute for Alternative Journalism
2025 I Street N, #1118
Washington, DC 20006
 Tel. 202/887-0022

International Gay Information Center
PO Box 2
Village Station, NY 10014
 Tel. 718/625-6463

The Kettering Foundation
200 Commons Road
Dayton, OH

The Kitchen
Center for Video, Music, Dance, Performance, Film, and Literature
512 West 19th Street
New York, NY 10011

Latino Collaborative
280 Broadway, #412
New York, NY 10007
 Tel. 212/732-1121

Lesbian Resource Center
1212 E. Pine Street
Seattle, WA 98122
 Tel. 206/322-3965

John D. and Catherine T. MacArthur Foundation
140 S. Dearborn Street, #1100
Chicago, IL 60603-5202

Media Access Project
2000 M Street NW, #400
Washington, DC 20036

Media Coalition
900 Third Avenue, #1600
New York, NY 10022
Tel. 212/891-2070

Media Democracy Project
c/o Made in USA Productions
330 West 42nd Street, #1905
New York, NY 10036
Tel. 212/695-3090

The Nation Institute
72 Fifth Avenue
New York, NY 10011

National Alliance of Artists' Organizations
918 F Street, NW
Washington, DC 20004
Tel. 202/347-6350

National Alliance for Media Arts and Culture
1212 Broadway, #816
Oakland, CA 94612

National Black Programming Consortium
929 Harrison Avenue, #104
Columbus, OH 43215

National Campaign for Freedom of Expression
1402 3rd Avenue, #421
Seattle, WA 98010

National Center for Nonprofit Boards
1225 19th Street NW, #340
Washington, DC 20036
Tel. 202/452-6262

National Coalition Against Censorship
275 7th Avenue
New York, NY 10001

*National Council of Churches/*Dept. of Communication
475 Riverside Drive, Room 850
New York, NY 10115
 Tel. 212/870-2048

National Council for Research on Women
Sara Delano Roosevelt House
47-49 East 65th Street
New York, NY

National Gay and Lesbian Task Force
1734 14th Street, NW
Washington, DC 20009
 Tel. 202/332-6483

National Gay Rights Advocates
540 Castro Street
San Francisco, CA 94114

National Institute Against Prejudice & Violence
31 South Greene Street
Baltimore, MD 21201
 Tel. 301/328-5170

Northwest Coalition Against Malicious Harassment
Box 16776
Seattle, WA 98116

People for the American Way
2000 M Street NW, #400
Washington, DC 20036

Union Producers and Programmers NETwork (UPPNET)
c/o UFCW Local 1442
PO Box 1750
Santa Monica, CA 90406

Appendix 3

Print Resources
for Media-Mediated Relationships
(A Partial Listing)

Adbusters Quarterly
Media Foundation
1243 W. 7th Avenue
Vancouver, Canada

The Advocate
1730 S. Amphlett
San Mateo CA 94402
Tel. 415/573-7100

American Film Institute
3 East 54th Street
New York, NY 10022

Anything That Moves
Bay Area Bisexual Network
2404 California Street, #24
San Francisco, CA 94115

Bad Attitude
Box 39110
Cambridge, MA 02139

Baltimore Magazine
131 E. Redwood Street
Baltimore, MD 21202
Tel. 301/752-7375

The Berkeley Monthly
910 Parker Street
Berkeley, CA 94710
   Tel. 415/848-7900

Black Lace
BLK Publishing Company
Box 83912
Los Angeles, CA 90083

Boston Magazine
31 St. James Avenue
Boston, MA 02116
   Tel. 617/357-4000

The Boston Phoenix
126 Brookline Avenue
Boston, MA 02215
   Tel. 617/267-1234

Brat Attack
Box 40754
San Francisco, CA 94140

Chico News and Review
120 W. 2nd Street
Chico, CA 95296
   Tel. 916/342-5604

Cineaste
200 Park Avenue South
New York, NY 10003-1503

City Paper
919 6th Street
Washington, DC 20001
   Tel. 202/289-0520

Creative Loafing
1011 W. Peachtree
Atlanta, GA 30309
Tel. 404/873-5623

The Dating Page
PO Box 310
Lynnfield, MA 01940
Tel. 508/535-6660

Des Moines Register
PO Box 957
Des Moines, IA 50304
Tel. 800/532-8141

Diseased Pariah News
c/o Men's Support Center
Box 30564
Oakland, CA 94604

Ecstasy: The Journal of Divine Eroticism
Box 862
Ojai, CA 93024

Entertainment Weekly
1675 Broadway
New York, NY 10019

Felix: A Journal of Media Arts and Communication
PO Box 184
Prince Street Station, NY

Film Comment
Film Society of Lincoln Center
140 W. 65th Street
New York, NY 10023

Film History
American Museum of the Moving Image
36-01 35th Avenue
Astoria, NY 11106

Film Quarterly
University of California Press
Berkeley, CA 94720

Friends Magazine
PO Box 372
Gales Ferry, CT 06335
    Tel. 203/464-2852

Friends and More
171 Park Street
West Springfield, MA
    Tel. 413/746-3283

frighten the horses: a document of the sexual revolution
Heat Seeking Publishing
41 Sutter Street, #1108
San Francisco, CA 94104

Future Sex
1095 Market Street, #809
San Francisco, CA 94013

Girljock
Rox-a-Tronic Publishing
Box 2522
Berkeley, CA 94702

Hartford Advocate
30 Arbor Street
Hartford, CT 06106
    Tel. 203/232-4501

Holy Titclamps
Box 591275
San Francisco, CA 94159

Hothead Paisan
Giant Ass Publishing
Box 214
New Haven, CT 06502

Intro Magazine
PO Box INTRO
Studio City, CA 91604
    Tel. 213/384-6876

Illinois Times
Box 3524
Springfield, IL 62708
    Tel. 217/753-1724

L.A. Weekly
5325 Sunset Blvd.
Los Angeles, CA 90027
    Tel. 213/462-6911

Lesbian & Gay Community Services Center
208 West 13th Street
New York, NY 10011
    Tel. 212/620-7310

Lesbian Herstory Archives
PO Box 1258
New York, NY 10116
    Tel. 718/768-3953

Libido: The Journal of Sex and Sensibility
Box 146721
Chicago, IL 60614

Lifestyle
2194 Palou Avenue
San Francisco, CA 94124
    Tel. 415/824-2901

Logomotive
Box 3101
Berkeley, CA 94703

Los Angeles Magazine
PO Box 49999
Los Angeles, CA 90049-0588
 Tel. 213/476-0588

Maine Times
41 Main Street
Topsham, ME 04086
 Tel. 207/729-0126

Miami Magazine
PO Box 340008
Coral Gables, FL 33114
 Tel. 305/374-5011

New Haven Advocate
1184 Chapel Street
New Haven, CT 06511
 Tel. 203/789-0010

New Republic
1220 19th Street, NW
Washington, DC 20036
 Tel. 202/331-7494

New Times Weekly
PO Box 2510
Phoenix, AZ 85002
 Tel. 602/271-0040

New York Public Library
20 West 53rd Street
New York, NY 10019
 Tel. 212/621-0618

The New Yorker Magazine
20 W. 43rd Street
New York, NY 10036

Newsweek
444 Madison Avenue
New York, NY 10022-6999

On Our Backs: Entertainment for the Adventurous Lesbian
526 Castro Street
San Francisco, CA 94114

Pacific Sun
PO Box 553
Mill Valley, CA 94942
 Tel. 415/383-4500

The Planet
PO Box 1171
Des Moines, IA 50311
 Tel. 515/274-1541

Premiere Magazine
5 Penn Plaza
New York, NY 10001
 Tel. 212/643-6420

Quim
Quim, BM 2182
London WCIN 3XX, England

Rolling Stone
1290 Avenue of the Americas
New York, NY 10104-0298
 Tel. 212/484-1616

The Sandmutopia Guardian
Box 410390
San Francisco, CA 94141

San Francisco Bay Guardian
2700 19th Street
San Francisco, CA 94110
 Tel. 415/824-7660

Santa Barbara News & Review
735 State Street, #222
Santa Barbara, CA 93101
  Tel. 805/963-9411

Singles Choice
E.J.G. Enterprises, Inc.
113 McHenry Road
Buffalo Grove, IL 60089
  Tel. 708/634-7700

Singles Connection
PO Box 11115
Tallahassee, FL 32302-3115

Singles' Personal Ads
PO Box 850
Needham Heights, MA 02194
  Tel. 617/444-2587

Spectator
Box 1984
Berkeley, CA 94701

Springfield Advocate
New Mass Media, Inc.
1127 Main Street
Springfield, MA 01103
  Tel. 413/781-1900

Spy Magazine
5 Union Square West
New York, NY 10003
  Tel. 212/633-6550

The Suttertown News
2791 24th Street
Sacramento, CA 95818
  Tel. 916/451-2823

Talkers
Box 60781
Longmeadow, MA 01116-0781

TANTRA: The Magazine
Box 79
Torreon, NM 87061-0079

Taste of Latex
Box 460122
San Francisco, CA 94146-0122

Thing: She Knows Who She Is
2151 W. Division Street
Chicago, IL 60622-3056

Time
Time & Life Building
Rockefeller Center
New York, NY 10020-1393

Tucson Weekly News
PO Box 50567
Tucson, AZ 85703
    Tel. 602/623-FREE

TV Guide
Box 500
Radnor, PA 19088

Utne Reader
1624 Harmon Place, #330
Minneapolis, MN 55403-1906

The Velvet Light Trap
University of Texas Press
PO Box 7819
Austin, TX 78713

The Village Voice
36 Cooper Square
New York, NY 10003
　Tel. 212/475-5555

The Washington Tribune
PO Box 12055
Washington, DC 20005
　Tel. 202/232-4900

The Washingtonian
PO Box 911
Annapolis, MD 21404
　Tel. 202/261-2447

The Weekly
17 E. University
Champaign, IL 61820
　Tel. 217/351-5144

Westword
1610 15th Street
Denver, CO 80202
　Tel. 303/534-4613

Whorezine
2300 Market Street, #19
San Francisco, CA 94114

Womyn Who Masturbate
Box 3690
Minneapolis, MN 55403

Worcester Magazine
475 Washington Street
Auburn, MA 01501
　Tel. 800/367-9898

Worcester Phoenix
314 Washington Street
Auburn, MA 01501
   Tel. 508/832-9800

Working Press of the Nation
National Register Publishing
PO Box 31
New Providence, NJ 07974-9903

Yellow Silk: Journal of Erotic Arts
Box 6374
Albany, CA 94706

Appendix 4

Magazines and Journals in Media-Mediated Relationships

Advertising Age
American Demographics
American Enterprise
American Journal of Sociology
Anything That Moves
Atlanta Business Chronicle
Atlantic City
The Australian and New Zealand Journal of Sociology
AV Communication Review
Baltimore Business Journal
Baltimore Magazine
Baton Rouge Business Report
Beijing Review
The Berkeley Monthly
Boston Business Journal
Boston Magazine
Broadcasting
The Business Journal—Milwaukee
Business Journal Serving Greater Sacramento
Business Week
Business West
California Business
Canadian Business
The Carolinas Speech Communication Annual
Chicago
Chocolate Singles Magazine
Cincinnati Business Courier

Cineaste
Colors
Communication Monographs
Communication Research
Communication Quarterly
Computerworld
Cosmopolitan
CQ Researcher
Crain's Chicago Business
Critical Studies in Mass Communication
D(allas) Magazine
The Dating Page
Details
Deviant Behavior
The Economist
Editor & Publisher
Elle
Entertainment Weekly
Family Coordinator
Family Planning Perspectives
Family Relations
Far Eastern Economic Review
Film Comment
Film Quarterly
Forbes
Fortune
Friends
Friends and More
Gay Books Bulletin
Genre
Harper's Bazaar
High Times
Human Communication Research
ImMEDIAte Impact
In Dublin
Insights on Global Ethics
Intro
Isthmus

Journal of Applied Social Psychology
Journal of Broadcasting & Electronic Media
Journal of Commerce and Commercial
Journal of Communication
Journal of Communication and Media Arts
Journal of Criminal Law and Criminology
Journal of Homosexuality
Journal of Marketing
Journal of Marriage and the Family
Journal of Personality and Social Psychology
Journal of Popular Culture
Journal of Sex Research
Journal of Social and Personal Relationships
The Law Journal
Living Single
Los Angeles Magazine
Maclean's
Mademoiselle
Match Book
Media Culture Review
Mensa Bulletin
Miami Magazine
Monthly Detroit
Movieline
National Geographic
National Review
National Singles Register
New England Journal of Medicine
New Media
New Perspectives Quarterly
New Statesman
New York
New York Journal
The New York Times Magazine
The New Yorker
Newsweek
New Woman
Out

Our World
Out and About
Out/Look
Person-to-Person
Personality and Social Psychology Bulletin
The Personals
Philadelphia Magazine
Premiere
Professional Psychology: Research and Practice
The Progressive (Madison, WI)
Psychiatry
Psychological Reports
Psychology Today
Public Opinion Quarterly
QW
Radio World
Raygun
Rolling Stone
Romantic Times
St. Louis Magazine
San Diego Business Journal
Savvy Woman
Self
Sex Roles: A Journal of Research
Sight and Sound
Single Life
Singles Choice
Singles Connection
Singles' Personal Ads
Singles Scene
Smithsonian
South Atlantic Quarterly
Spy
Style
Sweet 'n' Sexy Seniors
Talkers
Telematics and Informatics
Time

TV Guide
Unitarian Universalist Bisexual Network Newsletter
Utne Reader
Vanity Fair
The Velvet Light Trap
Washington Business Journal
The Washingtonian
Whole Life Times
The Wishing Well
Woman
Women's Studies in Communication
Worcester Phoenix
Working Woman
World Communication
World Press Review

Appendix 5

Newspapers in Media-Mediated Relationships

The Advocate
Arizona Republic/Phoenix Gazette
Boston Globe
Boston Phoenix
Charlotte (NC) *Observer*
Chicago Reader
Chicago Tribune
Christian Science Monitor
City Newspaper (NYC)
City Paper (Washington, DC)
Creative Loafing (Atlanta)
The Daily News (Durban, SA)
Des Moines Register
Detroit Metro Times
ELECTRICity (Philadelphia)
The Gazette (Montreal)
Illinois Times
International Herald Tribune
Ithaca (NY) *Times*
L.A. Weekly
Lifestyle (San Francisco)
London Times
Los Angeles Times
Maine Times
Metropolitan Almanac (NYC)
The Natal (SA) *Mercury*
National Review

National Singles Register
New York Journal
New York Post
The New York Times
News Herald (Panama City, FL)
Pittsburgh Pennysaver
Providence (RI) *Eagle*
San Francisco Bay Guardian
The Star (Johanesburg, SA)
The Spectator (North Carolina)
Talkers
Tucson Weekly News
Union-News (Springfield, MA)

Appendix 6

Broadcasting Resources
for Media-Mediated Relationships
(A Partial Listing)

ABC
77 West 66th Street
New York, NY 10023

A&E (Arts & Entertainment)
235 East 45th Street
New York, NY 10017

The Alliance for Community Media
666 11th Street NW, #906
Washington, DC 20001
    Tel. 202/393-2650

American Movie Classics (AMC)
150 Crossways Park West
Woodbury, NY 11797

Alternative Views
PO Box 7279
Austin, TX 87813

Black Entertainment Television (BET)
1700 North Moore Street, #2200
Rosslyn, VA 22209

Cable News Network (CNN, TBS, TNT)
One CNN Center, PO Box 105366
Atlanta, GA 30348

Cable Television Information Center
1800 N. Kent Street, #1007
Arlington, VA 22209

The Cable Television Public Affairs Association
414 Main Street
Laurel, MD 20707

CBS
51 West 52nd Street
New York, NY 10019

Chicago Access Corporation
322 S. Green Street
Chicago, IL 60607
   Tel. 312/738-1400

Cinemax
1100 Avenue of the Americas
New York, NY 10036

CNBC
2200 Fletcher Avenue
Fort Lee, NJ 07024

Comedy Central
1775 Broadway
New York, NY 10019

C-SPAN
400 North Capitol Street NW, #650
Washington, DC 20001

The Discovery Channel
7700 Wisconsin Avenue
Bethesda, MD 20814-3522

The Disney Channel
3800 West Alameda Avenue
Burbank, CA 91505

DIVA-TV
c/o ACT-UP
135 West 29th Street, 10th floor
New York, NY 10001
    Tel. 212/564-2437

Downtown Community Television
87 Lafayette Street
New York, NY 10013

ESPN
ESPN Plaza
935 Middle Street
Bristol, CT 06010

The Family Channel
1000 Centerville Turnpike
Virginia Beach, VA 23463

Fox Broadcasting Company
PO Box 900
Beverly Hills, CA 90213

Gay Cable Network
150 West 26th Street
New York, NY 10001
    Tel. 212/727-8850

Home Box Office (HBO)
1100 Avenue of the Americas
New York, NY 10036

The Independent Television Service
PO Box 65797
St. Paul, MN 55175

The International Radio and Television Society
420 Lexington Avenue, #1714
New York, NY 10170-1010
    Tel. 212/867-6650

Lifetime
36-12 35th Avenue
Astoria, NY 11106

The Movie Channel (TMC)
1633 Broadway
New York, NY 10019

MTV
1515 Broadway
New York, NY 10036

The Nashville Network
2806 Opryland Drive
Nashville, TN 37214

National Academy of Cable Programming
1724 Massachusetts Avenue, NW
Washington, DC 20036
    Tel. 202/775-3611

National Association of Broadcasters (NAB)
1771 N Street, NW
Washington, DC 20036
    Tel. 202/429-5300

National Association of College Broadcasters
71 George Street, Box 1824
Providence, RI 02912

National Citizens Committee for Broadcasting
PO Box 12038
Washington, DC 20005

National Coalition of Independent Public Broadcasting Producers
1 Donna Avenue
New York, NY 10956

National Community Network
3200 Cherry Creek Drive S., #500
Denver, CO 80209

National Federation of Community Broadcasters
666 11th Street NW, #850
Washington, DC 20001
   Tel. 202/393-2355

Native American Public Broadcasting Consortium
Box 83111
Lincoln, NE 68501

NBC
30 Rockefeller Plaza
New York, NY 10112

Nickelodeon
1515 Broadway
New York, NY 10036

The 90's
400 N. Michigan Avenue, #1608
Chicago, IL 60611
   Tel. 312/321-9321

Not Channel Zero
PO Box 805, Wakefield Station
Bronx, NY 10466
   Tel. 212/966-4510

Pacific Islanders in Communication
1221 Kapi'olani Blvd., #6A-4
Honolulu, HI 96814

Paper Tiger Television/Deep Dish TV
339 Lafayette Street
New York, NY 10012
  Tel. 212/473-8933

Public Broadcasting System (PBS)
1320 Braddock Place
Alexandria, VA 22314-1698

Response Television Corporation
PO Box 3358
Iowa City, IA 52240

San Francisco Community Television Corporation
1095 Market Street, #704
San Francisco, CA 94103-1630

Showtime
1633 Broadway
New York, NY 10019

USA Network
1230 Avenue of the Americas
New York, NY 10020

Video Hits One
1515 Broadway
New York, NY 10036

The Weather Channel
2600 Cumberland Parkway
Atlanta, GA 30339

Appendix 7

Communication Technology Resources for Media-Mediated Relationships
(A Partial Listing)

The Alliance for Public Technology
901 15th Street NW, #203
Washington, DC 20005

Alternative Media Information Center/"Media Network"
39 West 14th Street, #403
New York, NY 10011

Association Internationale dur Film d'Animation (ASIFA)
790 N. Milwaukee Avenue
Chicago, IL 60622

Audio-Visual Resources for Social Change
American Friends Service Committee
2160 Lake Street
San Francisco, CA 94121

Datalink
PO Box 100
Stratford-Upon-Avon CV37 3LE, England

Electronic Frontier Foundation
666 Pennsylvania Avenue SE, #303
Washington, DC 20003

Federal Comunications Commission
1919 M Street, NW
Washington, DC 20554

The Freedom Forum Media Studies Center
2950 Broadway
New York, NY 10027

Institute for Media Analysis
145 West 4th Street
New York, NY

Mass Learn Pike
Massachusetts Corporation for Educational Telecommunications
University Park at MIT
38 Sidney Street, #300
Cambridge, MA 02138

Mind Extension University
9697 East Mineral Avenue
Englewood, CO 80112

National Aeronautics and Space Administration (NASA)
300 E. Street, SW
2nd floor, Room 2L15
Washington, DC 20546

National Association of Telecommunications Officers and Advisors
c/o National League of Cities
1301 Pennsylvania Avenue NW
Washington, DC 20004

Recording Industry Association of America
1020 19th Street NW, #200
Washington, DC 20036

US Telecommunications Experts Center
University of Nebraska at Omaha
International Center for Telecommunications Management
Omaha, NE 68182

Andy Warhol Foundation for the Visual Arts
22 E. 33rd Street
New York, NY

X*Press Information Services, Inc.
Denver Corp. Center
4700 S. Syracuse Parkway
Denver, CO 80237

Appendix 8

Telephone Resources
for Media-Mediated Relationships
(A Partial Listing)

Brunch Buddies
Dating Service for Lesbians 800/2-FIND-US, ext. 1
Dating Service for Gay Men 800/2-FIND-US, ext. 2
Dating Service for HIV+ Men 800/2-FIND-US, ext. 3

CompuServe
Box 20212
Columbus, OH 43220
Tel. 614/457-8600

Echo
97 Perry Street, #13
New York, NY 10014
Tel. 212/255-3839

Gay Talk
PO Box 32592
Kansas City, MO 64111
Hotline: 816/931-4470

HOT GAY TALK
Voices International
Reno, NV
Tel. 900/976-2MEN

Lesbian Lust
Tropicana Ste. 318
Las Vegas, NV 89119
   Tel. 900/344-0333

Live Private Conversation
Theatre of the Mind
New York, NY
   Tel. 900/773-2837

Love Phones (WHTZ)
767 3rd Avenue
New York, NY
   Tel. 800/242-0100

National Singles Network
Avalon Communications
Ft. Lauderdale, FL
   Tel. 900/776-3033

New York's Nastiest
Swifty Communications
Los Angeles, CA
   Tel. 900/407-7700

Our Girls Give Great Phone!
A&R
Box 25001
Los Angeles, CA 90025
   Tel. 900/933-7473

Rick's Gay Dating Service
Ft. Myers, FL
   Tel. 900/288-HUNK

Michael Salem Ent., Inc.
300 E. 46th Street, #2E
New York, NY 10017
   Tel. 900/420-5677

Sex Connect (Gay Owned and Operated)
Advanced Communication Corp.
New York, NY
   Tel. 212/550-1212

Singles Dateline
Avalon Communication
Ft. Lauderdale, FL
   Tel. 900/787-4587, ext. 220

Talking Personals
Connections, USA
Ft. Lauderdale, FL
   Tel. 900/454-4500

24 Hr. HOT LIVE GIRLS
Telephun, Inc.
Los Angeles, CA
   Tel. 900/773-HOTT

WELL
27 Gate Five Road
Sausalito, CA 94966
   Tel. 415/332-4335

Appendix 9

A Filmography
on Media-Mediated Relationships

1904 *Personals.* Producer: Biograph
1904 *How a French Nobleman Got a Wife Through the New York Herald Personal Column.* Producer: Edison
1954 *Rear Window.* Director: Alfred Hitchcock
1958 *The Matchmaker.* Director: Gene Kelly
1960 *Peeping Tom.* Director: Michael Powell
1964 *Mail Order Bride.* Writer/Director: George Bassman
1964 *Sex and the Single Girl.* Director: Richard Quine
1968 *For Singles Only.* Director: Arthur Dreifuss
1969 *Hello, Dolly.* Director: Joseph Anthony
1970 *The Honeymoon Killers.* Director: Leonard Kastle
1971 *Fiddler on the Roof.* Director: Norman Jewison
1971 *Love Machine.* Director: Jack Haley, Jr.
1972 *Extreme Close-Up.* Director: Jeannot Szwarc
1977 *Citizens Band.* Director: Jonathan Demme
1977 *Looking for Mr. Goodbar.* Writer/Director: Richard Brooks
1980 *Atlantic City.* Director: Louis Malle
1980 *Death Watch.* Director: Bertrand Tavernier
1980 *Don't Answer the Phone.* Director: Robert Hammer
1980 *Private Lessons.* Director: Alan Myerson
1980 *Prostitute.* Director: Tony Garnett
1981 *I Sent a Letter to My Love.* Director Moshe Mizrahi
1981 *Not a Love Story.* Director: Bonnie Sherr Klein
1982 *Cafe Flesh.* Director: Rinse Dream
1982 *I Was a Mail Order Bride.* Made-for-TV movie
1982 *Eating Raoul.* Director: Paul Bartel
1982 *The Lonely Lady.* Director: Peter Sasdy

1983   *Lonely Hearts.* Director: Paul Cox
1983   *The Personals.* Director: Peter Markle
1983   *Risky Business.* Director: Paul Brickman
1983   *Scarred.* Director: Rose-Marie Turko
1983   *Star 80.* Director: Bob Fosse
1983   *Variety.* Director: Betty Gordon
1983   *Videodrome.* Director: David Cronenberg
1984   *Blind Date.* Director: Nico Mastorakis
1984   *Choose Me.* Writer/Director: Alan Rudolph
1984   *Crimes of Passion.* Director: Ken Russell
1984   *The Lonely Guy.* Director: Arthur Hiller
1984   *A Murder is Announced.* Director: David Giles
1985   *Desperately Seeking Susan.* Director: Susan Siedelman
1985   *Rate It X.* Directors: Paula de Koenigsberg and Lucy Winer
1986   *Beyond Therapy.* Director: Robert Altman
1986   *City in Panic.* Director: Robert Bouvier
1986   *Classified Love.* Made-for-cable television
1986   *Kamikaze Hearts.* Director: Juliet Bashore
1986   *Manhunter.* Director: Michael Mann
1986   *Mona Lisa.* Director: Neil Jordan
1986   *The Terroriser.* Director: Edward Yang
1986   *Working Girls.* Director: Lizzie Borden
1987   *Call Me.* Director: Sollace Mitchell
1987   *Family Viewing.* Director: Atom Egoyan
1987   *The Game of Love.* Director: Bobby Roth
1987   *Lady Beware.* Director: Karen Arthur
1987   *The Lonely Passion of Judith Hearne.* Director:
        Jack Clayton
1987   *Out of Order.* Director: Jonnie Turpie
1987   *Perfect Match.* Director: Mark Deimel
1987   *Personal Services.* Director: Terry Jones
1987   *Tough Guys Don't Dance.* Director: Norman Mailer
1988   *Call Me.* Director Sollace Mitchell
1988   *Cheap Shots.* Directors: Jeff Ureles and Jerry Stoeffhaas
1988   *Dangerous Love.* Director: Marty Ollstein
1988   *Freeway.* Director: Francis Delia
1988   *Fun Down There.* Director: Roger Stigliano
1988   *Heavy Petting.* Director: Obie Benz

1988 *I Saw What You Did*. Director: Fred Walton
1988 *Out of the Dark*. Director: Michael Schroeder
1988 *Party Line*. Director: William Webb
1988 *A Short Film About Love*. Director: Krysztof Kielowski
1988 *Talk Radio*. Director: Oliver Stone
1988 *Torch Song Trilogy*. Director: Paul Bogart
1989 *Monsieur Hire*. Director: Patrice Leconte
1989 *976-Evil*. Director: Robert Englund
1989 *The Rachel Papers*. Director Damien Harris
1989 *Sea of Love*. Director: Harold Becker
1989 *sex, lies, and videotape*. Director: Steven Soderbergh
1989 *Slaves of New York*. Director: James Ivory
1989 *Speaking Parts*. Director: Atom Egoyan
1990 *Bad Influence*. Director: Curtis Hanson
1990 *Crimes and Misdemeanors*. Director: Woody Allen
1990 *Elliot Fauman, PhD*. Director: Ric Klass
1990 *A Flame in My Heart*. Director: Alain Tanner
1990 *Lonely in America*. Director: Barry Alexander Brown
1990 *Lonely Woman Seeks Life Companion*. Director: Viacheslav Krishtofovich
1990 *Night Eyes*. Director: Jag Mundhra
1990 *Over Exposed*. Director: Larry Brand
1990 *Personals*. Director: Steven H. Stern
1990 *Pretty Woman*. Director: Garry Marshall
1990 *Pump Up the Volume*. Director: Allan Moyle
1990 *Scissors*. Director: Frank DeFelitta
1990 *Wild Orchid*. Director: Zalman King
1991 *Delirious*. Director: Tom Mankiewicz
1991 *Eating*. Director: Henry Jaglom
1991 *The Famine Within*. Producer/Writer/Dir: Katherine Gilday
1991 *Intimate Stranger*. Director: Alan Holzman
1991 *Julia Has Two Lovers*. Co-Producer/Director: Bashar Shbib
1991 *Lonely Hearts*. Director: Andrew Lane
1991 *My Own Private Idaho*. Exec. Prod./Dir./Writer: Gus VanSant
1991 *Night Eyes 2*. Director: Rodney McDonald
1991 *No Skin Off My Ass*. Director: Bruce LaBruce
1991 *Only the Lonely*. Director: Chris Columbus
1991 *Paris is Burning*. Co-Producer/Director: Jennie Livingston

1991 *The Phone Call.* Director: Allan A. Goldstein
1991 *Truth or Dare.* Director: Alek Keshisian
1991 *Until the End of the World.* Director: Wim Wenders
1992 *Animal Instincts.* Director: Blair Martin; Actors: Shannon Whirry, Mitch Gaylord
1992 *Are You Lonesome Tonight.* Director: E. W. Swackhamer
1992 *Basic Instinct.* Director: Paul Verhoeven
1992 *Blind Vision.* Director: Shuki Levy: Actors: Lenny Van Dohlen, Louise Fletcher
1992 *Consenting Adults.* Director: Gilbert Cates
1992 *The Crying Game.* Director: Neil Jordan
1992 *Damage.* Producer/Director: Louis Malle
1992 *Dance with Death.* Director: Charles Philip Moore
1992 *Deadbolt.* Director: Doug Jackson
1992 *I Don't Buy Kisses Anymore.* Director: Robert Marcarelli
1992 *The Lost Language of Cranes.* Producer: BBC Productions
1992 *Lonely Hearts.* Director: Andrew Lane
1992 *Love Crimes.* Director: Lizzie Borden
1992 *Man Trouble.* Director: Bob Rafelson
1992 *Night Rhythms.* Director: A. Gregory Hippolyte
1992 *976-Evil 2.* Director: Jim Wynorski
1992 *Pacific Heights.* Director: John Schlesinger
1992 *Sexual Response.* Director: Yaky Yosha
1992 *Single White Female.* Director: Barbet Schroeder
1992 *Singles.* Co-producer/Director: Cameron Crowe
1992 *Smooth Talker.* Director: Tom E. Milo
1992 *Straight Talk.* Director: Barnet Kellman
1992 *Sunset Strip.* Director: Paul G. Volk
1992 *Together Alone.* Prod./Writer/Dir./Editor: P. J. Castellaneta
1992 *Unlawful Entry.* Director: Jonathan Kaplan
1992 *Wild Orchid 2.* Director: Zalman King
1993 *Die Watching.* Actors: Christopher Atkins, Vali Ashton
1993 *Distinguished Gentleman.* Director: Jonathan Lynn
1993 *Dying to Love You.* Director: Robert Iscove
1993 *Fade to Black.* Actors: Heather Locklear, Timothy Busfield
1993 *Made in America.* Director: Richard Benjamin
1993 *Married People, Single Sex.* Producer/Director: Mike Sedan
1993 *Secret Games: The Escort.* Director: Gregory Hippolyte

1993	*Sex Is . . .* Director: Marc Huestis
1993	*Short Cuts.* Director: Robert Altman
1993	*Sleepless in Seattle.* Director: Nora Ephron
1993	*Sliver.* Director: Phillip Noyce
1993	*South Beach.* Director: Fred Williamson
1993	*Watch It.* Writer/Director: Tom Flynn
1993	*The Wedding Banquet.* Director: Ang Lee
1994	*Exit to Eden.* Director: Garry Marshall
1994	*Reality Bites.* Director: Ben Stiller
1995	*Boys on the Side.* Director: Herbert Ross

Appendix 10

Film/Video Resources
for Media-Mediated Relationships
(A Partial Listing)

Alliance for Community Media
666 11th Street NW, #806
Washington, DC 20001

American Film Institute
2021 North Western Avenue
Los Angeles, CA 90027

Angles: Women Working in Film & Video
PO Box 11916
Milwaukee, WI 53211

Association of Independent Video and Filmmakers
625 Broadway
New York, NY 10012

Berlin Film Festival
Budapester Str. 50, D-1000
West Berlin 30, Germany

Classic Productions
PO Box 952
Metairie, LA 70004
Specialty: Nude beauty & dance contests

Cineacion
346 9th Street
San Francisco, CA 94103
  Tel. 415/553-8135

Denver International Film Festival
Denver International Film Society
999 18th Street, #1820
Denver, CO 80202

El Salvador Media Project
335 West 38th Street, 5th floor
New York, NY 10018

Facets Multimedia
1517 West Fullerton
Chicago, IL 60614
  Tel. 800/331-6197

Film Arts Foundation
346 9th Street, 2nd floor
San Francisco, CA 94103
  Tel. 415/552-8760

Film in the Cities
2388 University Avenue
St. Paul, MN 55114

Frameline
Box 14792
San Francisco, CA 94114

Flying Focus Video Collective
2305 NW Kearney, #231
Portland, OR 97210

FM Concepts
Box 780
N. Hollywood, CA 91603
  Specialty: "Beautiful bare feet!"

GM Video
PO Box 1339
Sedona, AZ 86339
   Tel. 602/634-1285
   Specialty: Hottest nude and T&A videos available

The Hollywood Policy Center
10536 Culver Blvd.
Culver City, CA 90232

Latino Collaborative
280 Broadway, #412
New York, NY 10007

Lolita's
Brazil Video
PO Box 8572
La Jolla, CA 92038
   Specialty: Topless beaches of French Riviera

London Film Festival
National Film Theater
South Bank
London SE1, England

Los Angeles International Gay & Lesbian Film & Video Festival
Gay & Lesbian Media Coalition
8228 Sunset Blvd, #308
West Hollywood, CA 90046

Media Art
176 Duncan Street
San Francisco, CA 94110
   Specialty: Videos, laserdiscs, books

Melbourne Film Festival
GPO Box 2760 Ee
Melbourne, Victoria 3001, Australia

Montreal Film Festival
1455 Rue de Maisonneuve
Quest, Montreal, Quebec H3G 1M8, Canada

National Videotape Exchange
c/o Thurston Community TV
2940 Limited Lane
Olympia, WA 98502

Neighborhood Film/Video Project
3701 Chestnut Street
Philadelphia, PA

New York Film Festival
The Film Society of Lincoln Center
70 Lincoln Plaza
New York, NY 10023-6595

New York Lesbian and Gay Film Festival
The New Festival, Inc.
80 Eighth Avenue
New York, NY 10011

99 Cent Queer Video Festival
Allison Hennessy & Jeffrey Winter
Please Louise Productions
112 Albion Street
San Francisco, CA 94110
   Tel. 415/864-5453

Palm Springs Film Festival
401 S. Pavilion Way, Box 1786
Palm Springs, CA 92263

Public Interest Video Network
1642 R Street, NW
Washington, DC 29990

Recording Industry Association of America
1020 19th Street NW, #200
Washington, DC 20036

San Francisco Film Festival
San Francisco Film Society
1650 Fillmore Street
San Francisco, CA 94115

L. Scott Sales
PO Box 4430
College Point, NY 11365
    Tel. 800/582-4343
    Specialty: Erotic female fighting videos

Seattle International Film Festival
c/o Egyptian Theatre
801 E. Pine Street
Seattle, WA 98122

Sundance Film Festival
c/o Sundance Institute
Box 16450
Salt Lake City, Utah 84116

Sweet Majic
PO Box 164211
Miami, FL 33116
    Specialty: Bizarre Japanese adult videos

Telluride Film Festival
c/o National Film Preserve
535 S. Main Street, Box B1156
Hanover, NH 03755

Testing the Limits Collective
31 West 26th Street, 4th floor
New York, NY 10010

Third World Newsreel
335 West 38th Street, 5th floor
New York, NY 10018

Toronto Film Festival
69 Yorkville, #205
Toronto, Ontario M5R 1B8, Canada

USA Film Festival
2917 Swiss Avenue
Dallas, TX 97204

Venice Film Festival
C.A. Giustinian
San Marco, 30124
Venice, Italy

Video Data Bank
37 S. Wabash Street
Chicago, IL 60603

Video Project
5331 College Avenue, #101
Oakland, CA 94618

Video Software Dealers Association
303 Harper Drive
Mooretown, NJ 08057

Video Vamp
1483 N. Mt. Juliet Road, #142
Mt. Juliet, TN 37122
    Specialty: Erotic horror/cult video ("scream queens, imprisoned
    women, & psycho sluts")

Voyeur Vision
95 Christopher Street
New York, NY
    Tel. 212/924-4444

Women in the Director's Chair
3435 North Sheffield
Chicago, IL 60657
   Tel. 312/281-4988

Women Make Movies
225 Lafayette Street, #206
New York, NY 10012

Appendix 11

Songs About Media-Mediated
Relationships
(A Partial Listing)

1960s

Jimi Hendrix—*Burning of the Midnight Lamp*
("Loneliness is Such a Drag")
The Beatles—*Eleanor Rigby*
("All the lonely people, Where do they all come from?")
Otis Redding—*Sitting on the Dock of the Bay*
("This loneliness won't leave me alone")

1970s

James Taylor—*Fire and Rain*
("I've seen lonely times when I could not find a friend")
Pink Floyd—*Is There Anybody Out There?*
("Ooh, babe, don't leave me now/I need you . . . to beat to a
pulp")
    —*Empty Spaces*
("What shall we use to fill the empty spaces where we used to
talk?")
The Who—*Bargain*
("To win you, I'd stand naked, stoned, and stabbed")

1980s

The Police—*King of Pain*
("I will always be the king of pain")
Dire Straits—*Water of Love*
("I've been too long a-lonely/And my heart feels the pain")

Tina Turner—*What's Love Got to Do With It?*
("Who needs a heart when a heart can be broken?")

1990s
Guns'n' Roses—*Estranged*
("When you're whispering to yourself . . . ")
Madonna—*Express Yourself*
("You've got to make him express himself")
Paula Abdul—*Opposites Attract*
("You take two steps forward. I take two steps back/We get together 'cause opposites attract")
Wilson Philips—*Release Me*
("Come on baby, now hear me darlin'/'Cause you're a waste of time for me. I've got to make you see/That somehow you've just got to release me")
Seduction—*Two to Make it Right*
("It takes two to make a thing go right . . . to make it out of sight")
Janet Jackson—*Let's Wait a While*
("Let's wait a while/before it's too late . . . before we go too far. I really didn't know not to let all my feelings show/To save some for later so our love could be greater")
Madonna—*Justify My Love* ("I need to justify my love")
En Vogue—*My Loving' (You're Never Gonna Get)*
("What makes you think you can just walk back into her life? You had a good thing, oh yeah. Next time you got to give your woman a little respect/Or you're just wasting her time")
Blind Melon—*No Rain* ("I feel so plain")
Mariah Carey—*Dreamlover*
("I want a dreamlover/One that I can call my own")
Blur—*Modern Life is Rubbish*
("For Tomorrow"; "Advert"; "A Well Respected Man")
Marillion—*That Time of the Night*
("At that time of the night/When streetlights throw crosses through window frames/Paranoia roams . . . ")
    —*Going Under*
("Is it wrong to talk to myself even when there's nobody else?")

—Script for a Jester's Tear
("So here I am once more in the playground of broken hearts/
One more experience, one more entry in a diary, self-penned")
—The Rakes Progress
("What do you do when your roots have dissolved/And broken
down")
Bob Dylan—*World Gone Wrong*
("Unplugged"; "Ragged & Dirty"; "Blood in My Eyes")
KMFDM—*Angst* ("No justice, no peace")
Pink Floyd—*Paranoid Eyes*
("Button your lip; don't let the shield slip/Take a fresh grip on
your bulletproof mask")
Rush—*The Pass*
("Proud swagger out of the schoolyard, waiting for the world's
applause/Rebel without a conscience, Martyr without a cause")
Steve Perry—*For the Love of Strange Medicine* ("I am lost in a
world of emptiness")

Appendix 12

Media-Mediated Relationships: A Survey

In an effort to find out about your media uses in relationship formation and maintenance, I'd very much appreciate your filling out this survey. Please feel free to add extra comments. Thank you! Linda K. Fuller, Communications Department, Worcester State College, Worcester, MA 01602 USA.

A. *Print Media*
1. Have you ever placed a "personals" ad?
__1. No __2. Yes
    a. if yes, approximately how often:
    _Only once; _2-3 X; _4-24 X; _25-100 X;
    _100+ X
    b. If yes, where (check all appropriate)
    _Newspaper _Magazine _Other (be specific)
    c. Tell about your experience(s) with "personals."

2. Have you ever responded to a "personals" ad?
__1. No __2. Yes (If yes, tell about your experience(s)):

3. Are you, or have you ever been, a member of a reading group put together by an organization or a magazine?
__1. No __2. Yes (If yes, tell about your experience(s)):

B. *Broadcast Media*
1. Are you very familiar with radio call-in shows?
__1. No __2. Yes
    a. If yes, how often do you listen to them?
    _Only once; _Seldom; _Not very often; _Often
    b. If yes, which one(s):
    c. Have you ever called in? _No; _Yes (describe):

2. What are your experiences with, and opinions of, television shows like *Love Connection, The Dating Game, Prime Time Personals, Studs, Infatuation,* etc.?

C. *Movies*

What are your experiences with, and opinions of, movies dealing with mediated relationships, such as *Desperately Seeking Susan, Sea of Love, Paris is Burning, Single White Female, Consenting Adults, Sliver, My Own Private Idaho, Singles, Together Alone, Sleepless in Seattle,* etc.

D. *Communication technologies*

What are your experiences with, and opinions of, the following:
1. 900 telephone numbers
2. Computers
   a. Electronic mail
   b. Videodating
3. Virtual reality
4. Other (be specific)

Some information about you:
Gender: __M __F Sexual orientation:
Age: Race: Occupation:
Income level: __Less than $30,000/yr; __$30,000; __$30,000+
Hometown:

Appendix 13

Survey Comments
on Television Dating Shows
(Selected individual opinions)

1. Funny, entertaining—curious to see the conclusion.
3. Absolutely ridiculous, not only insulting to me but degrading of all human life.
8. They are garbage and offensive to people who actually think.
9. Wasted air time; need more documentaries.
11. Too funny and too predictable.
12. (M22) I was rejected on *The Dating Game* and now I think they're all lame!
13. They are fun to watch but you can't take them seriously.
16. Pointless.
21. Absolutely ludicrous.
26. Opinion: a big, big ZERO! Unstimulating—a waste to watch.
31. I find them very entertaining, especially when they fight.
35. I find them dull and uninteresting.
36. Entertainment only (glad you're not on show and seem as bad as guests).
41. I believe in different strokes for different folks.
42. (F22, Filipino) Fun to watch but don't take them too seriously. I don't think I would ever do it.
45. Good for people who are into that, or need it.
47. They're stupid 'cuz they make or try to make people believe they can just go on these shows and be set up with a "perfect match." People who date from same working areas or occupations tend to have short-term relationships.
51. Fun but tasteless at times.

55. Not a very good way to meet people.
57. I've watched *Love Connection* and *Studs*—only to get a good laugh—I especially like when the couple dislikes each other and look ridiculous on national TV.
58. I find them very funny, esp. if they didn't get along well together.
59. I watch them every once in a while. I personally think they are stupid. I'm not really interested in watching them.
60. I watch *Love Connection* every day at lunch because its very entertaining.
61. Most of these shows are demeaning to women.
64. They are hilarious to watch but all the contestants (except on *Studs)* seem like losers.
65. I very seldom watch these shows. I only watch them when there is nothing else on. I actually find them humorous.
68. Awful.
71. It's fun and light-hearted for entertainment value. It's a bit hyped and if anyone did find "true-love" I'd be surprised.
76. Good for a laugh. I can't believe people are so bored that they watch other people talk about their dates.
77. Personally find them comical.
83. (M20) All these TV shows are made up. The writers make it look more glamorous than it really is.
85. Just watch them on occasion, usually when there is nothing else on. Out of the list *Love Connection* is really the only show that I have watched. The host Chuck Woolery I think is pretty comical in some of the situations he puts himself in.
89. (M25) Mindless TV.
90. (M23) Seem really dumb. I can't see people going on a date with a complete stranger. It appears crazy to me to broadcast my personal life on TV.
91. (F20) Love these shows, just to see how people react to their experiences. I do know someone that went on *Love Connection* and she had fun doing it, but they didn't get along so they gave her a script for both of them (I never knew that).
95. Very interesting to see how people relate with different types of body gestures. Also verbally.

99. I know all of these shows and I love them, they are really funny, but I feel bad if the couple never works out. It's just another form of entertainment.
101. They're entertainment; they're funny; sometimes humiliating to the participants.
104. Amusing in a tabloid sort of way.
105. I have watched but these shows are for our entertainment not the participants' benefits.
107. These shows are boring. I think to myself, "People, get a life."
108. There is a large market for it.
109. They're fun to laugh at, but I feel bad for those that take them seriously.
111. (M19) Watch them if the girls are good looking or the couples fight a lot. They do have some value as they demonstrate what to do or not do in a new relationship.
112. While some of these TV shows are interesting to watch, I would never appear on one because I don't want the whole entire nation in on my personal life. They are interesting because of the different types of personalities you see on the shows, the different reactions, and responses people make.
113. (F26,AmInd) Watched occasionally for entertainment (i.e., to get a good laugh), but I don't think the participants know enough about each other to really be paired up suitably.
115. Personally think they are stupid, but do find myself tuning in from time to time. In other words, they're dumb but entertaining.
118. (M22) Watch them all the time.
122. Like them. They are different from other shows. It shows you how different some people are.
123. They are stupid beyond belief, tacky, and *unreal.* No one is like the people on these shows.
124. No experience. I'm not the type who would be involved with such nonsense.
127. I've watched them before, thought they were funny, but I don't have time to watch them anymore.
128. I think that for the most part they are a good way to meet people. I wouldn't do it.

134. They are very amusing. Especially when the date goes badly.
135. I think they are fun to watch but they're not for me. I would never go on a show like that. It's like a meat market.
136. They are just for fun. I don't think any long-lasting relationship has ever come from one of these shows.
137. I'm not particularly fond of them; however, they do satisfy a preoccuptation of people with other peoples' affairs. I think that these shows make people feel good about themselves or they help people to justify themselves in relationships.
138. I can't understand how people can give advice unless they are in the relationship. I can understand suggestion, but that's all.
139. A sexist view of dating, etc. Should be banned. . . .
143. For the most part those games are funny because some of the people they put on are complete morons.
145. I do not think someone on those shows would be worthwhile because they can't find anyone on their own.
150. I think they are ridiculous but Chuck Woolery is very well dressed.
151. They are, I'm sure, entertaining to many. Variety is great.
153. My opinion is that they only choose the best couples, i.e., argumentative, sappy, etc., for the network because of ratings.
155. Big business, not interesting.
171. (M35, homosexual) They always overplay everything.
174. Waste of brain power—if any is used watching these things.
176. OK to watch. Thought about becoming a guest.
177. I like the *Love Connection.* They pay for your dates and whoever the audience picks you get to go out with free.
178. For the bored and mindless.
179. I don't care for them. I think they are stupid but most of all they don't relate to me.
182. They are funny, and maybe some work for people, but my personal view is that they are a waste of time.
187. (M22) I think that they're senseless and for desperate people.
190. They stink, never watch 'em.
196. They are nuts!
198. (F36) Do not think *Studs* should be viewed by young people.

199. I think they are good for those people who want to be on the show. I like watching them but would never want to be on one.
200. Silly, funny sometimes—I guess they can be helpful to some contestants and people.
202. I find them amusing, don't take them very seriously, much too *superficial!*
205. Good clean fun.
207. Looks like a fun way to meet people if single.
208. They're cute at best—where do they find these people?
210. I hope people are only doing this for entertainment and not hoping to actually find their true loves.
211. Really boring, dull, insulting—similar to sale of cattle.
214. Farce.

Appendix 14

Survey Comments on Relationship Movies
(Selected individual opinions)

1. I loved *Singles* and *Sleepless in Seattle* because the situations were so real to life and they made the plots funny.
3. Movies are an art form not meaning to be belittled by my opinions but experienced and taken for what they are worth.
8. (GWM21) There should be more movies like them that explore interpersonal relationships.
11. Very sex oriented and very shallow.
16. *Private Idaho* was good, the rest sucked.
20. (BF20) I liked *SWF; Singles* was idiotic, chaotic, and worthless to watch. *Sleepless in Seattle* was interesting.
25. (BF23) Hollywood endings are so boring, unrealistic!
26. Have seen three or four—can't compare to TV's soaps.
29. (F36) Enjoyed some of these movies, can't identify with most.
33. (F22, Asian) Watching some of these movies has made me more leery of "personals" ads.
35. The list of movies given here is so long and varied I find it hard to make an overall sweeping judgment of them; i.e., some of these movies I enjoyed, others I didn't.
43. A very rare situation where someone will find a true love, but don't think that its entirely impossible.
44. Like them—very interesting and dramatic.
46. *Sea of Love* was very interesting, relationship between detective and female suspect formed through personal ad—trust lacking to a high degree.
48. Enjoy to see the right thing being done.
51. Unrealistic for me because none of these films represent any black love stories.

53. I prefer these movies over the action movies but my boyfriend calls these female movies.
54. (M22) Many I have seen exploit one sex or the other.
55. Entertaining and quite possibly may even serve as lessons, though I wouldn't use them as a basis for my love life.
56. (F20) I like seeing movies that deal with relationships especially when they are "realistic."
59. I love romantic movies. I would rather watch a romantic movie than one of those dating game shows.
61. Liked *Sleepless in Seattle* because it was refreshing—the relationship was not based on sex but love. Most of the other movies show relationships based on sex then love comes later, maybe.
64. It is really dependent on the characters themselves.
67. Some are better than others; the genre has very good and very bad movies.
68. When the characters are fresh, the concepts can be good for entertainment.
71. I've only seen one of these. I find that they are simply another theatre genre form of escapism.
73. *Sea of Love*-thumbs down; *My Own Private Idaho*-weird; *Sleepless in Seattle*—old-fashioned love story.
74. These movies are fun to watch and are fun to imagine, but in reality I feel that they are highly unlikely to be useful.
77. The films I've seen are good but nothing I really see in my life.
79. *Singles* was a great movie. It poked fun at relationships.
83. (M20) I like movies like this because my girlfriend has a shoulder to cry on.
85. Underlined *Desperately Seeking Susan, Single White Female, Consenting Adults, Singles,* and did enjoy them all. My choice of movie is usually because of the cast.
86. Provides something else than the "crash and burn" movies.
90. These movies are make believe, exaggerated, so don't deal with reality.
91. I love all these shows. I'm into romantic movies; favorite— *Sleepless in Seattle.* Great ending.

92. (M23) I've seen almost all and think that they're needed in today's society. Bring back good old relationships.

95. Good to learn how people interrelate with each other—through good and bad times.

99. (F20) *Sleepless in Seattle* the only one I saw and I loved it. I'm a romantic and love love stories. It's what I live for.

101. The thing about all of these movies that comes to mind is the realism in all of them. They are about issues that we don't often think about.

106. Some of these movies can actually give ideas to their audiences. It makes it kind of scary that there are some people who get ideas from movies.

111. I like the humorous relationship movies . . . that's really the only way to deal w/relat which are tough, that is, open minded and with a sense of humor.

113. Seen *Desperately Seeking Susan, Sea of Love* and thought that this way of meeting another person happens much more often than just simply dealing with each other without another's intervention. Someone else is always bound to butt in and try to help.

115. Haven't seen most, but most movies like these are entertaining if you can identify with the situation or if you can't and wish you could. Again—entertaining.

117. Unrealistic, but entertaining.

122. You need movies like these. People need to know how people really are.

126. The movies are too violent for today's young adults.

129. Some of these movies are good for entertainment but some should only be seen by adults.

134. I'm not really into relationship type films. The only one from here I've seen is *SWF*. I thought it was scary. That's one reason I wouldn't answer an ad.

135. I think that most of these movies were really good. I (loved) *Singles*. It was true to life. It's nice to see true love.

136. They show how, through the use of the media, people can get together for the better or the worst of it.

137. I think that most American-made films are tame in comparison to the cinematic world around us. Films like *My Own*

Private Idaho and *Paris is Burning* help show ignorant people who are truly out in our society. The problem is that they only come out in selected theaters or on video.

139. Only saw *SWF* and found it to be well done and entertaining; wouldn't want to find a roommate!

142. (BF19) Seen the ones circled *(Desperately Seeking Susan, Single White Female, Consenting Adults, Sliver, Singles)*. Enjoyed them all. But they had no influence on me.

143. Only seen three. I don't go for movies about love and care.

150. Only one I've seen is *SWF* and I thought it was predictable and silly.

151. Different talents make the world go round.

152. *Sleepless in Seattle*—cute movie, but not something that is likely to happen in reality.

153. Usually excellent thrillers are made with these but the real world is not like this—very few people realize that the person that places the ads holds the upper hand. They may choose the public place in which they meet, who they meet, and how often.

155. Interesting views but not always worth the time.

156. They are rare cases, Hollywood makes them look like it happens every day.

157. (M20) My girlfriend drags me to them (she pays) and I usually fall asleep.

161. These shows gave me a new sense of direction in response to open mindedness.

162. Interesting, entertaining, though formulated.

165. (Circled: *Sea of Love, Single White Female, Singles.*) They are good movies, only because they don't portray women as helpless beings.

171. (GM35) I believe we are all looking for that special love. So we tend to appreciate them deep down inside.

172. They are stupid but fun to watch. Creativity on one's behalf.

174. I like them much better than the TV dating shows, more substance.

175. Good, feel good movies.

177. (Circled: *Desperately Seeking Susan, Sea of Love, Consenting Adults, Sleepless in Seattle*) I liked them. I liked *Sleepless* the best. I thought that was the most realistic and fun.
181. It's nice to get lost for an hour or so in others' affairs—I do not take them very seriously though; when I walk out I leave them behind. Except for brief conversation.
182. I like these movies as long as they pertain to everyday life.
191. Depends on the director and cast. Some have meaning for me.
193. I've watched most of them, but they are not on the top of my list as far as a good story line and probably not something I'd watch again real soon!
196. (F51) Have seen only two of these. Very confusing and increase level of awareness of how screwed up people can be.
197. (Circled: *Sea of Love, Single White Female, Consenting Adults.*) Very entertaining movies—I thought *Sea of Love* was a real thriller. Relationships? Seem like a fine line between love/hate.
200. Depends on the theme of movie, my interest in it.
210. Purely entertainment.
211. Cute—typical Hollywood films—sex associated with establishing relationships.
212. Only saw *Sleepless in Seattle.* Loved it. I enjoy happy love stories.
213. They're only movies after all is said and done.

Appendix 15

Survey Comments
on 900 Telephone Numbers
(Selected individual opinions)

1. Rip off.
3. Unnecessary, promotes sociopathic behavior.
4. Get rid of them.
11. Waste of time.
12. Exploitation: preying on people's desperation.
13. Gross.
14. People who don't have a life.
15. Ridiculous, no experiences.
16. Never called, but I guess it gets some people off.
20. Never used. I know they charge.
21. Trash/garbage.
24. Crappy.
30. None, except I know that they're expensive.
34. Yuck, I don't approve of even the psychic friends.
36. No good—some people can be addicted.
37. Someone is making a good deal of money.
43. Waste of money.
44. Too expensive.
45. You never talk to a real person.
46. I have a block on my phone.
49. Sleazy.
50. Silly.
53. I feel these are harmless but should be kept only for adults.
55. Tacky.
57. If the lines are making money—good for them/the people that call are morons. (I have enough to worry about.)

64. They shouldn't be advertised on TV—but the money they rake in is phenomenal. My friend called the "Singles Line" and ran up a $500+ phone bill on my friend's phone. She met a 25-year-old blind white male and went to meet him at his house the next night in a town about 50 miles from here. We all begged her not to go. NOT SAFE!
76. No experience with them, but if adults want to use them, it's their own business.
78. (BM20) Never called, don't plan to.
80. Aimed at ripping off young kids.
86. Useless.
89. Hate them.
102. (M28) Never called but sex, money scams come to mind.
105. They roll big money and offer an outlet.
107. I have never used. They must serve a purpose.
108. Not socially acceptable according to my values.
109. It's new and it is a good money maker. We shall see what the outcome of 900 #s will bring.
110. No experience, not for me to judge.
112. Waste of money, quick fix need fulfillment.
113. Never called, think the ads for them are quite vulgar
115. Someone's making tons of of money—wish it were me. I think they are not really a good thing.
122. Never used them—I don't care for them—people can do without.
123. Con you out of money, for nothing. By the time you find out how much the call costs, you are already charged for it.
126. They just want to get your money.
127. Waste of time and money.
129. Not for very intelligent.
130. None, but commercials are entertaining.
135. They are *stupid* and take your money.
136. Never had an experience with. Great money making concept.
138. Not needed.
142. It is ridiculous and feeds the minds of sick people. However, it's a clever way to make money.
144. (M20) I like the dirty ones.
150. Expensive, insane, good business to get into.

151. (F41) People want to waste their money, fine—but have a check system so kids aren't using this.
155. Crap.
157. Fraud.
162. Get those ads *off* my TV.
163. Costly, only use with discrimination.
165. Don't find that I ever need to use these.
169. Safest sex you can have: unnecessary and a total rip off.
172. (BGM34) Promote, perpetuate perverts behavior.
183. (F25) Amusing but only called once.
190. Disapprove of preying on the weak.
196. Rip-off. Geared toward people who are lonely and can ill afford to use them.
197. (F25) No experience. Thank God.
203. They may be OK for some people who want to connect with this.
204. Bad idea (objectifies sex).
206. Stupid—used by gullible or uneducated people.
208. (M44) Trash—should be illegal or better controlled.
211. Never called. Waste of telephone line.

Appendix 16

Survey Comments on Electronic Mail
(Selected individual opinions)

1. Think it's a good idea, but tends to be a bit impersonal.
3. Pretty good.
4. Very useful.
9. Excellent communication pathway.
11. Never used it.
12. Sounds helpful and informative.
20. Interesting form of communication.
21. Can save money by using school's system.
23. Very expensive.
29. Am currentiy using/regularly.
32. Limited experience (just started). OK once I know how to use.
33. Very easy to use.
34. Fast way to communicate.
36. New to me but very interesting.
38. Experience minimal; I enjoy sending and receiving, especially quick responses.
39. Extensive knowledge. I am amazed at its growth rate.
41. Not much experience, but it's cool.
43. Just learning it; seems fun but a lot to remember.
44. A great way to contact others.
47. You can talk to people without having a visual idea of the person.
49. (M20, Indian) This is great. I had a girlfriend in Australia for a whole summer.
50. Annoying.
64. Fascinating because you can "write" to people all over the world.

66. Creative way of carrying news.
70. Too confusing to operate.
79. New way to communicate.
80. Wish I knew more about it.
97. Love it, great way to leave notes.
98. Use it often, very useful, saves time and money.
100. Use every day/I think that it will be the "thing" for communication in the future.
104. Inefficient, not useful.
105. Very useful. You *have* to know how to use in today's world.
107. Hate it and love it.
109. It's the future. It's a whole new way of life. So far it's been positive in most areas.
110. Used in class. Good and effective idea.
113. Amazing how easy you can talk to someone in another country.
121. Use daily at work—simplifies communication.
133. Now, this I've done and I think its great. I had a girlfriend in Australia. By doing this you find out about the person and don't care about their looks.
136. Excellent for handicapped or hearing impaired.
137. Good technology of the future.
147. I like and use E-mail to get information.
160. Good idea for communication over distance.
162. Fun to keep in contact with (or annoy) your friends.
163. Too much junk mail sent—probably good for business.
169. Good way to communicate quickly.
170. Handy.
171. Cheaper than 900#s.
172. Waste of money, electric, paper (trees).
174. Not for relationships.
175. Used it, liked it.
176. Need to be more acquainted.
177. Great idea, easy, fast, and very useful.
193. Use this all the time for business applications.
196. Gadget/status symbol.
198. Do not like for dating purposes.

199. OK if you're in a relationship already. I wouldn't want to meet someone this way.
202. Can be worthwhile.
208. Great stuff—use for business only.
211. Interesting—like it much—new.

Appendix 17

Survey Comments on Videodating
(Selected individual opinions)

3. Sociopaths easy escape from dealing with reality.
4. Stupid.
12. To each his/her own.
13. Desperate.
14. Whatever floats your boat.
15. Ridiculous.
21. Trash.
24. I'm poor, but good idea.
25. Not interested.
34. I don't know; I guess it's okay if it works, why not?
37. No experience/never used—I guess it works for some.
41. NUTS.
44. Not a bad way to meet people.
49. Never done it, don't know too much. Pretty weird, huh?
57. Why don't we just open shopping malls for people to pose in and we can just choose who we want?
64. Pul-lease.
66. Doesn't necessarily work, boring, and ineffective.
68. Waste of money.
78. Never used it; sounds interesting though; unfamiliar.
79. Waste of time.
84. Helpful.
86. Safer than the bars?
94. Waste of money. Go out and get a date yourself without paying someone to do it.
95. Always was curious, but would never do it.
96. Fine.

106. No good has ever come of it—everyone has something to hide. The self-absorption and protection people go through are amazing.
108. Promoting how we look instead of what's inside.
109. (M24 Hisp) It's not such a bad way to meet people.
110. No experience, not for me to judge.
113. Never done this, but I suppose it's a pretty good way for some (honest people) to meet.
129. I think these are pretty good for people who are single.
135. Dumb.
138. It depends on the person using it.
139. None—guess it's a choice and time efficient.

Appendix 18

Survey Comments on Virtual Reality
(Selected individual opinions)

3. Scary.
8. It's cool, but no experience with it.
11. Wild but tough on the eyes.
15. What do you mean?
25. N/A yet!
34. It's cool; I think that's a *true* step into the future!
37. Don't know much about.
49. Toooooo cooooool!
50. Overrated
54. Fascinating subject—would be *interested* in trying it.
58. I saw *The Lawnmower Man.*
62. Never used it.
66. The right way to go.
77. (M22) Try to keep up to date, but never used it, just seen shows.
79. Possibly the next "craze" in entertainment.
80. (M22) Went to see the virtual reality show in Boston. It was $25 per person and you had to wait in line for hours—virtual ripoff.
83. Seen a lot of programs about it. I think it looks like fun.
86. The video game of the future.
108. Saw in Boston this summer—awesome *escape* from *reality.*
109. Love it.
113. No one will ever get me to warp my mind in this fashion. Too much loss of control over the situation.
126. This is great. Can be educational and also entertaining at the same time.

132. Limited experience, but I think its very useful and interesting.
139. Looks like it could be useful in educational areas.
147. I love V.R. and wish it was more widespread.
149. Yes!
154. Queer.
155. O.K.
162. Neato.
175. Video game.
177. Great idea but if you live in virtual reality, where is reality?
178. Interested in continued developments/technology involved.
196. Sometimes too "real" is too "scary."
202. Sounds like lots of potential.
209. Would like to experience.
211. Seems pretty neat.

References

Adelman, Mara B. and Aaron C. Ahuvia, "Mediated Channels for Mate Seeking: A Solution to Involuntary Singlehood?" *Critical Studies in Mass Communication,* Volume 8, No. 3 (September, 1991): 273-289.

Adler, Jerry, "Sex in the Snoring '90s: A New Survey of American Men Shocks the Nation with What It Didn't Find." *Newsweek* (April 26, 1993): 55-57.

Alexander, Alison, Rodney Andrew Carveth, George Bohrer, and M. Sallyane Ryan, "College Student Soap Opera Viewing," in Suzanne Frentz (ed.), *Staying Tuned: Contemporary Soap Opera Criticism.* Bowling Green, OH 1992: Popular Press, 19-32.

Alexander, Kelly King, "Looking for Love in All the Right Places: Sports and Recreation Singles Connection." *Baton Rouge Business Report* (December 17, 1991): 19+.

Alexander, Ron, "A Face on TV Across a Lonely Room." *The New York Times* (August 25, 1991): 50.

Allen, Robert C., "The Guiding Light: Soap Opera as Economic Product and Cultural Document." In Horace Newcomb, *Television: The Critical View,* 4th ed. (New York: Oxford University Press, 1987): 141-163.

Ames, Katrine, "Domesticated Bliss: New Laws are Making It Official for Gay or Live-in Straight Couples." *Newsweek* (March 23, 1992): 62-63.

Andersen, Kurt, "Big Mouths: Populist and Popular, Radio's Right-Wing King and Gross-Out Wild Man Have New Mega-Best Sellers." *Time* (November 1, 1993): 60-66.

Angier, Natalie, "Bias Against Gay People: Hatred of a Special Kind." *The New York Times* (December 26, 1993): E4.

Armstrong, Cameron B. and Alan B. Rubin, "Talk Radio as Interpersonal Communication." *Journal of Communication,* Volume 39, No. 2 (Spring, 1989): 84+ .

Astor, David, "UM offering audiotex services for singles. How is 'Personally Speaking'—which combines free print ads with a paid 900-number system—doing? Two newspapers respond." *Editor Publisher,* Volume 124, No.16 (April 20, 1991): 46-49.

Attig, R. Brian, "The Gay Voice in Popular Music: A Social Value Model Analysis of 'Don't Leave Me This Way.' " In Michelle A. Wolf and Alfred P. Kielwasser, *Gay People, Sex, and the Media.* (Binghamton, NY: Harrington Park Press, 1991): 185-202.

Auletta, Ken, "The Electronic Parent," *The New Yorker* (November 8, 1993): 68-75.

Austin, Bruce, "Loneliness and Use of Six Mass Media Among College Students." *Psychological Reports,* 56 (1985): 323-327.

Auter, P. J., "TV That Talks Back: An Experimental Validation of a Para-Social Interaction Scale." *Journal of Broadcasting & Electronic Media,* Volume 36 (1992): 173-181.

Avery, Robert K. and Donald G. Ellis, "Talk Radio as an Interpersonal Phenomenon." In Gary Gumpert and Ray Cathcart (eds.), *Inter/Media* (New York: Oxford University Press, 1979): 108-115.

Avery, Robert K. and Thomas A. McCain, "Interpersonal and Mediated Encounters: A Reorientation to the Mass Communication Process." In Gary Gumpert and Robert Cathcart (eds.), *Inter-media: Interpersonal Communication in a Media World,* 3rd ed. (New York: Oxford University Press, 1986): 121-131.

Avicolli, T., "Images of Gays in Rock Music." In K. Jay and A. Young (eds.), *Lavender Culture.* (New York: Jove, 1979): 182-194.

Bad Object Choices (ed.) *How Do I Look: Queer Film and Video.* Seattle, WA: Bay Press, 1991.

Banerjee, Neela, "Still, it can't get very romantic if you have to go back to work." *The Wall Street Journal* (January 21, 1993): B1.

Barnouw, Erik. *A Tower in Babel: A History of Broadcasting in the United States to 1933.* New York: Oxford University Press, 1966.

Beck, Melinda, "Never Too Old to Go On Line: Computers Go Gray." *Newsweek* (June 15, 1992): 64.

"Becoming a Dream Girl: Training Manual for Operators of 970-LIVE, a Phone-Sex Service." *Harper's Magazine* (December, 1990): 26+.

Bell, Robert A. and Michael E. Roloff, "Making a Love Connection: Loneliness and Communication Competence in the Dating Marketplace." *Communication Quarterly,* Volume 39, No. 1 (Winter, 1991): 58-75.

Beniger, J. *The Control Revolution: Technological and Economic Origins of the Information Society.* Cambridge, MA: Harvard University Press, 1986.

Berchers, Hans. *Never-Ending Stories: American Soap Operas and The Cultural Production of Meaning.* Trier: WVT Verlag, 1992.

Berck, Judith, "Electronic Bulletin Boards: It's No Longer Just Techno-Hobbyists Who Meet by Modem." *The New York Times* (July 19, 1992): F12.

Berkman, Meredith, "Saturday Night Fever! How Date Movies Are Heating Up at the Box Office." *Entertainment Weekly* (May 7, 1993): 18-23.

Bernikow, Louise. *Alone in America: The Search for Companionship.* New York: Harper and Row, 1986.

Bernstein, S., "What Price True Happiness? Exactly $100,000 for the Execumatch Brand." *Canadian Business,* Volume 57 (September, 1984): 164-167.

Bloch, R. Howard. *Medieval Misogyny and the Invention of Western Romantic Love.* New Haven, CT: Yale University Press, 1991.

Block, Susan. *Advertising for Love: How to Play the Personals.* New York: Quill, 1984.

Bolig, Rosemary, Peter J. Stein, and Patrick C. McKenry, "The Self-Advertisement Approach to Dating: Male-Female Differences." *Family Relations* 33 (1984): 587-592.

Bouhoutos, J. C., J. D. Goodchilds, and L. Huddy, "Media Psychology: An Empirical Study of Radio Call-In Psychology Programs." *Professional Psychology: Research and Practice* 17: 408-414.

Brady, Lois Smith, "Vows: Susan Layton and William Palmer." *The New York Times* (November 28, 1992): V14.

Branwyn, Gareth, "Compu-Sex: Erotica for Cybernauts," *South Atlantic Quarterly,* Volume 92, No. 4 (Fall, 1993): 779-791.

Breen, Myles and Farrel Corcoran, "Myth in the Television Discourse." *Communication Monographs,* Volume 49 (June, 1982): 127-136.

Bright, Susie. *Susie Bright's Sexual Reality: A Virtual Sex World Reader.* Pittsburgh, PA: Cleis Press, Inc., 1992a.

Bright, Susie, "Sex in the Computer Age." *Elle* (February, 1992b): 56+.

Brody, E.W. *Communication Tomorrow: New Audiences, New Technologies, New Media.* New York: Praeger, 1990.

Brooks, Caryn, "Hand Jive." *Isthmus* (September 4, 1992): p. 169.

Brown, Mary Ellen. *Soap Opera and Women's Discourse: The Pleasure of Resistance.* Newbury Park, CA: Sage Publications, Inc., 1992.

Browne, David, "The Arts Hurtle (Limp?) Toward the Millennium." *The New York Times* (January 2, 1994): H30.

Buerkel-Rothfuss, Nancy L. and Sandra Mayes, "Soap Opera Viewing and the Cultivation Effect." *Journal of Communication,* Volume 31, No. 3 (Summer, 1981): 108-115.

Burros, Marian, "Eligible Bachelors and They Can Cook." *The New York Times* (January 3, 1990): B1.

Buss, A. H., "A Conception of Shyness." In J. A. Daly and J. C. McCroskey (eds.), *Avoiding Communication.* Beverly Hills, CA: Sage Publications, 1984.

Butterfield, F., "A Dating Service, but Not for Just Anyone." *The New York Times* (August 20, 1984): 8.

Buxton, Rodney A., "Dr. Ruth Westheimer: Upsetting the Normalcy of the Late-Night Talk Show." In Michelle A. Wolf and Alfred P. Kielwasser, *Gay People, Sex, and the Media.* (Binghamton, NY: Harrington Park Press, 1991): 139-153.

Califia, Pat, "Is their number up? The Supreme Court pulls the plug on phone-sex—line operators." *The Advocate,* No. 598 (March 10, 1992): 61.

Cambray, C. K. *Personal.* New York: Pocket Books, 1990.

Cameron, C., S. Oskamp, and W. Sparks, "Courtship in Style: Newspaper Ads." *Family Coordinator* 26 (1977): 27-30.

Cantor, Muriel G. and Suzanne Pingree. *The Soap Opera.* Beverly Hills, CA: Sage Publications, 1983.

Carter, Alan, " 'Swans Crossing': Young Love in the Afternoon." *Entertainment Weekly* (July 10, 1992): 46.

Carveth, Rod, "College Student Soap Opera Viewing and Perceptions of Love and Romance." *The Carolinas Speech Communication Annual*, Volume IX (1993): 21-34.

Carveth, Rodney and Alison Alexander, "Soap Opera Viewing Motivations and the Cultivation Process." *Journal of Broadcasting & Electronic Media*, Volume 29, No. 3 (Summer, 1985): 259-273.

Case, Tony, "Getting personal: *The Village Voice* is a good example of how personal ads have remained a moneymaker for newspapers despite the soft economy." *Editor & Publisher*, Volume 125, No. 5 (February 1, 1992): 16+.

Cate, R. M. and S. A. Lloyd, "Courtship." In Steve W. Duck (ed.), *Handbook of Personal Relationships*. New York: John Wiley (1988): 409-427.

Cathcart, Robert, "Our Soap Opera Friends." In Gary Gumpert and Robert Cathcart (eds), *Inter-Media* (New York: Oxford University Press, 1986): 207-219.

Chesebro, James W. and Donald G. Bonsall. *Computer-Mediated Communication: Human Relationships in a Computerized World*. Tuscaloosa, AL: The University of Alabama Press, 1989.

Clark, Charles S., "The Obscenity Debate." *CQ Researcher*, Volume 1, No. 31 (December 10, 1991): 969-992.

Cobb, Nathan, "Boy meets girl (whose weight is proportionate to height)." *Boston Globe Magazine* (November 18, 1990): 1+.

Colford, Paul D. *The Rush Limbaugh Story: Talent on Loan From God: An Unauthorized Biography*. New York: St. Martin's Press, 1993.

Comstock, George, "Today's Audiences, Tomorrow's Media." In Stuart Oskamp (ed.), *Television as a Social Issue* (Newbury Park, CA: Sage Publications, 1988): 324-345.

Coy, Peter and Michele Galen, "Let's not let phone pollution hang up free speech." *Business Week*, No. 3227 (August 19, 1991): 32.

Crabtree, Penni, "Matchmaker, Matchmaker Find Me a SWF Non-Smoker." *San Diego Business Journal* (November 9, 1992): 1-2.

Crichton, Sarah, "Sexual Correctness: Has it Gone too Far?" *Newsweek* (October 25, 1993): 52-56.

Crothers, Charles, "Community Radio: General and Focused Current Affairs Talk-Back." *The Australian and New Zealand Journal of Sociology,* Volume 11, No. 2 (ND): 54-59.

Cullison, A. E., "Searching for a Date in Japan." *Journal of Commerce and Commercial* (May 6, 1992): 8A.

Cvetkovich, Ann, "Dykes and Divas: Lesbianism and Fashion Photography." Paper presented at the Popular Culture Association, New Orleans, LA: 1993.

Darden, Donna K. and Patricia R. Koski, "Using the Personals Ads: A Deviant Activity?" *Deviant Behavior,* Volume 9, No. 4 (1988): 383-400.

Davidson, Alan G., "Looking for Love in the Age of AIDS: The Language of Gay Personals." *Journal of Sex Research,* Volume 28, No. 1 (February, 1991): 127-137.

Davidson, Keay, "Computer bulletin boards show upsurge in grass roots appeal." *Union-News* (April 23, 1993): 31.

Davis, Mark H. and Linda A. Kraus, "Social Contact, Loneliness, and Mass Media Use: A Test of Two Hypotheses." *Journal of Applied Social Psychology,* Volume 19, No. 12-13 (September, 1989): 1100-1124.

Deaux, Kay and Randel Hanna, "Courtship in the Personals Column: The Influence of Gender and Sexual Orientation." *Sex Roles* 11, Nos. 5/6 (1984): 363-375.

DeCecco, John P. (ed.) *Gay Relationships.* Binghamton, NY: Harrington Park Press, 1987.

della Cava, Marco R., "A night out on the town with Anka." *USA Today* (April 23, 1993): 1D.

D'Emilio, John, "The Irresistible Force of Gay Power." *Out* (April/May, 1993): 68-69.

DeMont, John, "Love and Fear in the Age of AIDS." *Maclean's,* Volume 105 (February 22, 1993): 40.

Denzin, Norman K. *The Cinematic Society.* Newbury Park, CA: Sage Publications, 1995.

Dervin, Brenda, "Communication Gaps and Inequities: Moving Toward a Reconceptualization." In Brenda Dervin and Melvin J. Voight (eds.), *Progress in Communication Sciences,* Vol. 2. (Norwood, NJ: Ablex, 1980): 73-112.

"Desperately seeking. . . ." *Entertainment Weekly* (March 26, 1993): 9.

DeWitt, Paula Mergenhagen, "All the Lonely People." *American Demographics,* Volume 14, No. 4 (April, 1992): 44-48.

Diamond, Todd, "Fairness Doctrine Battle Brews Over Regulating Airwaves." *Christian Science Monitor* (October 12, 1993).

Dixon, Wheeler Winston. *It Looks At You: The Returned Gaze of Cinema.* Albany, NY: State University of New York Press, 1995.

Dobnik, Verena, "Gay Students Get Own School." *Union-News* (December 23, 1991): 16+.

Doherty, Shawn, "How to find a mate in the wide open spaces: Rural Singles of America newsletter." *Newsweek* (December 2, 1985): 76.

Dolan, Carrie, "It's OK to be single, but marriage still is a touted possibility; many outfits are on the prowl for ways to serve market, whether it's happy or not." *The Wall Street Journal* (February 3, 1993): A1.

Dorsie, Mary Ann, "Research Targets Listeners, Not Just Listening." *Radio World,* Volume 17, No. 3 (February 10, 1993): 1+.

Doty, Alexander. *Making Things Perfectly Queer.* Minneapolis, MN: University of Minnesota Press, 1993.

Dutton, W. H., E. M. Rogers, and S. Jun, "Diffusion and Social Impacts of Personal Computers." *Communication Research,* Volume 14 (1987): 219-250.

Dyer, Richard, "Entertainment and Utopia." In Rick Altman (ed.), *Genre: The Musical: A Reader.* London: Routledge & Kegan Paul, 1981.

Dyer, Richard. *Gays and Film.* New York: Zoetrope, 1984.

Dyer, Richard. *Now You See It: Studies on Lesbian and Gay Film.* London: Routledge, 1990.

Eastman, Susan Tyler, Sydney W. Head, and Lewis Klein. *Broadcast/Cable Programming: Strategies and Practice*, 3rd Edition. Belmont, CA: Wadsworth Publishing Company, 1989.

Egan, Anne W., "The Myth and Reality of Meditation: Some Personal Reflections." Talk presented at the AF&PA Meeting, Sea Island, GA: 1993.

Ehrenreich, Barbara, "Burt, Loni and Our Way of Life." *Time* (September 20, 1993): 92.

"Electronic Orgasms: Love Games of the 90's You Should Know About," *Donahue* (May 25, 1993).

Elmer-DeWitt, Philip, "Orgies On-Line." *Time* (May 31, 1993): 61.

Emerson, Bo, "Romance, Friendship Blossoms by Computer." *Union-News* (November 5, 1992): L1.

Escoffier, Jeffrey, "Out of the Closet and Into History." *The New York Times Book Review* (June 28, 1992): 1+.

Faderman, Lillian. *Odd Girls and Twilight Lovers: A History of Lesbian Life in Twentieth-Century America.* New York: Columbia University Press, 1992.

Faludi, Susan, "The Man Shortage Myth." *Cosmopolitan* (July, 1992): 66+.

Fanning, Deirdre, "With This Headhunter, $10k Defines a Spouse." *The New York Times* (November 18, 1990): F27.

Farber, Jim, "We're Not Gonna Take It: Gay and Lesbian Activists Battle the Rise of Homophobia in Pop Music." *Rolling Stone* (May 13, 1993): 21.

Feirstein, Bruce, "I'm No Prude, But. . . ." *TV Guide* (January 1, 1994): 22-26.

Fejes, Fred and Kevin Petrich, "Invisibility, Homophobia, and Heterosexiam: Lesbians and Gays and the Media." *Critical Studies in Mass Communication,* 10 (1993): 396-422.

Fine, Marlene C., "Soap Opera Conversations: The Talk That Binds." *Journal of Communication,* Volume 31, No. 3 (Spring, 1981): 99-107.

Firestone, David, "The Last Romantics." *New York Times Magazine* (February 13, 1994): 44-47.

Fisher, Milton. *Haven't You Been Single Long Enough?* Green Farms, CT: Wildcat Publishing Co., 1992.

Fitzgerald, Mark and Debra Gersh, "Misuse of Classifieds." *Editor & Publisher* (April 11, 1987): 11+.

Flanders, Laura, "Ask, We'll Tell." *ImMEDIAte Impact,* Volume 1, No. 6 (Summer, 1993): 1+.

Foa, E. B. and U. G. Foa, "Resource Theory: Interpersonal Behavior as Exchange." In K. J. Gergen, M. S. Greenberg, and R. S. Willis (eds.) *Social Exchange: Advances in Theory and Research,* (New York: Plenum Press, 1980): 1-27.

Fogel, Alan. *Developing Through Relationships: Origins of Communication, Self, and Culture.* New Haven, CT: Yale University Press, 1993.

Foote, Jennifer, "From Russia—with Love? Mail-Order Brides for Lonely British Bachelors." *Newsweek,* Volume 117, No. 21 (May 27, 1990): 38.

Forester, Tom (ed.) *Computers in the Human Context.* Cambridge, MA: MIT Press, 1989.

Frentz, Suzanne (ed.) *Staying Tuned: Contemporary Soap Opera Criticism.* Bowling Green, OH: Bowling Green State University Popular Press, 1992.

Fretts, Bruce, "Do You Like to Watch?" *Entertainment Weekly* (October 8, 1993): 15-18.

Fretts, Bruce, "Hit Singles." *Entertainment Weekly* (January 27, 1995): 20.

Friendly, Fred W. *The Good Guys, The Bad Guys and the First Amendment: Free Speech vs. Fairness in Broadcasting.* New York: Vintage Books, 1975.

Fuller, Linda K., "International Propaganda via Shortwave: The Dutch Example from an American Perspective." *World Communication* ,Volume 15 (Fall, 1986a): 143-154.

Fuller, Linda K., "Television Games: Applications and Anecdotes." Paper presented to the 17th Annual International Simulation and Gaming Association, Toulon, France: 1986b.

Fuller, Linda K., "A Profile of Radio Listenership by Elderly, Educated Women." Paper presented to the Popular Culture Association, New Orleans, LA: 1988.

Fuller, Linda K., "Remembering Radio: Work in Progress on Oral History." Paper presented to the International Association for Mass Communication Research, Guaruja, Brazil: 1992a.

Fuller, Linda K., "Beyond Handbills, Hate Mail, and Harassment: 'Getting Gays' Through the Classifieds." Paper presented at the 22nd Annual Convention of the Popular Culture Association, Louisville, KY, 1992b.

Fuller, Linda K., "Desperately Seeking Meaning: 'Personals' in American Popular Film." In Paul Loukides and Linda K. Fuller (eds.), *Beyond the Stars III: The Material World in American*

Popular Film. (Bowling Green, OH: Popular Press, 1993a): 89-96.

Fuller, Linda K., "If Interactive Video is the Goal, What is the Best Educational Means to Achieve It?" *Telematics and Informatics,* Volume 10, No. 4 (1993b): 379-389.

Fuller, Linda K. *Community Television in the United States: A Sourcebook on Public, Educational, and Governmental Access.* Westport, CT: Greenwood Publishing, 1994.

Fuller, Linda K., "Intracinematology: A Sub-Contextual Model for Film Study." Working paper.

Fuller, Linda K., "Movie Mediations of AIDS." In Linda K. Fuller (ed.), *Media-Mediated AIDS* (Amherst, MA: HRD Press), forthcoming.

Fuller, Linda K. and Lilless McPherson Shilling (eds.). *Communicating About Communicable Diseases.* Amherst, MA: HRD Press, 1995.

Fuller, Linda K. "Women Producers of AIDS Films and Videos," in Nancy Roth and Linda K. Fuller (eds.) *Women's Ways of Acknowledging AIDS.* Binghamton, NY: The Haworth Press, forthcoming.

Furlong, Mary S., "An Electronic Community for Older Adults: The SeniorNet Network." *Journal of Communication,* Volume 39, No. 3 (Summer, 1989): 145-153.

Fury, Kathleen, "Dream Lovers." *Working Woman* (May, 1987): 192.

Gailey, Christine War, "Mediated Messages: Gender, Class and Cosmos in Home Video Games." *Journal of Popular Culture,* Volume 27, No. 1 (Summer, 1993): 81-97.

Gallimore, Timothy A. and Linda K. Fuller. *Telecommunications: Implicatins for Markets, Multiculturalism, and Media.* World Heritage Press, forthcoming.

Gandy, Oscar H., Jr. *The Panoptic Sort: A Political Economy of Personal Information.* Boulder, CO: Westview Press, 1993.

Ganley, Gladys D. *The Exploding Political Power of Personal Media.* Norwood, NJ: Ablex Publishing Corporation, 1992.

Gans, Herbert J., "The Famine in American Mass-Communication Research: Comments on Hirsch, Tuchman, and Gecas." *American Journal of Sociology,* Volume 77, No. 4 (January, 1972): 697-705.

Garcia, Guy, "Rock Finds Religion. Again." *The New York Times* (January 2, 1994): H1+.

Garcia, Guy, "O=Coy Banter, O=Nude Blondes." *The New York Times* (October 23, 1994), H17+.

Garrison, Deborah, "Phoning It In." *The New Yorker* (March 9, 1992): 93-96.

Gattiker, Urs. E. (ed.) *Technology-Mediated Communication.* Berlin: Walter de Gruyter, 1992.

Gelman, David, "Isn't It Romantic?" *Newsweek* (January 18, 1993): 59-61.

Geraghty, Christine. *Women and Soap Opera: A Study of Prime Time Soaps.* Cambridge, MA: Polity Press, 1991.

Gerbner, George, "Towards 'cultural indicators': The analysis of mass mediated message systems." *AV Communication Review* 17 (1969): 137-148.

Gerbner, George. "Violence in Television Drama: Trends and Symbolic Functions." In G. A. Comstock and E. A. Rubinstein (eds.), *Television and Social Behavior.* Washington, DC: Government Printing Office, Volume 1 (1972): 28-187.

Gerbner, George, Larry Gross, Michael Morgan, and Nancy Signorelli, "The 'Mainstreaming' of America: Violence Profile No. 11." *Journal of Communication,* 30 (1980): 10-29.

Gerbner, George, Larry Gross, Michael Morgan, and Nancy Signorelli, "Health and Medicine on Television." *New England Journal of Medicine* (October 8, 1981): 901-904.

Gerbner, George, Larry Gross, Michael Morgan, and Nancy Signorelli, "Living with Television: The Dynamics of the Cultivation Process." In Jennings Bryant and Dolf Zillman (eds.), *Perspectives on Media Effects* (Hillsdale, NJ: Erlbaum, 1986): 17-40.

Giddens, Anthony. *The Transformation of Intimacy: Sexuality, Love and Eroticism in Modern Societies.* Stanford, CA: Stanford University Press, 1992.

Gleiberman, Owen, "Exposing Himself [Howard Stern]." *Entertainment Weekly* (October 22, 1993): 66-67.

Goffman, Erving. *The Presentation of Self in Everyday Life.* New York: Doubleday Anchor, 1959.

Goldberg, Gary David and Jayne Anne Phillips, "The Intimacy of Mass Culture." *New Perspectives Quarterly,* Volume 7, No. 1 (Winter, 1990): 58-59.

Golding, Peter and Graham Murdock, "Unequal Information: Access and Exclusion in the New Communications Market Place." In Marjorie Ferguson (ed.), *New Communication Technologies and the Public Interest.* (Newbury Park, CA: Sage, 1986): 71-83.

Goldman, Robert. *Reading Ads Socially.* London: Routledge, 1992.

Goldstein, Harry, "The Dial-ectic of Desire." *Utne Reader,* No. 44 (March-April, 1991): 32-34.

Gonzales, Marti Hope and Sarah A. Meyers, "Your Mother Would Like Me: Self-Presentation in the Personals Ads of Heterosexual and Homosexual Men and Women." *Personality and Social Psychology Bulletin,* Volume 19, No. 2 (1993): 131-142.

Goodman, Walter, "Stern's Complaint." *The New York Times Book Review* (November 14, 1993): 7.

Gow, Joe, "Music Video as Persuasive Form: The Case of the Pseudo-Reflexive Strategy." *Communication Quarterly,* Volume 41, No. 3 (Summer, 1993): 318-327.

Graebner, Lynn, "Younger Men, Older Women." *The Business Journal Serving Greater Sacramento* (November 4, 1991): 1-2.

Gransden, Greg, "From Russia, with love; unhappy with prospects at home, Soviet women look West for husbands." *Los Angeles Times* (August 15, 1991): E1.

Greenberg, Bradley S., Robert Abelman, and Kimberly Neuendorf, "Sex on the Soap Operas: Afternoon Delight." *Journal of Communication,* Volume 31, No. 3 (Summer, 1981): 83-89.

Greenberg, Bradley and D. D'Alessio, "Quantity and Quality of Sex in the Soaps." *Journal of Broadcasting & Electronic Media,* Volume 29 (1985): 309-321.

Greenblatt, Stephen. "Kindly Visions." *The New Yorker* (October 11, 1993): 112-120.

Greenburg, Dan, "Looking for Like." *New York,* Volume 24, No. 39 (October 7, 1991): 72-77.

Grillo, R., "Gay Moments in Straight Music." *Gay Books Bulletin,* Volume 8 (1982): 22-26.

Grodin, Debra, "The Interpreting Audience: The Therapeutics of Self-Help Book Reading." *Critical Studies in Mass Communication,* 8 (1991): 404-420.

Gross, Jane, "Sex Educators for Young See New Virtue in Chastity." *The New York Times* (January 16, 1994): 1+.

Gross, Larry, "Out of the Mainstream: Sexual Minorities and the Mass Media." In Michelle A. Wolf and Alfred P. Kielwasser. *Gay People, Sex, and the Media.* (Binghamton, NY: Harrington Park Press, 1991): 19-46.

Gross, Larry, "The Contested Closet: The Ethics and Politics of Outing." *Critical Studies in Mass Communication,* Volume 8, No. 3 (September, 1991): 352-388.

Haag, Laurie L., "Oprah Winfrey: The Construction of Intimacy in the Talk Show Setting." *Journal of Popular Culture,* Volume 26, No. 4 (Spring, 1993): 115-121.

Hadleigh, B. *The Vinyl Closet: Gays in the Music World.* San Diego, CA: Los Hombres Press, 1991.

Hall, Carla, "Lonely hearts & the specter of AIDS: In L. A., a dating service for HIV-positive adults." *The Washington Post* (December 21, 1991): F1.

Halverson, Kim, "New Twist on Matchmaking: Rabbi Starts Service to Introduce Single Jews." *Union-News* (February 22, 1992): 18.

Harkison, Judy, " 'A Chorus of Groans,' notes Sherlock Holmes." *Smithsonian* (September, 1987).

Harrison, Albert A. and Laila Saeed, "Let's Make a Deal: An Analysis of Revelations and Stipulations in Lonely Hearts Advertisements." *Journal of Personality and Social Psychology,* 35 (1977): 257-264.

Hauser, Susan G., "No Bedfellows." *The New York Times Magazine* (May 31, 1992): 20+.

Hedges, Chris, "Looking for Love (Shh!) in Ads." *The New York Times* (May 9, 1993): V3.

Hendrick, Susan S. and Clyde Hendrick. *Romantic Love.* Newbury Park, CA: Sage Publications, Inc., 1992.

Hendrix, Harville. *Keeping the Love You Find: A Guide for Singles.* New York: Pocket Books, 1992.

Henneberger, Melinda, "Well, the Ukraine Girls Really Knock Them Out." *The New York Times,* Volume 142 (Nov 15, 1992): E6.

Henneberger, Melinda with Michael Marriott, "For Some, Youthful Courting has Become a Game of Abuse." *The New York Times* (July 11, 1993): 1+.

Herek, Gregory M. and Kevin T. Berrill (eds.) *Hate Crimes: Confronting Violence Against Lesbians and Gay Men.* Newbury Park, CA: Sage Publishers, 1992.

Hift, Fred, "Talk Shows Take Over." *Christian Science Monitor* (February 16, 1993): 13.

"High-Tech Sex," *CQ Researcher.* Volume 1, No. 31 (December 20, 1991): 983-985.

Himmelstein, Hal. *Television Myth and the American Mind.* New York: Praeger, 1984.

Hirschman, Elizabeth C., "People as Products: Analysis of a Complex Marketing Exchange." *Journal of Marketing,* 51 (January, 1987): 98-108.

Horton, Donald and R. Richard Wohl, "Mass Communication and Para-Social Interaction: Observations on Intimacy at a Distance." *Psychiatry,* Volume 19 (1956): 215-229.

Houlberg, Rick, "The Magazine of a Sadomasochism Club: The Tie That Binds." In Michelle A. Wolf and Alfred P. Kielwasser, *Gay People, Sex, and the Media.* (Binghamton, NY: Harrington Park Press, 1991): 167-183.

Hudson, Richard L., "Valentine videos seek Western beaus for Russian brides; Moscow matchmakers tell women to place boors on pedestal to win them." *The Wall Street Journal* (May 10, 1990): A1.

Illouz, Eva, "Reason Within Passion: Love In Women's Magazines." *Critical Studies in Mass Communication,* Volume 8, No. 3 (September, 1991): 231-248.

James, Caryn, "Lovelorn Hope Movies Have Just the Right Words." *The New York Times* (November 30, 1989): C19.

James, Caryn, "Love with Improper Strangers." *The New York Times* (April 22, 1990): H1+.

Jannot, Mark, "Love Brokers." *Chicago,* Volume 42 (February, 1993): 60+.

Jhally, Sut. *The Codes of Advertising*. New York: St. Martin's Press, 1987.

Joe, Susan Kim, "Socioemotional Use of Computer-Mediated Communication." Paper delivered at the International Communication Association conference, Washington, DC: 1993.

Johnson, Dirk. "Ken Hamblin: In Denver, the Surprising New Face of Right-Wing Talk Radio." *The New York Times* (January 2, 1994): E7.

Kahn, Marla J., "Factors Affecting the Coming Out Process for Lesbians." *Journal of Homosexuality,* Volume 21, No. 3 (1991): 47-70.

Kantrowitz, Barbara, "Sex on the Info Highway." *Newsweek* (March 14, 1994): 62-63.

Kantrowitz, Barbara, "Live Wires." *Newsweek* (September 6, 1993): 42-48.

Kaplan, E. Ann. *Women & Film: Both Sides of the Camera*. London: Metheun, 1983.

Kaplan, Janice, "Sex on TV '93: What's Taboo and What's Not." *TV Guide* (August 14, 1993): 8-13.

Kaplan, Justine, "Cupid's Tune: 'Buy, Buy Love.'" *Los Angeles Times* (November 20, 1992): E1.

Katz, Elihu, "On Conceptualizing Media Effects: Another Look." In Stuart Oskamp (ed.), *Television as a Social Issue* (Newbury Park, CA: Sage Publications, 1988): 361-374.

Katz, Jon, "Bulletin Boards: News from Cyberspace." *Rolling Stone* (April 15, 1993): 35+.

Katz, John, "The Tales They Tell in Cyber-Space Are a Whole Other Story." *The New York Times* (January 23, 1994): H5+.

Kauffman, L. A., "Queer Guerrillas in Tinseltown." *The Progressive* (July, 1992): 36-41.

Kelly, Ray, "The $elling of $ex," *Sunday Republican* (February 6, 1994): 1+.

Kendrick, Walter, "Increasing Our Dirty-Word Power: Why Yesterday's Smut Is Today's Erotica." *The New York Times Book Review* (May 31, 1992): 3+.

Kennedy, Dana, "Soaps on the Ropes." *Entertainment Weekly* (October 29, 1993): 37-38.

Kerr, E. B. and S. R. Hiltz. *Computer-Mediated Communication Systems.* New York: Academic Press, 1982.

Kidder, Rushworth M., "Sexual Values: Viewing Women as Partners, not Prey." *Insights on Global Ethics* (August, 1992): 3.

Kielwasser, Alfred P. and Michelle A. Wolf, "Mainstream Television, Adolescent Homosexuality, and Significant Silence." *Critical Studies in Mass Communication* 9 (1992): 350-373.

Klein, Hugh, "Content and Changes in Gay Men's Personal Ads, 1975 to the Present," work in progress.

Knickerbocker, Brad, "Gay Rights May Be Social Issue of 1990s." *Christian Science Monitor* (February 11, 1993): 1+.

Kolbert, Elizabeth, "An Open Mike, a Loudmouth Live, and Thou . . ." *The New York Times* (September 26, 1993): E2.

Konigsberg, Eric, "Love Means Never Having to Say Something That's Not in the Script. Amazing Revelation: *Studs* is Fake!" *Spy* (June, 1992): 26-27.

Laidlaw, Marc, "Virtual Surreality: Our New Romance with Plot Devices." *South Atlantic Quarterly,* 92, No. 4 (Fall, 1993): 647-668.

Laner, Mary Riege and G. W. Levi Kamel, "Media Mating 1: Newspaper Personal's Ads of Homosexual Men." In John P. DeCecco (ed.), *Gay Relationships.* (Binghamton, NY: Harrington Park Press, 1988): 73-89.

Larson, Erik. *The Naked Consumer: How Our Private Lives Become Public Commodities.* New York: Penguin, 1994.

Larson, Mark, "Singles magazine market heats up; *Singles Scenes* joins expanding field of publications aimed at local singles." *Business Journal Serving Greater Sacramento* (June 22, 1987): 12.

Lawyer, Gail, "Meeting a mate gets more creative: Marry Me, comedy dating show." *Washington Business Journal,* Volume 11, No. 20 (October 12, 1992): 1-2.

Lazier-Smith, Linda, "A Pilot Study of Personal Classified Ads Appearing in Capital-City Daily Newspapers: The Kinds, the Guidelines, the Trends." Paper presented at the Annual Meeting of the Association for Education in Journalism and Mass Communication, San Antonio, TX: August, 1987.

Lea, Martin (ed.). *Contexts of Computer-Mediated Communication.* London: Harvester Wheatsheaf, 1992.

Lederman, Diane, "Sex on the line: Sex easy to find on computer, phone." *Union-News* (Febrary 8, 1994): 1+.

Leland, John, "The New Voyeurism: Madonna and the Selling of Sex." *Newsweek* (November 2, 1992): 95-103.

Levy, David A, "Social Support and the Media: Analysis of Responses by Radio Psychology Talk Show Hosts." *Professional Psychology: Research and Practice,* 20: 73-78.

Lewis, Peter H., "The Next Tidal Wave? Some Call It 'Social Computing.' " *The New York Times* (September 19, 1993): F8.

Liebes, Tamar and Elihu Katz. *The Export of Meaning: Cross-Cultural Readings of Dallas.* New York: Oxford University Press, 1990.

Limbaugh, Rush. *See, I Told You So.* New York: Pocket Books, 1993.

Lindlof, Thomas and Timothy Meyer, "Mediated communication as ways of seeing, acting, and constructing culture: The tools and foundations of qualitative research." In Thomas Lindlof (ed.), *Natural Audiences* (Norwood, NJ: Ablex, 1987): 1-30.

Lindquist, R., "No bozos will be served by this matchmaker: Dating service owner seeks lonely singles w/$$ to spend." *Business Journal,* Volume 7, No. 1 (October 19, 1987): 19.

Linlin, Pang, "Matchmaking Via the Personal Advertisements in China Versus in the United States." *Journal of Popular Culture,* Volume 27, No. 1 (Summer, 1993): 163-170.

Lipkin, Mike, "Love, SEX and fear." *Style* (August, 1993): 74-80.

Livingston, Sonia. *Making Sense of Television: The Psychology of Audience Interpetation.* Oxford: Pergamon Press, 1990.

"Love is not a luxury in this recession: Great Expectations Creative Management, Inc." *California Business* (October, 1992): 16.

"Lovebytes." *The Economist,* Volume 320, No. 7723 (September 7, 1991): A28.

Lowry, Dennis T., Gail Love, and Malcolm Kirby, "Sex on the Soap Operas: Patterns of Intimacy." *Journal of Communication,* Volume 31, No. 3 (Summer, 1981): 90-96.

Lowry, Dennis T. and David E. Towles, "Soap Opera Portrayals of Sex, Contraception, and Sexually Transmitted Diseases." *Journal of Communication,* Volume 39, No. 2 (Spring, 1989): 76-83.

Lull, James (ed.). *Popular Music and Communication.* Newbury Park, CA: Sage Publications, 1987.

Lumby, M. E., "Men Who Advertise for Sex." *Journal of Homosexuality,* Volume 4 (1978): 149-162.

Lutz, Catherine A. and Jane L. Collins. *Reading National Geographic.* Chicago, IL: University of Chicago Press, 1993.

Lynn, Michael and Barbara A. Shurgot, "Responses to Lonely Hearts Advertisements: Effects of Reported Physical Attractiveness, Physique and Coloration." *Personality and Social Psychology Bulletin* Volume 10, No. 3 (September, 1984): 349-357.

McAllister, Celia F., "Dial-a-porn: Its Number Isn't Up Yet." *Business Week,* No. 3151 (March 26, 1990): 92C.

McCarthy, Anna, "Reach Out and Touch Someone: Technology and Sexuality in Broadcast Ads for Phone Sex." *The Velvet Light Trap,* No. 32 (Fall, 1993): 50-57.

Macero, Cosmo, Jr., "W. Mass stores tap profitable market." *Union-News* (February 7, 1994): 1+.

McKusick, Tom and Mike Tronnes, "Pathetic aesthetic." *Utne Reader* (November/December, 1992): 97-103.

MacLeod, Stewart, "Well-educated, dynamic man seeks. . . ." *Macleans* (May 29, 1989): 64.

Magiera, Marcy, "TV syndicators looking for love as 'Studs' sparks young adults." *Advertising Age,* Volume 63, No. 3 (January 20, 1992): 33-35.

Maio, Patrick J., "Matchmaker, Matchmaker." *Baltimore Business Journal* (July 10, 1992): 1-2.

Mano, Keith D., "Getting Personal." *National Review* (December 31, 1987): 52.

Marcus, Eric. *Making History: The Struggle for Gay and Lesbian Equal Rights, 1945-1990: An Oral History.* New York: Harper Collins, 1992.

Margolick, David, "For lawyers seeking another kind of partnership, a staid journal is loosening up with personal ads." *The New York Times* (September 29, 1989): B5.

Marin, Rick, "And So to Bed." *Entertainment Weekly* (May 7, 1993): 13-15.

Markoff, John, "The Latest Technology Fuels the Oldest of Drives." *The New York Times* (March 22, 1992): E5.

Marr, Bruce W., "Talk Radio Programming." In Susan Tyler Eastman, Sydney W. Head, and Lewis Klein, *Broadcast/Cable Programming: Strategies & Practices,* 3rd ed. (Belmont, CA: Wadsworth Publishing Company, 1989): 443-460.

Marsden, Michael T., "Television Viewing as Ritual." In Ray B.
Browne (ed.), *Rituals and Ceremonies in Popular Culture.*
(Bowling Green, OH: Bowling Green University Popular Press,
1980): 120-124.

Martin, Anya, "Let's Talk! Call-In Radio and TV Shows Are Transforming America." *BusinessWest* (Special Supplement, 1993): 29.

Martin-Barbero, Jesus. *Communication, Culture and Hegemony:
From the Media to Mediation.* Newbury Park, CA: Sage Publications, 1993.

Martinez, Al, "Lunch as a Way of Life." *Los Angeles Times* (March
4, 1993): B2.

Mason, M. S., "Love in the Movies." *Christian Science Monitor*
(March 12, 1991): 12.

Massey, Kimberly K. and Stanley J. Baran, "Mass Media and Sexual
Socialization: A Tale of Scientific Neglect." *Journal of Communication and Media Arts,* Volume 1, No. 1 (Spring, 1992): 17-34.

Masterman, Len (ed.) *Television Mythologies: Stars, Shows &
Signs.* London: Comedia Publishing Group, 1984.

"Matchmaker" (Dr. Barbara Chasen), *The New Yorker,* Volume 67,
No. 49 (January 27, 1992): 24-27.

Mathews, Jay, "From Closet to Mainstream: Upscale Gay Magazines Flood the Newsstand." *Newsweek* (June 1, 1992): 62.

Maupin, Armistead, "A Line That Commercial TV Won't Cross."
The New York Times (January 9, 1994): H29.

Meeks, Fleming, "Dating for Dollars." *Forbes,* Volume 147, No. 1
(January 7, 1991): 296.

Metz, Robert. *The Today Show: An Inside Look . . .* Chicago, IL:
Playboy Press, 1977.

Meyer, Josh, "Dating service fights solitude of HIV-infected: Being
Alive dating service for people with AIDS, or with virus that
causes it." *Los Angeles Times* (December 24, 1991): B3.

Meyrowitz, Joshua. *No Sense of Place: The Impact of Electronic
Media on Social Behavior.* New York: Oxford University Press,
1985.

Minsky, Terri, "Mating for Ratings on Dating Games." *The New York Times* (April 4, 1992): H29.

Mitchell, Kathleen, "Bachelors Strut Their Stuff." *Union-News* (March 30, 1993): 25+.

Modelski, Tania, "The Search for Tomorrow in Today's Soap Operas." *Film Quarterly,* Volume 32, No. 1 (Fall, 1979).

Modelski, Tania. *Loving with a Vengeance: Mass-Produced Fantasies for Women.* Hampden, CT: Archon Books, 1982.

Moffatt, Susan, "Real Estate's Role as Tokyo Cupid." *Fortune* (December 17, 1990): 12.

Moore, Martha T., "Advertisers: Business, not Politics." *USA Today* (April 23, 1993): 1B.

Moran, Barbara B. and Susan Steinfirst, "Getting Personal about Personals: What Happens After You Place That Ad?" Paper presented at the Popular Cultural Association conference, Toronto: 1990.

Morris, Geoffrey, "Talk of the Town." *National Review* (July 29, 1991): 53.

Morrison, Joy, "Network Q: The Broadcast 'samizdat' of the American Gay and Lesbian Community." Paper presented to the International Communications Association, Sydney, Australia, 1994.

Morrow, Lance, "Advertisements for Oneself." *Time,* Volume 126 (September 2, 1985): 74.

Mosco, Vincent. *The Pay-Per Society: Computers and Communication in the Information Age.* Toronto: Garamond Press, 1989.

Munson, Wayne. *All Talk: The Talkshow in Media Culture.* Philadelphia, PA: Temple University Press, 1993.

Murstein, B. I. *Paths to Marriage.* Beverly Hills, CA: Sage Publishers, 1986.

Nasaw, David. *Going Out: The Rise and Fall of Public Amusements.* New York: Basic Books, 1994.

Nauer, Kim, "Meet the Renta Yentas." *Crain's Chicago Business* (August 26, 1991): 35.

Nicholls, Marc, "Lonely in the Lab: Seduction and Scientists Just Don't Mix." *World Press Review,* Volume 40, No. 3 (March, 1993): 25.

Nimmo, Dan. *Mediated Political Realities,* 2nd edition. White Plains, NY: Longman Publishing Group, 1990.

Noble, Barbara Presley, "The Unfolding of Gay Culture." *The New York Times* (June 27, 1993): F23.

Nochimson, Martha. *No End to Her: Soap Opera and the Female Subject.* Berkeley, CA: University of California Press, 1993.

Nordgren, Sarah, "Singles just aren't swinging: Study finds subdued habits." *Union-News* (October 7, 1994): 1+.

Nordheimer, Jon, "No. 1 Activity of Today's Lovers? Worrying." *Union-News* (March 2, 1992): 14-15.

Obermiller, Tim Andrew, "Sex by the Numbers." *University of Chicago Magazine* (October, 1994): 34-37.

O'Connor, John J., "American Family Values? Not on Late Night TV." *International Herald Tribune* (July 1, 1992): 8.

Ognibene, Peter J., "Be My Classified Valentine." *Psychology Today,* Volume 18 (February, 1984): 70.

O'Neil, Kerry, "Gritty, Clubby Mags Cater to 20-Somethings." *Christian Science Monitor* (December 13, 1993): 17.

O'Neill, Molly, "Words to Survive Life With: None of This, None of That." *The New York Times* (May 27, 1990): 1+.

O'Toole, Lawrence, "Heart of Stone." *Entertainment Weekly* (November 5, 1993): 72-73.

Ouellette, Laurie, "Video Wars." *Media Culture Review,* Volume 2, No. 3 (July/August, 1993): 1+.

Ozick, Cynthia, "Puttermesser Paired." *The New Yorker* (October 8, 1990): 40+.

Pauly, Brett, "Love at First Byte. . . . " *Union-News* (September 1, 1992): 23-24.

Peale, Cliff, "At 62, Schumacher finds date with destiny as entrepreneur." *The Cincinnati Business Courier* (September 28, 1992): 4.

Perry, David K. "Assessing the Import of Media. Related Effects: Some Contexualist Considerations." *World Communication,* Volume 21, No. 2 (December, 1992): 69-82.

Perse, Elizabeth, "Soap Opera Viewing Patterns of College Students and Cultivation." *Journal of Broadcasting & Electronic Media,* Volume 30 (1986): 175-193.

Perse, Elizabeth M., Pamela I. Burton, Elizabeth S. Kovner, Margaret E. Lears, and Ruma J. Sen, "Predicting Computer-Mediated

Communication in a College Class." *Communication Research Reports,* Volume 9, No. 2 (December, 1992): 161-170.

Potter, W. James, "Cultivation Theory and Research: A Conceptual Critique." *Human Communication Research,* Volume 19, No. 4 (June, 1993): 564-601.

Powers, Ann, "Queer in the Streets, Straight in the Sheets." *The Village Voice* (June 29, 1993).

Preissl, Brigitte, "Determinants of Strategic Use of Communication Technology." Paper delivered at the Programme on Information and Communication Technologies national conference, Newport, UK: 1992.

Preston, J. and F. Brandt. *Classified Affairs: A Gay Man's Guide to the Personal Ads.* Boston: Alyson Publications, 1984.

Priest, Patricia J. *Public Intimacies: Talk Show Participants and Tell All TV.* Cresskill, NJ: Hampton Press, 1995.

Rakow, Lana F., "Looking to the Future: Five Questions for Gender Research." *Women's Studies in Communication,* 10 (Fall, 1987): 79-86.

Rapaport, Matthew. *Computer Mediated Communications: Bulletin Boards, Computer Conferencing, Electronic Mail, and Information Retrieval.* New York: John Wiley, 1991.

Rapping, Elayne, "Daytime Inquiries." *The Progressive* (October, 1991): 36-38.

Rapping, Elayne. *The Movie of the Week: Private Stories, Public Events.* Minneapolis, MN: University of Minnesota Press, 1992.

Rasak, Phillip E., "Talkers vs. The Callers." *Talkers* (Mid-July, 1993): 8.

Rawlins, William K. *Friendship Matters: Communication, Dialectics, and the Life Course.* New York: Aldine de Gruyter, 1992.

Reid, Michael A.D., "Matchmaking: Art not Science." *Atlanta Business Chronicle* (September 16, 1991): 30A+.

Reveaux, Tony, "Let the Games Begin." *New Media* (January, 1994): 48-53.

Rheingold, Howard. *The Virtual Community: Homesteading on the Electronic Frontier.* Reading, MA: Addison-Wesley, 1993.

Rice, Ronald E., "Mediated Group Communication." In Ronald E. Rice (ed.), *The New Media: Communication, Research, and Technology.* (Beverly Hills, CA: Sage Publications, 1984): 129-154.

Rice, Ronald E., "New Media Technology: Growth and Integration." In Ronald E. Rice (ed.), *The New Media: Communication, Research, and Technology* (Beverly Hills, CA: Sage Publications, 1984): 33-54.

Rice, R. E. and G. Love, "Electronic Emotion: Socioemotional Content in a Computer-Mediated Network." *Communication Research,* Volume 14 (1987): 85-108.

Rich, B. R., "New Queer Cinema." *Sight and Sound,* Volume 2, No. 5 (1992): 30-39.

Rich, Frank, "Public Stages: Burn, Baby, Burn!" *The New York Times Magazine* (November 28, 1993): 40.

Roan, Shari, "Computer, Telephone Counseling: Therapy for Yuppies." *Union-News* (December 13, 1992): A1.

Roberts, Dorothy H., "Love in the Morning Edition: Valentine Messages in the Newspaper." Unpublished paper, 1986.

Roberts, James C., "The Power of Talk Radio." *American Enterprise* (May/June, 1991): 59.

Rogers, Everett M. *Diffusion of Innovations.* New York: The Free Press, 1962, 1971, 1983.

Rogers, Everett M. *Communication Technology: The New Media in Society.* New York: Free Press, 1986.

Roth, Nancy and Linda K. Fuller. *Women's Ways of Acknowledging AIDS: Communication Perspectives.* Binghamton, NY: The Haworth Press, forthcoming.

Rubens, Suzanne D., "First Amendment—Disconnecting Dial-a-porn." *Journal of Criminal Law and Criminology,* Volume 80, No. 4 (Winter, 1990): 968-995.

Rubin, A. M., E. M. Perse, and R. A. Powell, "Loneliness, Parasocial Interaction, and Local Television News Viewing." *Human Communication Research,* Volume 12 (1985): 155-180.

Rubin, Mike, "Love is on the Air: Studs Like Me." *The Village Voice* (April 28, 1992): 45-46.

Rupp, Carla Marie, "Promoting 'personals': New York weekly surveys personal ad users and aggressively promotes their use by readers." *Editor & Publisher* (March 24, 1984): 16+.

Russo, Vito. *The Celluloid Closet: Homosexuality in the Movies,* revised ed. New York: Harper & Row, 1987.

Sarch, Amy, "Making the Connection: Single Women's Use of the

Telephone in Dating Relationships With Men." *Journal of Communication,* Volume 43, No. 2 (Spring, 1993): 128-144.

Schemo, Diana Jean, "A Matchmaker's Niche: Mentally Ill Couples." *The New York Times* (December 14, 1992): A1.

Schiller,Herbert I. *Who Knows: Information in the Age of the Fortune 500.* Norwood, NJ: Ablex, 1981.

Schneider, Howard, "The Low Expectations Dating Club." *The Washington Post* (February 14, 1993): F1.

Seligman, Jean, "The HIV Dating Game." *Newsweek* (October 5, 1992): 56-57.

Semeiks, Jonna G., "Sex, Lawrence, and Videotape." *Journal of Popular Culture,* Volume 25, No. 4 (Spring, 1992): 143-152.

"Sex Talk on the Radio With Dr. Judy." *The New York Times* (May 9, 1993): V4.

Shaffer, Jeffrey, "Worlds of Love." *The New Yorker* (June 27, 1988): 25.

Shannon, L. R. "Older Americans Conversing On Line." *Union-News,* Springfield, MA (December 2, 1993): 14+.

Shaw, Charla Markham. "Video Dating: A Return to Sentimental Culture?" Paper presented to the Popular Culture Association, 1992.

Shenon, Philip, "Brash and Unabashed, Mr. Condom Takes on Sex and Death in Thailand." *The New York Times* (December 20, 1992): E7.

Shenon, Philip, "Where single women are in big demand." *Union-News* (August 22, 1994): 20-21.

Sheridan, Geoffrey, "Clever, handsome, witty man seeks . . . " *New Statesman,* Volume 112 (August 15, 1986): 22.

Shipman, David. *Caught in the Act: Sex and Eroticism in the Movies.* London: Elm Tree Books, 1985.

Shoemaker, Pamela and Stephen Reese. *Mediating the Message: Theories of Influences on Mass Media Content.* White Plains, NY: Longman Publishing Group, 1991.

Signorelli, Nancy and Michael Morgan (eds.) *Cultivation Analysis: New Directions in Media Effects Research.* Newbury Park, CA: Sage Publications, Inc., 1990.

Silverstone, Roger. *The Message of Television: Myth and Narrative in Contemporary Culture.* London: Heinemann Educational Books, 1981.

Sklar, Robert. *Movie-Made America: A Cultural History of American Movies,* Revised and Updated. New York: Vintage Books, 1994.

Smillie, D., "Talking to America: The Rise of Talk Shows in the '92 Campaign." In Everett E. Dennis (ed.), *An Uncertain Season: Reporting in the Postprimary Period* (Arlington, VA: Freedom Forum, 1992): 17-27.

Smith, Corliss, "Sex and Genre on Prime Time." In Michelle A. Wolf and Alfred P. Kielwasser, *Gay People, Sex, and the Media* (Binghamton, NY: Harrington Park Press, 1991): 119-138.

Smith, Jane E., V. Ann Waldorf, and David L. Trembath, "Single white male looking for thin, very attractive . . . " *Sex Roles: A Journal of Research,* Volume 23 (December, 1990): 675-685.

Smith, Katrin, "Hi-tech heart-throbs: Peking singles turn to computer, television." *Far Eastern Economic Review,* Volume 150, No. 49 (December 6, 1990): 36-38.

Sneider, Julie, "Love and matchmaking in the time of AIDS: As sexual mores change, more singles embrace dating services." *The Business Journal-Milwaukee* (August 8, 1992): 1-2.

Spayde, Jon, "A salon by any other name: Study circles emerge to tackle social problems." *Utne Reader* (November/December, 1993): 40.

"Stations hanging up on party lines: More and more stations are rejecting ads for 900 services." *Broadcasting,* Volume 118, No. 10 (March 5, 1990): 61.

Stefanac, Suzanne, "Sex & the New Media." *New Media* (April, 1993): 38-45.

Stein, M. L., "Audiotex personal ads bring in revenues." *Editor & Publisher,* Volume 124, No. 48 (November 30, 1991): 22.

Stein, M. L., "In praise of Voice Personals: They continue to be a top moneymaker in newspaper audiotex but some guidelines must be followed to make them a success." *Editor & Publisher,* Volume 126, No. 14 (April 3, 1993): 14.

Stein, Ruthe. *The Art of Single Living: A Guide to Going it Alone in the '90s.* New York: Shapolsky Publishers, Inc., 1990.

Steinfirst, Susan and Barbara B. Moran, "The New Mating Game: Matchmaking Via the Personal Columns in the 1980s." *Journal of Popular Culture* 22, No. 4 (Spring, 1989): 129-140.

Stern, Aimee L., "Relationship Marketing: Courting Consumer Loyalty With the Feel-Good Bond." *The New York Times* (January 17, 1993): F10.

Stern, Howard. *Private Parts.* New York: Simon & Schuster, 1993.

Sterngold, James, "Why Japan Is in Love With Vending Machines." *The New York Times* (January 5, 1992); 1+.

Stewart, Steve. *Gay Hollywood: Over 75 Years of Male Homosexuality in the Movies.* Laguna Hills, CA: Companion Publications, 1993.

Stifel, Vicki, "The Romance of Romance." *Worcester Magazine* (October 20, 1993): 15-18.

Surlin, Stuart H., "Uses of Jamaican Talk Radio." *Journal of Broadcasting & Electronic Media,* 30 (Fall, 1986): 459-466.

Surlin, Stuart H. and Walter C. Soderlund, "Jamaican Call-In Radio: An Analysis of Callers and Hosts." Paper presented to the Association for Education in Journalism and Mass Communication, Kansas City, MO: 1993.

Surra, C. A., "Research and theory on mate selection and premarital relationships in the 1980s."*Journal of Marriage and the Family,* Volume 52 (November, 1990): 844-865.

Svetkey, Benjamin, "Up Close and Personals." *Entertainment Weekly* (August 9, 1991): 44.

Swartz, Mimi, "The Joy of Tapes." *Entertainment Weekly* (December 18, 1992): 16.

"Talk Radio Networks Pursue Role of AM 'White Knight.'" *Broadcasting* (August 27, 1990): 41.

Tannen, Deborah, "Gender Gap in Cyberspace." *Newsweek* (May 16, 1994): 52-53.

Tannen, Mary, "Mr. Clean." *The New York Times Magazine* (February 12, 1995): 52-53.

Tasker, Yvonne. *Spectacular Bodies: Gender, Genre and the Action Cinema.* London: Comedia, 1993.

Tempest, Rene, "Minitel: Miracle or Monster?" *Los Angeles Times* (October 24, 1989): A1.

Thomas, Lisa, "Here's an Expensive Love Connection: J. Wingo International." *San Diego Business Journal* (April 8, 1991): 12.

Thornton, Emily, "Japan's new Cupid: Vending Machines." *Forbes,* Volume 125, No. 7 (April 6, 1992): 13.

Tichenor, P. J., G. A. Donohue, and C. N. Olien, "Mass Media Flow and Differential Growth in Knowledge." *Public Opinion Quarterly,* Volume 34 (1970): 159-170.

Tierney, John, "Porn, the Low-Slung Engine of Progress." *The New York Times* (January 9, 1994): H1+.

Tierney, John, "Picky, Picky, Picky." *The New York Times Magazine* (February 12, 1995): 22+.

"TLC for DWMs and SWFs: Classified love ads are a booming business." *Time* (January 10, 1983).

Tuchman, Gaye, "Realism and Romance: The Study of Media Effects." *Journal of Communication,* Volume 43, No. 4 (Autumn, 1993): 36-41.

Tucker, Ken, "*Studs* and the Decline of Western Civilization." *Mademoiselle* (November, 1992): 90.

Turkle, Sherry, "Computational Seductions: The Roots of Computer Holding Power." In John V. Pavlik and Everett E. Dennis (eds.), *Demystifying Media Technology* (Mountain View, CA: Mayfield Publishing Company, 1993): 18-25.

Turner, John R., "Interpersonal and Psychological Predictors of Parasocial Interaction with Different Television Performers." *Communication Quarterly,* Volume 41, No. 4 (Fall, 1993): 443-453.

"TV programme helps in finding a spouse." *Beijing Review,* Volume 33, No. 25 (June 18, 1990): 38.

Tyler, Parker. *Screening the Sexes: Homosexuality in the Movies.* New York: DaCapo Press, Inc., 1993.

Underwood, Nora, "Lust at the end of the line." *Maclean's,* Volume 106, No. 6 (February 8, 1993): 52-54.

Valeriano, Lourdes Lee, "It's a match! Revenue-hungry dailies discover the appeal of voice personals." *The Wall Street Journal* (January 14, 1993): A1.

Valle, Paul Della, "Talk Dirty to Me—$2.99 a Minute." *Worcester Magazine* (November 17, 1993): 18.

Viles, Peter, "Talk Radio Riding High." *Broadcasting* (January 15, 1992): 24.

Wade, Betsy, "Growing Market For Gay Travel." *The New York Times* (December 20, 1992): XX3.

Walker, Richard, "Tied Up on the Phone." *New Statesman & Society,* Volume 3, No. 128 (November 23, 1990): 12-14.

Wallach, Van, "Monitoring the Personal Touch." *Advertising Age* (July 25, 1985): 44.

Walsh, Jim, "The New Sexual Revolution: Liberation at last? Or the same old mess?" *Utne Reader* (July/August, 1993): 59-65.

Walther, Joseph B., "Interpersonal effects in computer-mediated interaction: A relational perspective." *Communication Research,* Volume 19, No. 1 (1992): 52-90.

Walther, Joseph B. and Judee K. Burgoon, "Relational Communication in Computer-Mediated Interaction." *Human Communication Research,* Volume 19, No. 1 (September, 1992): 50-88.

Wasko, Janet and Vincent Mosco (eds.) *Democratic Communications in the Information Age.* Norwood, NJ: Aglex, 1992.

Weir, John, "Gay-bashing, Villainy and the Oscars." *The New York Times* (March 29, 1992): H17-18.

Weir, John, "Bent out of Shape." *Details* (February, 1994): 131-133.

Weiss, A., "From the Margins: New Images of Gays in the Cinema." *Cineaste,* Volume 15, No. 1 (1986): 4-8.

Weiss, Andrea. *Vampires & Violets: Lesbians in Film.* New York: Penguin Books, 1992.

Wexler, Joanie M., "Great Expectations for Multimedia Courtship." *Computerworld,* Volume 26, No. 41 (October 12, 1992): 65.

Wexman, Virginia Wright. *Creating the Couple: Love, Marriage, and Hollywood Performance.* Princeton, NH: Princeton University Press, 1993.

"Where Do We Stand On Pornography?" *Ms.* (January/February, 1994): 32-41.

White, Armond, "Outing the Past." *Film Comment* (July/August, 1992): 21-25.

White, Armond, "The Blinding of the Light." *Film Comment* (September/October, 1993): 58+.

Wilkinson, Peter, "The Meet Market." *Savvy Woman* (July/August, 1990): 53+.

Willey, George A., "End of an Era: The Daytime Radio Serial." *Journal of Broadcasting,* Volume 5 (Spring, 1961): 109-110.

Wilson, Edmund. *Memoirs of Hecate County.* Boston, MA: David R. Godine, 1942, 1980.

Wober, Mallory and Barrie, Gunter. *Television & Social Control.* New York: St. Martin's Press, 1988.

Wolf, Michelle A. and Alfred P. Kielwasser. *Gay People, Sex, and the Media.* Binghamton, NY: Harrington Park Press, 1991.

Wolf, Sharon. *Guerilla Dating Tactics: Strategies, Tips and Secrets for Finding Romance.* New York: Dutton, 1993.

Woll, Stanley B., "So many to choose from: Decision strategies in videodating." *Journal of Social and Personal Relationships,* Volume 3 (1986): 43-52.

Woll, Stanley B. and P. Chris Cozby, "Videodating and Other Alternatives to Traditional Methods of Relationship Initiation." In Warren H. Jones and Daniel Perlman (eds.), *Advances in Personal Relationships: A Research Annual* (Greenwich, CT: JAI Press, 1987): 69-108.

Woll, Stanley B. and Peter Young. "Looking for Mr. or Ms. Right: Self-Presentation in Videodating. *Journal of Marriage and the Family,* Volume 51, No. 2 (May, 1989): 483-488.

Wood, Julia P. and Steve Duck (eds.), *Under-Studied Relationships.* Thousand Oaks, CA: Sage Publications, 1995.

Woodward, Kenneth L., "Angels: Hark! America's Latest Search for Spiritual Meaning Has a Halo Effect." *Newsweek* (December 27, 1993): 52-57.

Wright, Robert, "Life on the Internet." *New Republic* (July 12, 1993).

Yamaguchi, Mari, "Japanese Espouse Import of Brides." *Union-313 News* (June 19, 1993): 23.

Zerbinos, Eugenia, "Talk Radio: Motivation or Titillation?" Paper presented to the Association for Education in Journalism and Mass Communication, Kansas City, MO: 1993.

Zoglin, Richard, "Bugle Boys of the Airwaves." *Time* (May 15, 1989): 88.

Zoglin, Richard, "The Shock of the Blue." *Time* (October 25, 1992): 71-72.

Index

Page numbers followed by an "n" indicate a reference note.

Acharya, Dharmendra, 22
ACT-UP, 18
Adelman and Ahuvia, 26,29n,132
Adler, Jerry, 16
Advertising/advertisements, 13,40,
    83,110,112-114,153,168
Advertising Age, 62
Advocate, The, 64,70,141,142
AIDS, 2-3,9,14,16,18,20,33,37,54,
    70,71,72,108,139,156-158,
    160,168,170n
Alan Guttmacher Institute, 16
Alexander et al., 101
Alexander and Carveth, 104-105
Alexander, Kelly King, 8
Alexander, Ron, 109
Algeria, 71
Allen, Robert C., 103-104
Alternative media, 37,43,50,65,72,
    73,111
American Association of University
    Women Educational
    Foundation, 7
American Newspaper Publishers
    Association, 64
Ames, Katrine, 29n
Andersen, Kurt, 91
Angier, Natalie, 29n
Anka (Radakovich), 37
"Anonymous" programs, 12
Antioch College, 17
Armstrong and Rubin, 88-89
Arts & Entertainment (A&E), 23
Astor, David, 62

Attig, R. Brian, 167
Auletta, Ken, 135-136
Austin, Bruce, 26
Australia, 21,111,151
Auter, P. J., 25
Avery and Ellis, 88,89
Avery and McCain, 26
Avicolli, A., 167-168

Bad Object Choices, 156
Baker, Nicholas, 33
Banerjee, Neela, 11
Barbach and Guisinger, 36
Barnouw, Erik, 81
Barry, John A., 125,144n
Bartlett, David, 92
Bay Area Youth Positives, 9
Baywatch, 108
Beavis and Butt-head, 17
Beck, Melinda, 130
Beijing Review, 21
"Being Alive," 9
Belgium, 111
Bell and Roloff, 26,131
Beniger, J., 118
Berchers, Hans, 102
Berck, Judith, 145n
Berkman, Meredith, 158
Bernikow, Louise, 26
Bernstein, S., 21
Berry, Bertice, 99
Bisexuals, 9,19,38-39,57-58,72,98
Bittner, Bob Miles, 52

Bloch, R. Howard, 28n
Block, Susan, 34-35,60,61
Blood Brothers, 9
Bloomfield, Dr. Harold, 36
Bolig, Stein, and McKenry, 40-41,67
Books, 32-36
Bordwell, Staiger, and Thompson,
        147-148
Bouhoutsos, Goodchild and Huddy,
        114n
Brady, Lois Smith, 28n,44
Branwyn, Gareth, 125-126,136-137,
        145n
Breen and Corcoran, 97
Bright, Susie, 32,136
Broadcasting, 81-115,227-232
Broadcasting, 114n
Broadcasting/cablecasting
        technologies, 135-136
Brody, E. W., 120
Brooks, Caryn, 33,122
Brown, Caryn, 102
Brown, Helen Gurley, 154
Brown, Les, 99
Brown, Tina, 9
Browne, David, 171-172
Brunch Buddies, 11
Buckley, Bill, 91
Buerkel-Rothfuss and Mayes, 105,106
Bush, George, 100
Business/Agency Resources, 201-206
Buss, A. H., 89
Butterfield, F., 131
Buxton, Rodney A., 85

California Business, 7,28n
Callen, Michael, 20,29n
Cambray, C. K., 35-36
Cameron and Sparks, 67
Campbell and Rebello, 147,170n
Canadian Business, 21
Cantor and Pingree, 101
Carter, Alan, 106-107
Cartoons, 58-59

Carveth, Rod, 102,104,106,114n
Carveth and Alexander, 106
Case, Tony, 50
Cate and Lloyd, 26
Cathcart, Robert, 102
Chase, Chevy, 99
Chasen, Dr. Barbara, 9
Chesebro and Bonsall, 26,122
Chicago, IL, 11,72,75,109,132
China, 21,23,71
Christian Science Monitor, 11
Christina, 99
Cincinnati Business Courier, 7
Clark, Charles S., 139
Clark, Mary Higgins, 36
Clinton, President Bill, 18,84,92,100
Cobb, Nathan, 86
"Cocooning," 4
Communication technologies,
        117-145,233-235
Computers, 66,121-130
Computer-mediated communication,
        122
Comstock, George, 143-144
Correspondence/Introduction
        Resources, 189-199
Court TV, 108-109
Crabtree, Penni, 8
Crichton, Sarah, 17
Crothers, Charles, 90
Crystal, Billy, 97
C-SPAN, 100
Cullison, A. E., 21
"Cultivation Analysis," 24-25,97,
        106,172,173,183
Cultural Environment Movement,
        1,25,29n
Cvetkovich, Ann, 113-114
Cybersex. *See* Lovebytes

Darden and Koski, 67,68-69
"Date checking," 8
Davidson, Alan G., 70,127
Davis and Kraus, 13,26
Deaux and Hanna, 67

DeCecco, John P., 19,20
DeCecco and Elia, 20
della Cava, Marco R., 37
Demarest, Michael, 80n
D'Emilio, John, 18
DeMont, John, 3
Denzin, Norman K., 153
Dervin, Brenda, 118
Dery, Mark, 144n
DeWitt, Paula Mergenhagen, 3,4
Diamond, Todd, 92
Dixon, Wheeler Winston, 153
Dobnik, Verena, 18
Dolan, Carrie, 26,144n
Donahue, 99,138,145n
Donohoe, Amanda, 97
Dordick, Herbert S., 27
Doty, Alexander, 156
Douglas, Suzanne, 61-62
Dutton, Rogers, and Jun, 26,122
Dworkin and MacKinnon, 185
Dyer, Richard, 155,156,182-183

Eastman, Head, and Klein, 88
Editor and Publisher, 71,80n
Egan, Anne W., 12
Ehrenreich, Barbara, 26
Elmer-DeWitt, Philip, 126,127
E-mail, 129,180,277-279
Emerson, Bo, 26,129
Entertainment Weekly, 41,79n,114n,
        153,172
Escoffier, Jeffrey, 17
Etheridge, Melissa, 168

Faderman, Lillian, 18
Fairness Doctrine, 83,91,92
Faludi, Susan, 3,27
Family Planning Perspectives, 16
Fanning, Deirdre, 12
Far Eastern Economic Review, 21
Farb, Peter, 125,144n
Farber, Jim, 19

Feirstein, Bruce, 184
Fejes and Petrich, 19,155,156
Fine, Marlene, 103
Firestone, David, 43
Fisher, Milton, 27
Fitzgerald and Gersh, 80n
"Flame wars," 125
Foa and Foa, 26
Fogel, Alan, 26
Foote, Jennifer, 21
Forbes, 34,142
Forester, Tom, 122
Forster, E. M., 133
Fortune, 72,80n
Fox network, 110,111
Frentz, Suzanne, 102,114n
Fretts, Bruce, 108,112,114n
Friendly, Fred, 81
Friends, 26,107,112
Friends for Life, 9
Friendship Exchange, 8
Fuller, Linda K., 2,19,25,79,80,82,
        83,90,109,118,144,148,169,
        170n
Fuller and Shilling, 3
Furlong, Mary, 130
Fury, Kathleen, 63

Gailey, Christine War, 134
Gallimore and Fuller, 144
Gaming and simulations, 169
Gandy, Oscar, 27,118,144
Ganley, Gladys, 26
Gans, Herbert J., 12-13
Garber, Marjorie, 110
Garcia, Guy, 153,167
Garrison, Deborah, 33
Gattiker, Urs E., 26,117-118,122
Gays/lesbians, 11,17-20,29n,38-39,
        58,67,69-70,71,91,96-97,109,
        111,132,137,155-157,167-168,
        183-184
Gay Academic Union, 18
Gay and Lesbian Alliance Against
        Defamation (GLAAD), 18

Gay Games, 19
Gelman, David, 21
Geraghty, Christine, 102
Geraldo, 99
Gerbner, George, 24,25,27,29n,103,
    105,106,183,187n
Gerbner,Gross, Morgan, and
    Signorelli, 103
Germany, 111
Giddens, Anthony, 14
Gleiberman, Owen, 92-93
Goffman, Erving, 26,171,186n
Goldberg, Whoopi, 99,157
Goldberg and Phillips, 14,99
Golding and Murdock, 118
Goldman, Robert, 40
Goldstein, Harry, 139
Gonzales and Meyers, 69-70
Goodman, Ellen, 65
Goodman, Walter, 93,94,114
Gordon, Eric A., 168
Gow, Joe, 108
Graebner, Lynn, 8
Gransden, Greg, 21
Graves, Gay, 145n
Great Expectations, 7
Green, Jesse, 169n
Green, Michele, 97
Greenbaum, Bruce, 8
Greenberg and D'Alessio, 102
Greenberg, Abelman, and D'Alessio,
    102
Greenblatt, Stephen, 39
Greenburg, Dan, 29n
Grillo, R., 167
Grodin, Debra, 34
Gross, Jane, 186
Gross, Larry, 19
Grossman, Ed, 45-46,47,48,79n

Haag, Laurie L., 99
Hadleigh, B., 156
Hall, Arsenio, 99,100
Hall, Carla, 9,19

Halttunen, K., 131
Halverson, Kim, 8
Hamblin, Ken, 92
Harkison, Judy, 80n
Harlequin Publishers, 34
Harpers, 139
Harris, Louis and Associates, 7
Harrison, Michael, 94,95,114n
Harrison and Saeed, 66-67
Hate/homophobia, 19,71-72,132,
    156,157,168
Hauser, Susan G., 15
Haworth Press, 21
Hedges, Chris, 71
Hendrick and Hendrick, 26
Hendrix, Harville, 27
Henneberger, Melinda, 21
Henneberger and Marriott, 7
Herzog, Herta, 101,103,115n
L'Heureux, John, 79n
Hift, Fred, 98
Himmelstein, Hal, 97-98
Hirsch, P. M., 25
Hirschman, Elizabeth C., 66,68
HIV+, 11
Holbrook, Hal, 97
Horton and Wohl, 25
Houlberg, Rick, 39
Hudson, Richard L., 21

Illouz, Eva, 41-42
India, 21,22,151
Information Please Almanac, 5
Interactive media, 122,133-134
International Directory of Bisexual
    Groups, 9
International Society of Introduction
    Services, 4
Internet, 124,126
Intimacy, 14
"Intracinematology," 148
Introductions Club, 9
Ireland, 76-77,151

Isabora, 74
"It's *just* Lunch," 11

Jamaica, 90
James, Caryn, 62,158
Jannot, Mark, 132
Japan, 21,23,139
Jewish dating/matchmaking, 8,86
Jhally, Sut, 13
Joe, Susan Kim, 26,122
John, Elton, 168
Johnson, Dirk, 92
Jones, Jenny, 99
Journal of Homosexuality, 21

Kamen, Paula, 15
Kaminer, Wendy, 28n
Kantrowitz, Barbara, 124,125,128
Kaplan, E. Ann, 151
Kaplan, Janice, 108
Kaplan, Justine, 12
Katz, James, 27
Katz, Jon, 122,124
Kauffman, L. A., 156
Kendrick, Walter, 32,185
Kennedy, Dana, 107
Kenya, 21
Kerr and Hiltz, 122
Kidder, Rushworth, 4
Kielwasser and Wolf, 97
King, Larry, 85,99,177
Klein, Hugh, 70
Knickerbocker, Brad, 18
Kolbert, Elizabeth, 84-85
Konigsberg, Eric, 111
Korea, 21
Kuriansky, "Dr. Judy," 85

Laidlaw, Marc, 136
Lake, Ricki, 99
Landers, Ann, 53
Laner and Kamel, 67

Lang, k.d., 168
LaRose, Robert, 27
Larson, Erik, 26
Larson, Mark, 36,131
Lasswell, Harold, 117,144n
Lawyer, Gail, 110
Lazier-Smith, Linda, 43-44
Lea, Martin, 26,122,144n
Leach, Bob (Single Booklovers),
    56-57
Lederman, Diane, 54
Leland, John, 14
Lesbians. *See* "Gays/lesbians"
Levy, David A., 89
Lewis, Peter H., 26,123
Liebes and Katz, 115n
Limbaugh, Rush, 83,91-92,100,177,
    184
Lindlof and Meyer, 26,28
Lindquist, R., 131
Linlin, Pang, 71
Lipkin, Mike, 15
Lipsitz, George, 170n
Lloyd, Joan, 36
London Times, The, 60,74
Loneliness, 13,62,65,75,149,
        151-152,156,159,161,
        163,167,171
Los Angeles, CA, 9
Loukides, Paul, 2
Love, Patricia, 36
Lovebytes, 123-127,136
Lovephones, 85
Lowry and Towles, 102
Lowry, Love, and Kirby, 102,105
Lull, James, 166
Lumby, M. E., 67
LunchDates, 11
Lutz, John, 35
Lutz and Collins, 39-40
Luxembourg, 111
Lynn and Shurgot, 68

Macero, Cosmo, Jr., 54,130
MacLeod, Stewart, 74

Mad About You, 112
Madonna, 14,152,160,168
Magazines, 36-42,219-223
Magiera, Marcy, 109
Maio, Patrick J., 8
ManMate, 19
Mano, D. Keith, 62,66
Mapplethorpe, 14
Margolick, David, 80n
Markey, Edward, 91-92
Markoff, John, 26,123-124,133
Marr, Bruce, 83
Marsden, Michael T., 97
Martin, Anya, 94,114n
Martin-Barbero, Jesus, 185-186
Martinez, Al, 28n
Massey and Baran, 13,26
Masterman, Len, 97
Matchmaking/matchmakers,
        8,12,20-21,28n,61,
        71,131,153-154
Mathews, Jay, 19,38
Maupin, Armistead, 97
McCarthy, Anna, 112-113,121,139
McDonagh, Maitland, 170n
McLuhan, Marshall, 84
Media-mediated relationships
    broadcasting, 81-115
    communication technologies,
        117-145
        broadcasting/cablecasting,
            135-136
        computers, 121-130
        interactive media, 133-134
        telephony, 139-144
        video, 130-133
        virtual reality, 136-139
    considerations
        international considerations,
            20-24
        media considerations, 12-14
        sexual considerations, 14-17
        sexual orientation
            considerations, 17-20
        societal considerations, 2-12

Media-mediated relationships,
    communication technologies,
    (continued)
        theoretical considerations,
            24-26
    methodology, 27-28
    motion pictures, music, and more,
        147-170
    print media, 31-80
    review of the literature, 26-28
    survey, 173-182,259-284
Meeks, Fleming, 142
Mercury, Freddie, 168
Messinger, Eric, 79n
Metz, Robert, 98
Meyer, Josh, 9
Meyrowitz, Joshua, 26,27,172
Miller, Dennis, 99
Miller, Michael Vincent, 28n
Milton, John, 31
Minsky, Terri, 109,115n
Mitchell, Kathleen, 7
Modelski, Tania, 79n,101,103
Moffat, Susan, 23
Mondo 2000, 138
Moore, Martha T., 19
Moran and Steinfirst, 69
Morocco, 21
Morris, Geoffrey, 88
Morrison, Joy, 38,111
Morrow, Lance, 61
Mosco, Vincent, 26,122
Motion pictures, 13,147-166,
        178-179,267-271
    dating/mating, 153-158
    filmography, 241-245
    film/video resources, 247-253
    personals, 158-161
    phone sex, 161-163
    psycho-sociological angst,
        148-153
    radio relationships, 163-165
    video and variations, 165-166
Movieline, 75,147
Moyers, Bill, 91

MTV, 14,17,100,107,108
Munson, Wayne, 82
Murdoch, Rupert, 108
Murphy, Eddie, 140
Murstein, B. I., 27
Music, 166-168,255-257

Nader, Ralph, 83
Nasaw, David, 184
Nashe, Carol, 114n
National Association of Radio Talk
    Show Hosts (NARTSH),
    89,114n
National Gay and Lesbian Task
    Force, 18
National Geographic, 39-40,114
National Opinion Research Center
    (NORC), 16
Nauer, Kim, 8
New London, CT, 9
New Media, 124,134
New York Times, The, 9,12,15,44,71,
    80n,84,92,93,114n,131
New Yorker, 9,28n,58-59,63
Newcomb, Horace, 103
Newlywed Game, The, 8
Newsletters, 54-58
Newspapers, 42-54
Newsweek, 14,17
Nicholls, Marc, 7-8
Nimmo, Dan, 26
Noble, Barbara Presley, 19
Nochimson, Martha, 102
Nordgren, Sarah, 16
Nordheimer, John, 29n
Norville, Deborah, 85

Obermiller, Tim Andrew, 16
Obscenity, 54,138
O'Connor, John J., 110
Offit, Avodah, 33
Ognibene, Peter J., 74
O'Neil, Kerry, 37

O'Neill, Michael J., 135
O'Neill, Molly, 12
O'Toole, Lawrence, 153
Ouellette, Laurie, 132
Out/Look, 18
"Outing," 17
Ozick, Cynthia, 63-64

"Parasocial Interaction," 25
Pauly, Brett, 128
Pavlik and Dennis, 19
Peale, Cliff, 7
Perry, Robert, 26,183
Perse et al., 26,122
Persian Gulf War, 84
Personals, The, 31,60-80,141-142,
    158-161,175-176
    content, 62-64
    economics, 64-66
    history, 60-62
    media, 72-79
    sociology, 66-72
Peru, 21
Phillipines, 21
"Plump Partners," 7
Poole, Ithiel deSola, 123
Popcorn, Faith, 21
Potter, W. James, 25
Povich, Maury, 99,139-140
Powers, Ann, 20
Preissl, Brigitte, 117
Premiere, 75
Preston and Brandt, 67
Priest, Patricia J., 100
Print media, 31-80,207-217

Radio, 82-95,163-165,176-178.
    See also Talk Radio
Radio-TV News Directors
    Association, 92
Rakow, Lana F., 2
Rapaport, Matthew, 26,122
Rapping, Elaine, 98-99,108,114n
Rasak, Phillip E., 83

Rawlins, William K., 27
Regis and Kathie Lee, 99
Reid, Michael A. D., 24
"Relationship marketing," 12
"Relationship" shows on TV,
    107-112
Relationship surrogates, 169
Reveaux, Tony, 134
Rheingold, Howard, 126-127
Rice, Ronald E., 26,27,144
Rice and Love, 122
Rich, B. R., 156
Rich, Frank, 131
Rivers, Joan, 99
Roan, Shari, 143
Roberts, Dorothy H., 74
Roberts, James C., 88
Rogers, Everett M., 118,142
Roiphe, Katie, 17
Rolling Stone, 8,28n,38,75,182
Romantic Times, 33
Rooney, Andy, 91
Roseanne, 97,112
Roth and Fuller, 3,157
Rowland, Willard, 27
Rubens, Suzanne D., 141
Rubin, Mike, 110-111
Rubin, Perse, and Powell, 25
Rupp, Carla Marie, 80n
Russo, Vito, 156

Sadomasochism, 39,65
Saenz, Mike, 137,138
Sarch, Amy, 139
Schemo, Diana Jean, 8
Schiller, Herb, 118
Schneider, Howard, 27
Science Connection, 7
Seinfeld, 26,96,112,150
Seligman, Jean, 3,9
Semeiks, Johanna G., 165
Senior citizens, 37,43,128,129-130
Sex-on-line. *See* Lovebytes
Sex surveys, 16

Sexual correctness, 17
Sexual literacy, 15
Sexual socialization, 13
Shaffer, Jeffrey, 63
Shannon, L. R., 128
Shaw, Charla Markham, 131-132
Sheen, Martin, 97
Shenan, Philip, 21,23
Sheridan, Geoffrey, 66
Shilling, Lilless, 3
Shipman, David, 148
Shoemaker and Reese, 26
Silverstone, Roger, 97
Simpson, O. J., 96,109
"Singles," 3-6,36-37,44,54-56,86,
    151,154-155,182
Singles Choice, 44-48
Sirius, R. U., 138
60 Minutes, 98
Smillie, D., 83,114n
Smith, Katrin, 21
Smith, Waldorf, and Trembath, 68
Sneider, Julie, 3
Snyder, Tom, 85
Soap operas, 100-107
Social Network, 8
South Africa, 77
Southern Poverty Law Center, 19
Soviet Union, 21
Spain, 111
Sports & Recreation Singles
    Connection, 8
Stacy, Carol, 33
*Statistical Abstract of the United
    States*, 5
Stefanac, Suzanne, 124,137,145n
Stein, M. L., 144n
Stein, Ruthe, 27
Steinfirst and Moran, 62,69
Stern, Aimee L., 12
Stern, Howard, 17,83,91,92-94,135,
    177,184
Sterngold, James, 23
Stewart, Steve, 156
Stiegel, Vicki, 79n

Stonewall 25, 97
Studs, 1,110-111
Surlin and Soderlund, 90-91
Surra, C. A., 3
Svetkey, Benjamin, 109
Swartz, Mimi, 133
Sweden, 111
Syatt, Dick, 85-87

Talk radio, 83-91
Talk Soup, 100
Talkers, 94
Telephony, 112-113,114n,139-144,
    179-180,237-239,273-275
Television, 96-114
Television dating shows (e.g.,
    *Dating Game, Infatuation,
    Love Connection, Prime Time
    Personals, Studs*), 109,
    177-178,261-265
Theroux, Paul, 36
thirtysomething, 97
Thomas, Lisa, 12
Tichenor, Donohue, and Olien, 118
Tierney, John, 4,119,141,187n
Time, 80n,91
Today, 98
"Together," 9,10
Townsend, Peter, 168
Travel magazines, 11
Trust, 14
Tuchman, Gaye, 26
Tucker, Ken, 110
Turkle, Sherry, 122-123
Turner, John R., 25
TV Guide, 57,107,115n,182
Tyler, Parker, 156

Union-News (Springfield, MA), 43,
    53-54
United Kingdom, 76,111,154
USA Today, 19,72
U.S. Bureau of the Census, 4,5

U.S. Department of Commerce,
    Economics, and Statistics, 5
Utne Reader, 16-17,37,42

Valentines, 74-75,139-140
Valeriano, Lourdes Lee, 144
Valle, Paul della, 140
Versace, Gianni, 40,114
Video, 130-133,164-166
Videodating, 7,127-128,131-133,
    165,180-181,281-282
Village Voice, The, 50-51,61,66,70,
    73,110,142
Virtual reality, 136-139,181,283-284
Voice Introduction Personals, 141-142
Vox, 1,32-33
Voyeurism, 14,33,40,62,112,113,134,
    137,152-153,166

Wade, Betsy, 19
Walker, Richard, 142
Wall Street Journal, 21,57,80n
Wallach, Van, 72
Walsh, Jim, 16,96,117
Walther, Joseph B., 26,27
Walther and Burgoon, 26,122
Warner, Marina, 79n
Washington Post, 27,72,74
Wasko and Mosco, 118
Webb, Don, 81
Weir, John, 155
Weiss, A., 156
Westheimer, Dr. Ruth, 32,85,177
Wexler, Joanie M., 128
Wexman, Virginia Wright, 13
White, Armond, 166
Whitney, Jane, 99
Wilkinson, Peter, 12
Willey, George A., 100-101
Williams, Jerry, 84
Williams, Montel, 99
Wilson, Edmund, 60-61
Winfrey, Oprah, 99-100
Wober and Gunter, 97
Wolf and Kielwasser, 20,168

Woll, Stanley B., 131
Woll and Cozby, 131,185
Woll and Young, 132
Wood and Duck, 26
Woodiwiss, Kathleen, 33
Woodward, Kenneth L., 185
Worcester, MA, 76,79n,140-141
World Health Organization (WHO), 15
Wright, Robert, 124

Yamaguchi, Mari, 23
Yellow journalism, 43

Zerbinos, Eugenia, 89
"Zines," 37
Zoglin, Richard, 88,114n